CERAMICS   OF   DERBYSHIRE

Ceramics of
DERBYSHIRE
1750-1975

An illustrated guide edited by

H.G.Bradley

COPYRIGHT

Some of the illustrations printed in this guide are official museum photographs. Grateful acknowledgement, both for the prints and permission to reproduce them, is made to:-

Victoria & Albert Museum.

Nos. 2, 8, 13, 14, 17, 18, 30, 41, 43, 45, 70, 71, 80, 83, 118, 124, 141, 146, 166, 167, 197, 233, 239, 461.
Wirksworth shards.

Derby Museum & Art Gallery.

Nos. 49, 57, 61, 93, 99, 122, 143, 144, 157, 163, 211, 218, 220, 264, 433, 435, 437, 438, 439, 441, 442, 443, 444, 446, 447, 450.
Salt-glazed fragments.

Royal Crown Derby Museum.

Nos. 133, 269, 283, 305, 306.

Holborn of Menstrie Museum, Bath.

No. 89.

Cecil Higgins Art Gallery, Bedford.

No. 48.

City of Birmingham Museum.

No. 138.

City Art Gallery, Bristol.

Nos. 119, 246, 247, 248, 249.

Astley Hall, Chorley.

Nos. 414, 421, 467.

Leeds Art Galleries.

Nos. 209, 227, 384, 389, 395, 410, 413, 415, 419, 420.

City of Manchester Art Galleries.

Nos. 108, 109, 408, 468.

Northampton Museum & Art Gallery.

Nos. 393, 394, 416.

Norfolk Museum Service
(Castle Museum, Norwich)

Nos. 47, 50, 53, 140, 181, 182, 231, 232, 387, 407, 409, 411, 457, 469, 470.

Western Park Museum, Sheffield.

Nos. 359, 364, 378.

National Museum of Wales.

Nos. 51, 55, 59, 63, 107, 148, 165, 282.

G. Godden, Worthing.

Nos. 225, 373, 463, 464.

This edition © 1978 by Gilbert Bradley, 14 Dorset Square, London, N.W.1., 1st printing 1978, 1SBN 0 9506165 0 8.

Manufactured in Great Britain by Maslands Ltd., Fore Street, Tiverton, Devon. Lithographic Reproduction by Isca Litho, Haven Road, Exeter.

IN MEMORIAM

H.C.B.

FOREWORD

The theme of this Illustrated Guide and of the Seminar and
Exhibition which gave birth to it is an interesting one: the
ceramic products of a small land-locked country far away from
any great centres of fashion or markets. How did the extremely
varied ceramics, here illustrated, come to be produced where
they were?

With the benefit of hindsight it seems a pity that the
Exhibition and Seminar could not have begun with the slipware
of the County, problematical though the identification of
these remains. Slipwares, with their reliance on contrasting
qualities and colours of clay would have helped emphasise the
basis of the Derbyshire industry in the County's geology, with
its wide range of clays and its seams of coal, natural advantages
shared with the ceramic industry of North Staffordshire. On the
adverse side, a heavy soil and hilly terrain made the roads in
much of the County virtually impassable for much of the year.
Gradually, as in neighbouring Staffordshire, turnpike roads,
canals and finally railroads facilitated the expansion of
markets and encouraged the production of wares like cream-
coloured earthenware and porcelain that could neither be made of
local materials nor disposed of locally.

Derbyshire ceramics should not be considered in isolation. The
County's slipwares and creamwares clearly owed much to the
proximity of Staffordshire and William Duesbury I of the Derby
porcelain factory was not the only figure in the ceramic history
of Derbyshire who started his career in the Staffordshire
Potteries. Nor did skills and influences all flow from Derbyshire to Staffordshire: Haslem quotes an admiring saying 'a Derby
man has an extra wheel' as current in the Staffordshire Potteries.
'Crouch ware' the name used in eighteenth century Staffordshire
for brown salt-glazed wares, seems to derive from Crich in Derbyshire and one of the contributors to the Illustrated Guide rightly
points out the influence of Derby porcelain figures on the
Staffordshire pottery figure. On the other hand Derby porcelain
figures would themselves never have come into existence without
influences from London and overseas; in studying 'the second
Dresden' we must not forget the first.

A Seminar or an Exhibition devoted to ceramics can be welcomed in
several differing ways: as an opportunity to clarify problems of
attribution; to identify modellers and designers; to study the
economic and social life of the potters or their customers. Each
of these approaches was to some degree in evidence at the 1976
Morley College Seminar, but I think it was above all the
Exhibition that brought us back from the by-ways of research to
the first reason for our interest in ceramics: the beauty of the
ware itself. This Exhibition is commemorated in the Illustrated
Guide that follows.

J.V.G. Mallet
Keeper,
Department of Ceramics,
Victoria & Albert Museum.

C O N T E N T S

ILLUSTRATIONS

Colour Plates

A C K N O W L E D G E M E N T S

As Editor I should like to thank Morley College Ceramic Circle for permission to catalogue and illustrate the items in the exhibition held in the Morley College Art Gallery in connection with their 1976 Seminar. This, by kind permission of Barry Till, the Principal, was on "Ceramics of the Derbyshire Area".

Due to security reasons, it is not possible to mention the names of the individuals who lent pieces from their collections, but I should like to record my thanks to them for their assistance and co-operation. I should especially like to thank John Mallet, Keeper of Ceramics and Gaye Blake-Roberts, Museum Assistant in the Department of Ceramics at the Victoria and Albert Museum and Timothy Clifford, Assistant Keeper, Prints and Drawings Department of the British Museum, for their help and co-operation.

In addition I should like to thank:-

Roy Hughes and Rosemary Bowers of the Derby Museum and Art Gallery.
John Twitchett, Curator, and
Betty Bailey, Assistant Curator at the Royal Crown Derby Museum.
Ann Linscott, Public Relations Officer of Royal Doulton Tableware Ltd.
Peter Walton, Keeper, Lotherton Hall, Leeds,
Michael Parkinson, Keeper and
Emeline Leary, Assistant Keeper, Decorative Arts, City of Manchester
                                        Art Gallery.
Sheenah Smith, Assistant Keeper of Art, Castle Museum, Norwich,
Cleo Witt, Curator, Applied Art, City of Bristol Museum and Art Gallery.
Dr. Mary Holbrook, formerly Curator, Holburne of Menstrie Museum, Bath.
Peter Hughes, Assistant Keeper, Department of Art, National Museum
                                        of Wales,
Glennys Wild, Deputy Keeper, Department of Art, City of Birmingham
                                        Museum and Art Gallery.
Molly Pearce, Keeper of Applied Arts, Western Park Museum, Sheffield,
William Terry, Curator, Museum and Art Gallery, Northampton,
Gordon Haworth, Amenities Officer, in charge of the collection at
                                        Astley Hall, Chorley, Lancashire,
and Geoffrey Godden, all of whom have given me every assistance and answered my many requests. Also I am most grateful to my many friends in the antiques trade for their help.

In the preparation of this Guide, I owe particular thanks to Gaye Blake-Roberts, who has been most generous with her time, knowledge and help. Others who have assisted in the preparation are, Joanna Whiteley, of Messrs. Sotheby Parke Bernet and Co., Marjory Biedermann, J.C. Holdaway and Dr. W.A.M. Holdaway of Morley College Ceramic Circle, who have helped to check and proof read the entries, and Martin O'Rourke who has given his assistance. Thanks are also due to Messrs. Artco Ltd, London, who have photographed many of the pieces illustrated.

EDITORIAL

This guide is based on the pieces which were on display in the
exhibition held at Morley College, London, in November 1976 and
therefore the mediaeval pottery or later slipware which were
made in the pot works scattered around the country are not
included.

In selecting the pieces, I followed the recommendations of the
lecturers at the seminar who have written the introductions to
the various sections. All museum references have been included
where appropriate. The number of pieces in the blue and white
section was the largest ever assembled and, although not fully
comprehensive, when taken in conjunction with those illustrated
in "English Blue & White Porcelain of the 18th Century" by Dr.
Bernard Watney, it represents most of the known shapes and
patterns produced at Derby. An attempt has been made to ascribe
an accurate date to denote when all of the pieces illustrated
were first produced. However, in any commercial undertaking the
successful lines may have been continued well beyond the dates
specified.

Since the time of the earlier exhibition held in Derby in 1870,
when one case was filled with pieces which were ascribed to
Wirksworth, almost all trace of this factory has disappeared; it
is omitted from many of the usual books of reference and the only
examples on display at Morley College were fragments kindly lent
by the Victoria and Albert Museum. It is hoped that, if and when
an excavation can be carried out on the site of this factory, it
will again be possible to ascribe pieces to Wirksworth. It should
be remembered that all knowledge of the kiln at Melbourne had been
completely lost until the shards and fragments were excavated
there in 1957 but, unlike Wirksworth where there are documents
concerning the ownership and production, no documents, other than
the references in contemporary newspapers, have been traced referring
to Melbourne.

One of the main objects of an exhibition is to take a fresh look
at the objects on display, and it will be seen that in the section
on other factories there are a number of pieces originally thought
to be of Derbyshire origin. In some cases an attribution has been
agreed - in others there is still uncertainty. It is hoped that
this will prompt both collectors and scholars to take up the
challenge.

14, Dorset Square,   H. Gilbert Bradley.
London N.W.1.

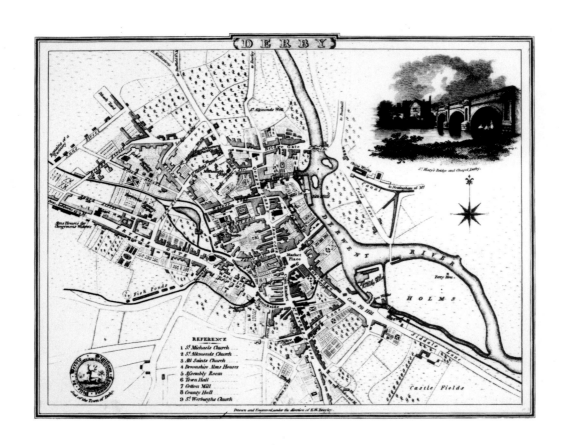

REFERENCE

1 St Michaels Church
2 St Alkmonds Church
3 All Saints Church
4 Devonshire Alms Houses
5 Assembly Room
6 Town Hall
7 Cotton Mill
8 County Hall
9 St Werburghs Church

St Mary's Bridge and Chapel Derby.

Drawn and Engraved under the direction of E.W. Brayley.

EARLY HISTORY OF THE DERBY FACTORY

The first indication of a ceramic industry within the city of Derby is confirmed by the existence of several cream jugs inscribed with the date 1750. This is corroberated by a passage in the 'Derby Mercury' for January 26th, 1753, concerning the drowning of a workman from the China Works near Mary Bridge, on Christmas Eve. Other early references to the existence of a factory are contained in the Parish Registers of St. Alkmund's Church in Derby, which record the baptism of Andrew Planché's sons in 1751 and 1754; and the marriage of William Whitehall, 'labourer at the China House' in the Register of St. Werbergh's Church in Derby, in 1754.

Proof of the successful manufacture of china at Derby is given in the London Account Book of William Duesbury, the independent decorator, working in London. This volume covers the period from November 22nd 1750 to August 1753, and includes such entries as: May 5th, 1753, 'Mr. Foy 1 pr of Darbey figars large (to enamell)'.

The site of the porcelain works has been open to much speculation. If the newspaper advertisement is assumed to be correct, then the first site was probably 100 yards eastwards of St. Mary's Bridge, (see later map of 1806, opp.). An advertisement in the Derby Mercury' for July 30th, 1756, states, 'Occupied by Mr. Heath and Company in the China Manufactory and let at £10 per annum exclusive of all taxes'. The property was not sold and was re-advertised for sale by public auction on October 25th, 1756, when it was bought by the tennants, Mr. Heath and Company.

Both John Heath and Andrew Planché had been resident in Derby before the arrival of William Duesbury of Longton. The association of the three of them is indicated in a surviving, unsigned, draft Partnership Agreement of 1756. There is no evidence as to whether Andrew Planché continued with the Derby China Works much after the agreement, but the Works, under the guidance of William Duesbury I (1756-1786) expanded and flourished.

Gaye Blake-Roberts.

DERBY FIGURES AND VASES. 1750-1848

In this brief introduction it is not possible to give a thorough survey of the figures and vases at Derby from the experimental early 1750's until the factory's closure in 1848. The century or so covered by these figures demonstrates a remarkable series of technical and stylistic developments in ceramics, and reflects a turbulent phase, philosophically, economically and sociologically. The riches resulting from the Industrial Revolution produced a new class of patron who required different ornaments for their homes.

Many Derby figures, recent descendants of confectioners' sugar paste sculpture, were at first intended to garnish dining tables and desserts. Porcelain boars rootled amongst drifts of parsley for plovers' eggs, the 'Elements' on high <u>rocaille</u> bases triumphed over truffles, larks' tongues, roast capons and magnums of champagne. Other figures and vases were intended as '<u>garniture de chiminée</u>' for stressing the architecture of chimney-pieces and often drawing together at the room's focal point a combination of the colours used in the room. The curious palette colours of pea-green, claret, flesh pink and gold appearing on Derby vases of the 1770's nicely reflects the colour schemes used in contemporary interiors by such designers as Adam, Chambers, and Wyatt. No such unity appears in rooms of the late 1780's and 90's dominated by Henry Holland's French preference for gold and white, while by the 19th century, such ideas would have appeared absurd both to the manufacturer and patron.

The history of porcelain figures is partly governed by different manufacturing techniques. Derby figures all appear to have been slip cast. The first group, which include such figures as the 'Kitty Clive' in the Schreiber Collection, and 'The Actor' (see No.1), are somewhat doubtfully Derby productions and bear little resemblance in paste and modelling to the well known group of cream jugs incised 'D 1750' or 'Derby'. We do know that figures were in early production, for William Duesbury in his London decorating establishment in 1752 and 1753 itemised 'Derby' and 'Derbyshire' figures. The chief, if not sole manufacturer of porcelain figures before 1756 at Derby appears to have been Andrew Planché (b. 1728; apprenticed goldsmith 1740-47; documented Derby 1751-6; d. Bath 1809). (See Nos. 2-6).

The early figures are usually classed as 'dry-edge' for they are made of a soft porcelain with a thick glassy glaze that was applied leaving an area bare of glaze around the lower sides of the base.

The excellent figures of this period like the 'St. Thomas', 'St. Philip' 'Chinese Groupe of the Senses', 'Charging Bulls' and 'Boars' (No.6) are usually attributed to Planché, but we have little or no evidence that Planché was the modeller. It has been plausibly suggested by John Mallet that these figures may have been modelled in London and the models sent up to Derby, as was the practice common in later years at the factory.

In 1756 William Duesbury, the former London decorator now described
as 'enameller of Longton', with John Heath, 'banker', drew up a draft
agreement with Planché, 'china maker' to manufacture porcelain.
Planché was apparently soon dropped from the partnership leaving
Duesbury the chief proprietor who ran the factory with success until
his death in 1786.

In 1756 the new Derby proprietors began to manufacture figures in a
different lighter paste and with an improved more governable glaze.
Figures were now placed in saggars on balls of clay which resulted
in the dry rough 'patch' marks usually found on Derby figures until
c.1811. Derby added to the earlier 'dry-edge' repetoire, a large
number of figures copied from Meissen, advertising them as the 'Second
Dresden', (see Nos. 10, 12, 13, 14 & 15). These early figures are
usually known as the 'pale family' after the distinctive palette of
yellow, dull turquoise, and pinkish crimson. By the later 1750's there
is a marked tendency for the glaze to become increasingly bluer and the
flower painting on the costumes to become of the distinctive 'cotton
stalk' variety. In the 1760's the figures tend to be larger and more
robust with a plethora of rococo 'S' or 'C' scroll ornament, forests
of bocage and generous gilding in emulation of their competitors,
Chelsea. Faces often have high colouring with distinctive brick-red
cheeks.

In 1770 William Duesbury bought the ailing but immensely prestigious
Chelsea porcelain factory. He ran it, in conjunction with the Derby
concern, until Chelsea's closure in 1784. By acquiring the Chelsea
works he inherited much Royal and aristocratic patronage. Chelsea's
associations with the modellers and painters of the Tournai factory
were beneficial, for, not only did the Tournai painters Duvivier and
Willems work for Duesbury, but soon the modellers Pierre Stephan and
Nicolas Gauron joined the factory (see Nos. 21, 22, 23 & 24). As
Duesbury had previously re-used the 'dry-edge' models, he now re-used
many of the earlier Chelsea models (No.18) and added new ones by
employing sculptors such as John Bacon R.A. (1740-99). Derby c.1773
appear to have benefitted from an excellent designer, perhaps an
architect, for from about this time appear a series of remarkably
ambitious well modelled figures and vases often deriving from recherché
designs and in the most advanced taste (like Nos. 27-30). Derby made
use of the rich claret and mazarine blue of Chelsea, and added to the
repetoire a striking pea-green and opaque blue colour. They were
clearly marketing these new lavish ornaments in direct competition
with Boulton's ormolu and Wedgwood's agates and basalts.

In 1771 Derby produced figures and vases in a fine white unglazed
biscuit body resembling marble like those of Sèvres. This, they
continued to use with variations of paste until the factory's closure.
They continued to copy Meissen (No.26) and Sèvres (No.27) but also
acquired plaster models probably from John Cheere (No.37) and other
dealers like Peter Donati and Sarti. Engravings were the usual source
for the figures and during the late 1770's compositions after Angelica
Kauffmann (1741-1807) enjoyed a great vogue. The Chelsea factory closed

down in 1784, when the lease came to an end. In two years Duesbury I died and the factory was taken over by his son, William Duesbury II. During his father's last years the factory gained an important client, Benjamin Lewis Vulliamy, the King's clockmaker. Vulliamy used Derby biscuit figures on his clocks, acting as a go-between for Duesbury to acquire models by the best London modellers and even retailed much of Duesbury's most ambitious porcelain. Vulliamy continued as a client with the younger Duesbury. It was through him that the modeller J.J. Spängler from Zürich came to Derby (Nos. 38-40). Spängler was the son of the proprietor of the Zürich porcelain factory who was a friend of Fussli and Lavater. During the years 1790-95, Spängler produced models of the highest standard and not only modelling them but also supervising their assembly. The other figure modeller William Coffee, working at Derby during this period appears to have been less talented (No.41).

William Duesbury II survived his father by ten years and during this period he continued the policies of his father. He took into partnership the Irish miniature painter Michael Kean. When Duesbury died, Kean married his widow and carried on the concern. Kean is given credit for introducing smear glazing to biscuit (see Nos. 39-40). He allowed the factory to decline, became financially embarrassed, and eventually sold out to his former clerk Robert Bloor, in 1811.

Figures during the 'Bloor' period were made in a dry chalk-like paste and, when decorated, were painted in a bright palette dominated by ultramarine and chrome green. For the new figures, often crude and doll-like, Bloor relied on members of the factory personnel like the Keys brothers, John Whitaker and George Cocker (No.46). Bloor became insane in 1828, but his representatives maintained the factory until its closure in 1848.

Derby from the late 1770's until the second quarter of the 19th century had the virtual monopoly of English porcelain figure production and this was largely due to the acumen of William Duesbury I. The figures, at their worst, were dull, anaemic and weakly repetitive, but at their best achieved a very high technical and artistic level. As an indication of the factory's considerable success, it is indeed true to say that most English pottery figures c.1780-1820 were imitations of figures manufactured by Derby.

Timothy Clifford.

1. AN ACTOR   c.1750-51

Standing figure of a headless man, with his left arm to his breast in a
declamatory gesture and his right arm by his side. He wears a shirt
with wide frilled cuffs, a long-sleeved tunic, a cloak pinned at his
throat, a kilt and boots.
On a shaped octagonal base ornamented with two strawberry flowers in
relief.
White glazed.

    16.4 cm.   Private Collection.

Note: It has been argued that this primitive figure on its distinctive
      base belongs to the earliest class of Derby figures like the non-
      phosphatic 'Kitty Clive', (see B.M.Watney, 1972, A Hare, A Ram,
      Two Putti and Associated Figures, Trans. E.C.C., Vol.8, Pt.2,
      pp.224-27, Pl.183d). On the present evidence, both these
      attributions appear unpersuasive. The applied strawberry flowers
      on the bases do not bear a particularly close resemblance to
      those on the earliest Derby wares, and the paste, glaze, and
      style of modelling, are difficult to parallel closely with any
      generally admissible Derby pieces. A rather closer relationship,
      at any rate, for 'Kitty Clive', is found with some of the
      'Snowman' Longton Hall figures, which may suggest, for this
      class, a Staffordshire origin.
      Actors similarly dressed appear in G.Bickham, Jr. 1739,
      Musical Entertainer, London, (e.g. head piece to p.100 'On
      Gallant Moor of Moor Hall').

2. TASTE

Girl seated wearing a linen cap, frilled blouse, laced bodice, paniered
skirt and full petticoat. She holds, with her left hand, a basket of
fruit on her lap and lifts a pear to her mouth with her right hand.
On circular mound base.
Painted in enamel colours with sparse gilding.
'Dry-edge'.

    15.4 cm.   Victoria & Albert Museum.
                                         (C.1410-1924).

See. No.3.
Note: This figure forms part of a set of the Five Senses. Four are
      reproduced in F.B.Gilhespy, 1965, Derby Porcelain, London
      Fig.14. The modeller is unrecorded but the type is attributed
      to Andrew Planché, although no signed Planché models are known.
      The type of decoration is thought to have been executed outside
      the factory, probably in William Duesbury's London decorating
      studio. (Mrs. Donald MacAlister, 1931, William Duesbury's
      London Account Book, 1751-1753, E.P.C.Monograph, London). The
      same model is represented in the Schreiber Collection (No.1,
      286) as a white glazed figure. It was re-issued a little later
      on a smaller scale as a 'pale family' figure with alternations
      in the arm positions and a lute in place of the basket of
      fruit (Victoria and Albert Museum; C.678-1925). The figure
      re-appears later with a companion seated male playing the
      flute, both with candle branches (pair with Denis Vandekar,
      1975).

2

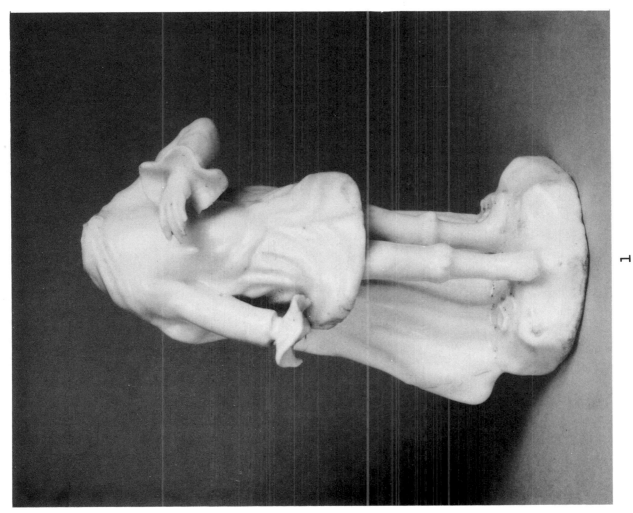

1

3. TOUCH   c.1751-56

Girl seated wearing a linen cap, ruff, frilled blouse, laced bodice
with sleeves, and a full skirt. She sits with her legs crossed,
looking over her left shoulder and faces profile to right, exposing
her right ear, and gestures with both hands towards a parrot on a
perch to her right.
On a circular mound base.
Painted in polychrome enamel colours with sparse gilding.
'Dry-edge'.

    16.4 cm.   Private Collection.

      Note: Forms part of the same set of 'Senses' as No.2.
           Another example in the Fitzwilliam Museum, Cambridge
           (F.A.Barrett & A.L. Thorpe, 1971, Derby Porcelain, Pl.8).

4. CHINESE BOYS REPRESENTING 'AIR' AND 'WATER'   c.1751-56

Boy as 'Water', wearing broad brimmed straw hat and seated frontally,
his legs crossed, holding in his hand a fishing rod (missing).
His companion, as 'Air', with shaved head wearing ruff, wide-sleeved
tunic and trousers. He looks up to the left and gestures upwards
with his outstretched right arm. Both on round bases with pierced
air holes.
Sparsely enamelled.
'Dry-edge'.

Mark: 'WATER' incised under the base of water.

    10.3 cm.   Private Collection.

      See. No.5. where figure of 'Air' is incorporated in 'Taste'.
      Note: These figures are discussed and reproduced in G.A.Godden,
           1974, 'British Porcelain, an Illustrated Guide', London
           p.204, Fig.225. They form part of a set of the 'Elements'
           represented by Chinese children. They may have been
           decorated in William Duesbury's London decorating
           establishment. For another pair, with candle sconces
           and gilt metal bocage with porcelain flowers see Barrett
           & Thorpe, 1971, op. cit., p.11, 196, Pl.13. Similar gilt
           metal bocage recurs on a white glazed Derby group of
           birds on branches in the Victoria and Albert Museum,
           (c.67-1929).

3   4

5 & 6 THE CHINESE SENSES : TOUCH AND SMELL   1751-56

'Touch' represented by a Chinaman about to chastise a boy. The bearded
Chinaman wearing a broad brimmed straw hat, tunic and cloak raises a ?
cane (missing) in his right hand to strike the hands of a small boy who
kneels to the right.   'Smell' represented by a woman standing, wearing
a small conical hat and flowing robe tied at the waist. She holds a
flower (missing) to her nose in her left hand, whilst a boy to the
left, with clean shaven head, leans over backwards to reach out for
the flower.   Both on pad bases.
White glazed with a 'dry-edge'.

    Touch, 23.9 cm.   Smell, 21.6 cm.   Private Collection.

See. No.4 for figure of small child.
Note: The two figures form part of a set of the Chinoiserie 'Senses',
      discussed in Barrett & Thorpe, 1971, op. cit., pp.196-7, Pl.6'
      'Sight', Pl.17 'Smell'. Examples are recorded glazed in the
      white ('Touch' with traces of cold colours, Victoria & Albert
      Museum, Schreiber I, 284), decorated in a pale palette with
      washes of colour ('Taste' and 'Sight', Untermyer collection
      Metropolitan Museum, New York) and with scattered flowers
      of the type associated with Duesbury's London decorating
      establishment, ('Smell', Metropol. Mus.). A mould for the
      head of the female figure in 'Sight' was found among the old
      Derby moulds at Copeland-Spode (Stoner, 1924, Chelsea Moulds -
      an Important discovery, Connoisseur, Vol. May, p.7, Pl.5).
      The style is strongly reminiscent of the Chinoiseries of
      François Boucher (1703-1770) but an engraved source has not
      been discovered. They may have something to do with the
      'Livre de six feuilles représentant les cinq Sens par
      différents amusements chinois sur les dessins de F.Boucher'
      which were announced by Gabriel Huquier in the Mercure for
      1740.

7. SEATED BOAR   c.1751-53.

    The animal seated to the right on his hind legs with his head turned
    fiercely towards the spectator.
    On an oval mound base ornamented with oak leaves and acorns.
    White glazed with 'dry-edge'.

        10.3 cm.   Private Collection.

    Note: This figure with its companion, a trotting boar, are
          represented in the Victoria & Albert Museum (white glazed,
          C.166 & A-1935) and the British Museum (sparsely enamelled,
          Gilhespy, 1965, op. cit., p.14). The seated boar is taken
          from the celebrated antique marble in the Uffizi, Florence,
          of which bronze reproductions are known, many from the
          workshop of Giovanni Francesco Susini (d.1644). The model
          was re-issued in France during the 18th century for ormolu
          andirons, with companion stag (Country Life, 1969, August 14th);
          another pair at Château Compiegne. The boar differs from the
          Antique in that the head of the Derby figure has a more
          pronounced turn, the hindquarters are stouter and acorns
          have been added to the base. Boars are listed in William
          Duesbury's London Accounts (MacAlister 1931, op. cit.)
          1752/October 27/Mr. Mitchell/1 pr of Boars 5s.0d'.

5   7   6

8. DANCING BOY ON PIERCED BASE   ?c.1755

Boy wearing broad-brimmed hat, frilled shirt tied with bows,
tattered sleeveless jacket, waistcoat, breeches and hose. He
dances with his weight on his left foot and holds his arms out
in front of him with his right arm raised.
On a pierced rococo scroll base with shaped pedestal support.
Painted in enamel colours.

Mark: Incised circle surrounding a triangle sub-divided by
      lines and dots.   (See opposite).

    18.5 cm.   Victoria & Albert Museum.
                                          (C.540-1921).

       Note: This belongs to a distinctive class of figures, often
             beribboned, and modelled with sharp noses and receding
             chins. The group appear usually on pierced rococo-scroll
             bases. They are of a light-weight paste with a tendency
             to dirty black specks in the body.
             The group consists of:
             (1)   'Cat up a tree' (Victoria & Albert Museum C.162-1929)
                   with incised mark similar to the above.

             (2)   'Seated youth with a Dog' (Fitzwilliam Museum,
                   Cambridge, 3069-1928; Barrett & Thorpe, 1971, op. cit.,
                   pp. 14-15, Pl.26).

             (3 & 4) 'Pair of Seated Youth and Girl with Dogs and a
                   Parrot' (British Museum; A. Lane, 1961, English
                   Porcelain Figures of the 18th Century, Exhibition
                   Catalogue, London, p.100, Pl.62a.)

             (5)   'Crested Pheasant' (Untermyer Collection, Y.
                   Hackenbroch, 1957, Chelsea and other English
                   Porcelain... in the Irwin Untermyer Collection.
                   Harvard, p.211, Pl.106, Fig.280).

       They have been thought to be Derby, of transitional type,
       c.1755, but this attribution is by no means satisfactory.

8   8a

9. MARS   c.1756

Mars standing wearing cuirass, thronged kilt, buskins and a plumed
helmet his right hand on his hip and his left grasping his sword hilt.
The figure on a low wide rococo scroll base is supported, to the left by
a shield and, to the right, by a bundle of flags and other martial
trophies.
Painted in enamel colours and gilt.
'Dry-edge'.

    34.5 cm.   Private Collection.

    Inscribed on filling to firing crack on base in purple enamel:
'Marsicus non Musecum' and at right angles 'F.C.?B.' (See 9a).
A firing crack in precisely the same place appears on a figure
of Mars of the same model with W.H.Newby, Knightsbridge, 1976.
That figure appeared to be inscribed 'More words more'.

    Note: The 'Mars' first appeared at Derby c.1751-3, height 6 in.,
          on a plain circular pad base (E.C.C., 1948, Commemorative
          Exhibition,London, Catalogue, Pl.67, No.306). At much the
          same time it was issued on a broad circular base with the
          addition at the back of a leafy tree-trunk supporting a
          candle sconce (sparsely enamelled, height 22.8 cm.,
          Gilhespy, 1965, op. cit., Fig.27). The distinctive baroque
          pose may have been taken from the destroyed statue of
          'Louis XIV' by Martin Desjardins (1640-94). Henry Cheere
          (1703-81) had used a similar pose for his statues of the
          'Duke of Ancaster' (1728), 'Christopher Codrington' (1732),
          and the 'Duke of Ormonde' (1737).(M.Whinney, 1964, Sculpture
          in Britain 1530-1830, London, pp.98-101, Pl.72). The pose
          was adapted by J.J.Kändler for a figure of 'Mars' at
          Meissen before 1747 (K.Berling, 1911, Königlich, Sächsische
          Porzellan Manufaktur Meissen, 1710-1910, Dresden, Pl.9,
          Fig.4). It was later used with reversed leg positions and
          the omission of a helmet at Chelsea, R.W.Blunt, ed.1924,
          (Cheyne Book of Chelsea China and Pottery, London, Pl.10,
          Fig.151). 'Mars', paired with 'Britannia', 'Minerva', or
          'Venus', remained popular at Derby until c.1800.

10. MINERVA   c.1756.

Standing figure wearing a plumed helmet, cuirass, long-sleeved tunic
and a cloak caught by a sash and hanging from her shoulder. She holds
in her right hand a spear (missing) and rests her left on a shield
moulded with the head of Medusa.
On a low wide rococo scroll base.
Painted in enamel colours.
'Dry-edge'.

    31 cm.   Private Collection.

    Note: The 'Minerva' is related to the lead garden statues of
          John Cheere (1709-87) M.Whinney, 1964, op. cit., Pl.107b).

10

9

9a

11. GIRL DANCING HOLDING A POSEY   c.1758

Girl wears small circular hat, blouse with frills at the neck and
sleeves, laced bodice, jacket and skirt. She looks half right and
holds a posey in her left hand and lifts her skirt in her right.
On a pad base ornamented with flowers.
Painted in enamel colours.
'Pale family'.
Mark: Three patches and a small hole.

     15.5 cm.   Private Collection.

          Note: For the pose the modeller referred to the 'dry-edge'
                'Dancing Shepherdess' (Victoria & Albert Museum,
                C.115-1938; enamelled, Barrett & Thorpe, 1971, op. cit.,
                Pl.4).
                This figure was issued at Derby with a companion
                'Scotsman playing the bagpipes' (E.C.C., 1948, op. cit.,
                (Exhib. Cat.) No.307).
                The girl later appears on a scroll base (photograph,
                Ceramic Department, Victoria & Albert Museum).

12. BOY PLAYING PIPE   c.1760

Small boy wearing broad-brimmed hat, shirt, waistcoat, jacket,
breeches and bare feet. The figure, with his right foot forward,
stands playing a pipe with both hands. A large dog is seated
behind him on the pad base.
Painted in enamel colours.
Mark: Three patches and a small hole.

     17 cm.   Private Collection.

          Note: The figure is copied faithfully from one made at
                Meissen, by J.J. Kändler, c.1760, (R.Rückert,1966,
                Meissener Porzellan 1710-1810, Munich, No.922, Pl.225).

12   11

13. BOY HOLDING A COCKEREL. c.1758   Colour Plate No. Frontispiece.

Boy standing looking over his right shoulder holding a cockerel in his arms. The figure wears a cocked hat, shirt with frilled cuffs, jacket and striped trousers. He stands on a pad base with flowery tree stump support.
Painted in enamel colours.

     15.3 cm.   Victoria & Albert Museum.
                                          (C.673-1925).

Note: Taken from a Meissen figure for which the original wax survives (M.Sauerlandt, 1925, Eine Wachsfigur nach Meissener Modell, Der Kunstwanderer, VII, pp.430-431, Figs.1-3). The figure was made a little later at Derby on a more elaborate base (see No.13) and also copied in Italy at Doccia (Victoria & Albert Museum, C.470-1921; Lane, 1954, Italian Porcelain, London, Col.Pl.C.).
The companion figure of a 'Woman holding a Hen' is in the Victoria and Albert Museum (C.674-1925).

14. BOY HOLDING A COCKEREL c.1763-65

Similar model to No.13 but on an elaborate rococo scroll base with flowering bocage support.
Painted in enamel colours and gilded.

     20.4 cm.   Victoria & Albert Museum.
                                          (C.1002-1917).

Note: A larger model of No.13. The richer style of decoration is an early reflection of Derby's competition with the contemporary Chelsea 'Gold Anchor' figures.

15 WELCH TAILOR AND WIFE   c.1763-65
&
16 Tailor wearing tricorn hat, coat and breeches mounted on a billy goat holding on to its left horn. Strapped to his back is a basket containing two kids. The Tailor's wife wears a straw hat, shawl, bodice, and full skirt. She is mounted on a nanny goat and holds on to its left horn while clasping a child, with her right arm, to her bosom. A basket containing two further children is strapped to her back. Both on mound bases with applied leaves and flowers.

   Tailor 25.3 cm; Wife, 26 cm.   Private Collection.

Note: This pair of satirical figures is copied from those modelled at Meissen in 1740 by Kändler (Tailor) and Eberlein (Wife) (Rückhert, 1966, op. cit., No.885, 978, p.216). According to legend they were made originally in mockery of von Brühl's tailor who had asked to be present at a court banquet but instead he was represented, modelled as a table decoration. The Derby title 'Welch Tailor' does not denote the tailor's nationality but appears to be a corruption based upon a mistranslation of the Meissen title : Schneider, welcher auf einem Ziegenbock reutet (Tailor who rides on a goat...).
This pair in several sizes with various attributes, and pedestal styles remained popular at the factory until its closure.

13   (16, 15)   14

17. MARS   c.1765-68

Similar model to No. 9, but in a later palette and on a smaller mound with applied rococo scrolls.
Painted in enamel colours.

    36 cm.   Victoria & Albert Museum.
                                                    (28-1874).

        Note: A companion 'Britannia' is also in the Victoria & Albert
              Museum (Schreiber 1, 303).

18. MARS CANDLESTICK   c.1765-68

Similar model to No.17, but on a wide base silhouetted at the bottom with 'S' and 'C' scrolls and with a flowering tree at the centre back supporting a candle sconce.
Painted in enamel colours.

    25.2 cm.   Victoria & Albert Museum.
                                                    (C.2595-1910).

        See. Notes to Nos. 9 and 17.
        Note: A severe octagonal shield has now replaced the former
              asymetrical rococo example.

19. VASE WITH SATYR HANDLES c.1775

Vase on flared foot, pear-shaped body with elongated neck. The handles formed by horned satyr heads, their horns twisting back and slotting inside a ring on the neck of the vase. The body ornamented with applied grapes and vine leaves.
Painted in enamel colours.

    23 cm.   Private Collection.

        Note: In February 1770 Duesbury bought the Chelsea factory and
              immediately started to use the existing Chelsea moulds.
              This vase is taken from a model commonly met with during
              the Gold Anchor period. (Pair, Victoria & Albert Museum,
              C.78 & 79-1948). It has been shown previously that, the
              design is taken from an etching by R.Vien after Joseph
              Marie Vien (1716-1809), a source also copied by Wedgwood
              and Bentley ('Agate' vase, Victoria & Albert Museum,
              2387-1901).

20   BUCK AND DOE   c.1775-80
&   Buck with antlers (replaced) seated to the right looking over his
21. right shoulder towards the spectator. Doe seated to the left facing
     quarter left. Both on shaped mound base.
     Painted in enamel colours.

     Buck, 15.8 cm.   Doe, 12.8 cm.   Private Collection.

        See. No.220, where it appears transfer printed on a jug.
        Note: This model was made at Derby from c.1753 (?London decorated,
              Gilhespy, 1965, op. cit., Pl.5). They were adapted from a
              pair modelled at Meissen by Kändler (Carl Albiker, 1935,
              Die Meissner Porzellantiere im 18 Jahrhundert, Berlin,
              p.123, Pl.42, Fig.182). A pair, in an early palette, are
              at Derby Museum (Barrett & Thorpe, 1971, op. cit., p.198,
              Pl.21). They seem to have been popular especially locally
              as a 'Stag at Lodge' is the blazon of the town of Derby.
              An example of the doe in enamel colours with bocage
              c.1780-90 was with Mrs. Donovan, Kensington, 1975, and
              a biscuit example of the stag c.1790-1800, with sockets
              for metal antlers (missing) was in a Kentish private
              collection.

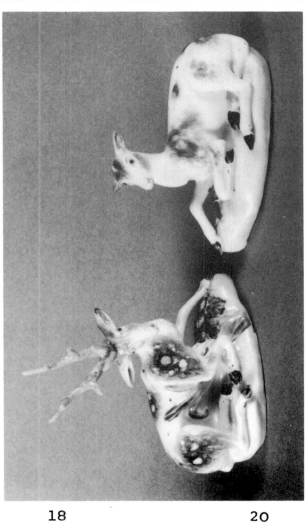

17   19   18   20

22. AIR   c.1773

A girl running forward wearing a blouse, loosely laced bodice, flowing
skirt and thonged sandals. She looks up to the right towards a dove
perched on her outstretched left hand and holds a hunting horn in her
right hand.
On a cloud-shaped base.
Painted in enamel colours and gilt.

    22.7 cm.   Private Collection.

      See. No.23.
      Note: 'Air forms part of a set of the 'Four Elements' (Gilhespy,
           1965, op. cit., Fig.143) which are described in the undated
           factory price list, J.Haslem, 1876, Old Derby China Factory,
           London, as 'No.3 The Elements, Stephan'. The numbers in the
           price list correspond to the incised numerals under the
           bases of the figures. These appear to have been used first
           some time in or after 1773 when William Wood, the clerk from
           Derby, took over the Covent Garden warehouse. This figure is
           dated 1773 on the basis of the strong similarity of palette
           to a group of 'Arithmetic' in the Victoria and Albert Museum
           (Sch.1, 345) in which one of the putti holds a ledger dated
           'Apr.6 1773'. It bears no incised numerals under the base.
           The set originated at Tournai in the 1760's where the figures,
           somewhat plumper, are met with on tall rockwork bases beside
           perfume burners (Brussels, Musée Cinquantenaire). 'Air'
           appears on an unsigned sheet of pen studies attributed to
           Lecreux (Belgium, private collection).
           By 1773 there were two modellers working for Duesbury who
           had been at Tournai, Pierre Stephan and Nicolas Gauron. They
           both earned the same high salary of 8s. 9d. a day. On the
           basis of Gauron's documented work at Tournai (the Oultremont
           'Apotheosis'), it is likely that 'Air' is by Stephan.

23. AIR   c.1775-80.

Similar model to No.22, but smaller and on a straight sided rectangular
base with canted corners, moulded with key fret.
Biscuit.

Mark: Incised 'No.3'.

    18.1 cm.   Private Collection.

      See. Note to No.22.
           The set enamelled on this base (Barrett & Thorpe, 1971, op.
           cit., Pl.25). A similar base with key fret is found on the
           'bust of an unidentified woman' in the British Museum
           (L.II.32) which bears the incised name 'Stephan'.
      Note: Biscuit porcelain was first advertised at Derby in 1771,
           following the fashion set by Sèvres and Tournai. It was
           always more expensive than that enamelled and gilt; for
           example, this set, according to the factory lists (Haslem,
           1876, op. cit.,) in the third size, cost £1.16s. enamelled
           and £2.2s. in biscuit.

22   23

24. FIRE   c.1775.

Two putti on a tall rockwork base with a central tree support. A naked
boy putto to the left wearing a broad-brimmed hat, works the treadle
of a grindstone with his right foot and holds, with both hands, an
arrow (missing) against the stone for sharpening. His girl companion,
a fur around her midrift, is seated to the right. She raises her right
hand and holds in her left, a flaming torch.
Biscuit.

Mark: Incised 'No.48'.

    21.9 cm.   Private Collection.

      Note: The group forms part of the set of the 'Four Elements' in
            groups of two figures each (C.M.Scott & G.R.Scott, Jr. 1961.
            <u>Antique Porcelain Digest</u>, Newport, Pl.169, Fig.619).
            A set was offered for auction by Mr.Christie, February 9th,
            1773, Lot 5. They were conceived originally to be seen from
            all sides for 'dressing desserts' down the centres of
            dining tables or on buffets, often standing on looking-glass
            plateaux.

            'Fire' was originally modelled with variations at Tournai in
            the 1760's. The style is reminiscent of Nicholas Gauron's
            documented group of 'The Apotheosis of Charles d'Oultremont,
            Prince Bishop of Liège' in Tournai biscuit (1764, Belgium,
            Château Warfusée).
            It is likely to be this modeller, or a relative of the same
            name, who worked for Duesbury, C.1770-73.

25. PASTORAL GROUP WITH SHEPHERD PLAYING HIS PIPE TO A SLEEPING
    SHEPHERDESS.   c.1780.

A shepherd in contemporary costume, stands to the right playing his
pipe to a shepherdess left. The shepherdess lies asleep, her head
resting on her left hand, a wreath in her right. A dog walking at the
shepherd's side, a sheep sitting by hers. The figures supported by a
rocky mound on which stands a classical vase and cover. To the left of
the vase's pedestal, water gushes from the mouth of a dolphin and falls
into two shell-shaped basins.
Painted in enamel colours and gilt.

Mark: Incised 'No.12'.

    32.6 cm.   Private Collection

      Note: Described as 'No 12 Pastoral Group' in the factory price
            lists (Haslem, 1876, <u>op. cit</u>.,) and in the mould lists
            (W.Bemrose, 1898, <u>Bow Chelsea and Derby Porcelain</u>, London)
            as 'Fountain Group'.
            An example was offered by Mr. Christie, February 9th
            1773, lot 19.
            The type ultimately derives from a painting by François
            Boucher (1703-70) and may have been modelled by Pierre
            Stephan.

24   25

26. VENUS   c.1773-75

The goddess wearing loose flowing robe belted at the waist standing
with her weight on her left foot and resting her right foot on a
dolphin. She holds an apple in her hand and is restraining Cupid,
who tugs at her skirt to the right.
On rocky base ornamented with seaweed, a cowrie and other shells
Painted in enamel colours and gilt.

Marks: None.

    27.3 cm.   Private Collection.

        Note: Another example of this rare figure is in the British
              Museum (W.King, 1925, English Porcelain Figures of the
              18th Century, London, Fig.51).

27. DANCING GROUP   c.1775

Boy to right wearing tricorn hat, shirt, waistcoat, jacket, breeches
and hose, walks forward and puts his arms around the waist of his
companion. Girl to left wearing blouse, bodice, skirt and pinafore
places her left arm on her partner's shoulder and clasps his left
hand.
On rococo scroll base with tree stump support.
Painted in enamel colours and gilt.

Mark: Incised 'No.16' and 'US'.

    18.5 cm.   Private Collection.

        Note: This group is copied from a Meissen model by J.J.Kändler
              of 1770 (W.Doenges, 1921, Meissner Porzellan, Dresden,
              p.105, Fig.49).
              Another example, without the incised marks, in the Victoria
              & Albert Museum (Herbert Allen Collection, Cat. No 96,
              Pl.25).
              The group remained popular up to the closure of the factory.

26   27

28. DRAPED VASES (Pair)   c.1778-80

Pair of Vases, their bodies hung with festoons of drapery in reliefs,
the necks contracted upwards and are decorated with spiral fluting.
Below the beaded rims lions masks in relief and gilt foliage festoons.
On spreading feet resting on octagonal plinths which stand on shaped
pedestals ornamented in relief with satyr masks terminating on hoof
feet, and foliage festoons.
Painted in enamel colours and gilt.

Mark: Gold Anchors on the plinths. 'No.38' incised.

    32.5 cm.   Private Collection.

        Note: These vases first appear described in Christie's sale of
9 February 1773 and again in the undated Trade Catalogue
(?1772-74; reprinted Bemrose. 1898, op. cit., pp. 52-65).
They are not listed in either Haslem's 1876, op. cit.,
list of figures, groups and vases or in 'Bemrose's list
of models and moulds. The model is taken from Sèvres, the
vase flacon à mouchoir of c.1765-6 (A.Troude, 1897, Choix
de Modeles de...Sèvres, Paris, Pl.95; S.Eriksen, 1974,
Early Neo-Classicism in France, London, p.372, Pl.279).
A Derby vase following faithfully the Sèvres form is in
a private collection, Ampthill. This pair have additions
not found in the French prototypes like the covers, lion
masks and foliage festoons at the necks and elaborate
pedestals. They are discussed : M.C.F.Mortimer, 1972,
The Antique Taste: The Neo-Classical Vases of Derby in
the 1774 Catalogue, The Antique Collector, August,
pp.205-210, Fig.4.

29. FOUNTAIN VASE   c.1773-74

Urn shaped two handled vase; the handles formed as putti riding
dolphins, the sides with putti holding swags, the gadrooned rim with
satyr masks, the cover with cupids fighting, the lower part with
infant mermen, the whole standing on a plinth supported by four
sphinxes.
Painted in enamel colours and gilt.

Mark: Gold Anchor on the plinth. Incised 'No.19'.

    40.7 cm.   Private Collection

        Note: First described in Christie's sale of 9 and 10 February
1773 where one sold for £17.17s. and again in the undated
Trade Catalogue (Bemrose, 1898, op. cit., pp.52-65). It
remained popular, others were described in the sale of
5 May 1778 and another in Lygo's letter to Duesbury of
13 March 1790. Presented in Bemrose's list of moulds as
'No.19 Large Fountain Vase'. Bemrose attributed the model
to J.C.F.Rossi, but in 1773 he would have been only eleven
years old. It has not been demonstrated before that it is
faithfully copied from an unsigned etching by Jacques
Saly (1717-1776); an impression in Victoria and Albert
Museum; 29778.7).
      Lit. M.C.F.Mortimer, 1972, op. cit., p.208, n.2. Fig.2.

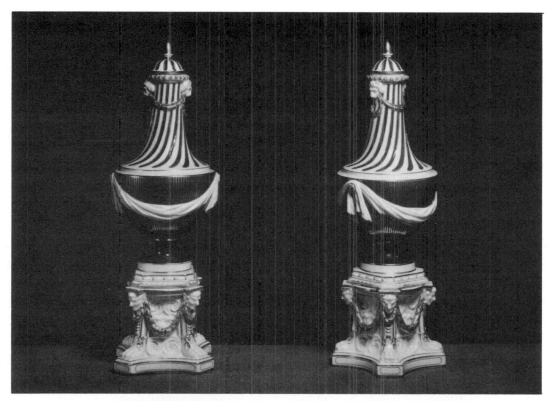

28

29

30. ANTIQUE VASES WITH SCROLL HANDLES (Pair)   c.1778-80.   Colour Plate P.5

Oviform vases on spreading feet and square plinths. The shoulders
formed of incurving acanthus which meets the neck at a band of
moulded studs. Covers with global knops.
Painted in 'Smith's blue', enamel colours and gilt, the classical
subjects en grisaille.

Mark: 'No.68' incised.

   25.4 cm.   Victoria & Albert Museum.
                                                 (C.240, C.241-192).

   Note: These are rare examples of Derby's direct borrowing
        from the Antique. The grisaille decoration is taken
        from frescoes discovered at Pompeii and Herculaneum
        (Le Antichità di Ercolano Esposte, I, Naples 1757
        part 2). In this instance Duesbury almost certainly
        had the plates copied from T. Martyn and J. Lettice,
        1773, The Antiquities of Herculaneum, London, for his
        name appears among the subscribers with his competitors
        Matthew Bolton and Josiah Wedgwood.
        A pair that may have resembled these, was offered by
        Christie and Ansell in a sale of Chelsea porcelain,
        May 5th, 1778, 'One pair Etruscan vases enamel'd with
        Herculean (sic) figures' (J.E. Nightingale, 1881,
        Contributions towards the History of English Porcelain
        Salisbury, p.53).

30

31-35. GARNITURE OF FIVE VASES   c.1782

The central vase (31) with compressed loop handles standing on
flaring feet with square plinth. The lower zone of the body
moulded with ogee fluting which is repeated on the cover. The
flanking vases (32 and 33) with imbricated loop handles standing
on flaring vertically fluted feet, with vertical mouldings on the
lower zone of the body repeated on the waisted necks, matching
covers (one missing). Pair of Ewers (34 and 35) of ovoid form
standing on flaring vertically fluted feet, with stiff leaf
ornament on the lower zone of the bodies, shell-shaped lips,
high loop handles terminating in satyr masks.
Painted in enamel colours and gilt.

Marks: Central vase, incised 'No.72'; side vases, incised 'No.97',
        ewers, incised 'No.98'.
        All with Gold Anchors on the plinths.

Central vase, 25.5 cm.
Side vases, without covers, 12.7 cm.
Ewers, 23.6 cm.   Private Collection.

Note: This is a very rare complete example of a Derby
      garniture de cheminée. It can be dated with precision
      for it was offered by Christie and Ansell in a sale of
      Derby and Chelsea Porcelain, 7 May 1782 and the four
      following days (Nightingale, 1881, op. cit., p.71):
      'A set of 5 superbly elegant vauses enamel'd in
      compartments with figures and landscapes, gold stripes
      richly ornamented with fine blue and gold, the central
      vause is enamel'd with a figure of 'Maria', the 2 side
      pieces with figures of 'Damon and Delia', 'Paris and
      Oenone' and the 2 end pieces with a shepherd and lamb
      and shepherdess with a bird cage £2. 12s.' The figure
      of 'Maria', illustrating Sterne's Sentimental Journey,
      is after a composition by Angelica Kauffmann (1741-1807),
      engraved in red stipple by W.W. Ryland and published
      April 12, 1779, after a Kauffmann composition engraved
      by Francesco Bartolozzi, 1780, illustrating a poem by
      George, Lord Lyttleton in Vol. II of Dodsley's
      Collection of Poems by Several Hands.
      The type of figure painting at Derby is usually
      attributed to Richard Askew and the landscapes to
      Zachariah Boreman, but on insufficient evidence.

34, 32, 31, 33, 35

36. MARS   c.1780-85

   Similar pose to Nos. 9, 17 and 18, but on a simple square plinth.
   Biscuit.

   Mark: Incised 'No.114'.

      16 cm.   Private Collection.

         Note: About 1780 Derby re-issued several of the early 'dry-
               edge' figures such as the 'Mars', 'Apollo' and 'Venus',
               and the very large 'Jove' and 'Juno' of c.1760. They
               were reduced to heights varying from 15.3 cm. to 20.4
               cm., placed on simple square plinths and usually marketed
               in biscuit. In this way the démodé rococo models were
               shrewdly transformed to become acceptable to neo-classical
               tastes.

37. MILTON   c.1780-85

   Standing figure of Milton in 'Van Dyck' costume. He draws his cloak
   about him with his right hand, his left elbow resting on a pile of
   books which stand on a pedestal. The pedestal decorated in bas-relief
   with the expulsion of Adam and Eve (Paradise Lost).
   Biscuit.

   Mark: Incised 'No.297'.

      25.4 cm.   Private Collection.

         Note: This figure with its companion 'Shakespeare' were originally
               issued during the 'dry-edge' period. They continued in
               production at Derby up to the closure of the old works.
               Later they were re-issued in Parian from the Derby moulds
               by Copeland.
               The original model in plaster was almost certainly
               purchased from the sculptor, John Cheere (1709-87) of
               Hyde Park Corner.
               Josiah Wedgwood bought plasters from the same source rather
               later and an example of the Milton in bronzed plaster, on
               loan to the City Art Gallery, York, is signed 'J.Cheere,
               fecit/1749'.
               For a more detailed discussion see T.Friedman & T.Clifford,
               1974, 'The Men at Hyde Park Corner, Sculpture by John
               Cheere, 1709-1787', Temple Newsam, Leeds and Marble Hill,
               Exhibition Catalogue, Twickenham, Nos.54, 55, Pl.11 & 13.

36   37

38. PIPING SHEPHERD   c.1791-95

Shepherd wearing loose shirt, short jacket, breeches and hose,
stands cross-legged leaning against a tree stump.He plays the
flute resting with his left elbow on the stump. A sheep lies at
his feet.
Biscuit.

Mark: Incised 'No.369' and star (*).

   26.7 cm.   Private Collection.

          Note: The model is a clothed adaptation of a celebrated
               antique 'The Piping Faun' (closest to Vatican example,
               reproduced in S.Reinach, 1903, Répétoire de la
               Sculpture Grecque et Romaine, Paris, Tome II, Vol.I,
               p.135, Fig.5). The style of modelling is completely
               consistent with the seated boy piper on the 'Russian
               Shepherd Group' (Lane, 1961, op. cit., p.110, Pl.75).
               This model appears to be referred to in a letter from
               Joseph Lygo to Duesbury, 10 January 1791.
               Examples of the above figure with his companion
               'Shepherdess' are in the British Museum (1936. 7-15.
               17, 18).
        Exh. E.C.C., 1977, English Ceramics 1580-1830. Exhibition
               Catalogue No.151.

39. THE PROPOSAL   c.1795

Young man wearing his hair tied en queue, cravat, double-breasted
frock coat, breeches and hose. He stands his right foot forward,
his left arm clasped to his breast, gazing upwards at his companion.
40. Young woman, her hair elaborately arranged, wearing laced bodice,
scarf, jacket, petticoat and overskirt, hanging in a short train
at the back.
Biscuit.

Marks: Both incised 'No.372', cursive 'D' crossed batons and crown
       and X *.

   Man, 17.5 cm. Woman, 18.8 cm.   Private Collection.

          Note: This rare pair of figures are probably by J.J.Spängler.
               The style is consistent with such documented works as
               'Pair of Figures with a Dead Bird' (Lane, 1961, op. cit.,
               Pl.74b) and 'Palemon and Lavinia' (W.M.Binns, 1906,
               The First Century of English Porcelain, London, facing
               p.132).

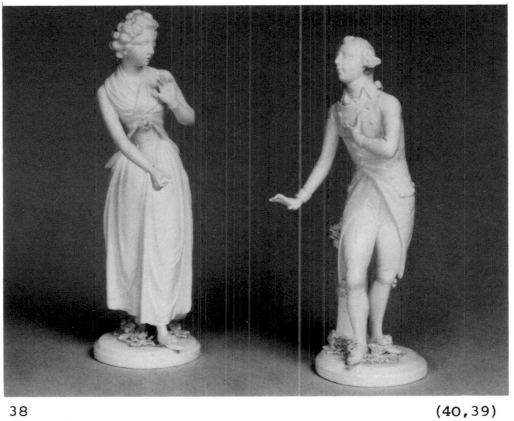

41. ADMIRAL HOWE.   c.1795

Standing, wearing a wig, cocked hat, naval uniform with ribbon and star of the Bath, his left arm on his hip, his right resting on the muzzle of a cannon. On a rocky base, with an anchor, shells, and seaweed.
Biscuit, pipe clay or possibly unglazed creamware.

Mark: Incised 'Stephan' on the base.

    27.3 cm.   Victoria & Albert Museum.
                                          (C.134-1937).

Note: The admiral represented is not Rodney, as is popularly
       supposed, but Howe. The likeness is taken from Mather
       Brown's portrait of 'Admiral Howe on the deck of the
       Queen Charlotte at the battle of the Glorious First of
       June' 1794. (National Maritime Museum, Greenwich).
       After Stephan left Derby c.1773/4 he continued to supply
       models freelance.
       This figure was not made as an original maquette for a
       Derby figure but was made in a mould, of which five
       others are recorded, three in pale buff clay and two
       in black basalts.
       For figures of 'Rodney' and 'Hood' by Stephan, conceived
       en suite see R.T.H.Halsey, 1916, Ceramic Americana of
       the 18th Century, Part IV, Art in America, pp. 55-6,
       Figs. 10 & 11. The Admirals are conceivably by Stephan's
       son who modelled for Wirksworth and later for Chamberlain's
       Worcester.

42. SETTER LYING DOWN   c.1798-1810

The dog lying curled up facing the spectator, its legs out in
front, resting its throat on its left paw. On a straight-sided
rectangular base.
Biscuit, possibly unglazed creamware.

Mark: Incised 'W.Coffee' on the upper surface. (See 42a).

Base L. 9.3 cm. W. 5.3 cm.   Private Collection.

> Note: To judge from the paste this animal, signed by William
> Coffee (working 1791-died 1846), is not from the main
> Derby factory. The model was certainly issued in
> porcelain by Rockingham (D.G.G.Rice, 1965, Rockingham
> Ornamental Porcelain, London, Pl.115b.). Coffee
> modelled at Derby c.1793-96 but left to work at Pinxton
> and Church Gresley, returning to set up on his own
> account in Derby c.1798. He continued in the modelling
> business in Derby until certainly 1810. Judging from
> his signed models, he had little talent at human figure
> modelling but was more competent with animals. Haslem,
> 1786, op. cit., pp.156-7 related that the handsome
> Shepherd No.396 (Lane, 1961, op. cit., p.110, Pl.76)
> was by Coffee, but this was clearly a misunderstanding.
> The Shepherd, on the basis of style, was Spängler's,
> although the sheep, and perhaps the dog, may have been
> additions by Coffee.

43. OVAL BROOCH ENCRUSTED WITH FLOWERS   c.1830-50

Biscuit, mounted in gold.

Mark: Incised 'S.S/DERBY' on the back.

L. 4.3 cm.   W. 2.9 cm.   Victoria & Albert Museum.
                                          (M.16-1973).

> Note: The brooch is probably the work of Susana Stephan
> (b. Madeley c.1811 - working 1861). Flower modelling
> was the usual reserve of women and children. She was
> the wife of Peter Stephan (b. Stoke c.1796 - working at
> Derby 1870), who was the son of John Charles Stephan
> (working at Wirksworth 1773, supplied models to
> Chamberlain's Worcester 1793) and grandson of Pierre
> Stephan (fl. 1769-1819; see No.41). She had a daughter
> Hannah, born at Broseley c.1842, a son George born
> about 1844, and another son Edward born 1847, both
> 'apprentice china potters' (G.A. Godden, 1970, Coalport
> and Coalbrookdale Porcelains, London, pp.127-8; Haslem,
> 1876, op. cit., p.155).
> Bemrose 1898, op.cit., recorded (p.120) that Derby in
> the 18th and early 19th century was an important centre
> of the jewellery trade. This simple gold mount might
> have been supplied by a firm like Severne & Co who
> apparently gave employment to eighty or ninety hands,
> beside outworkers.

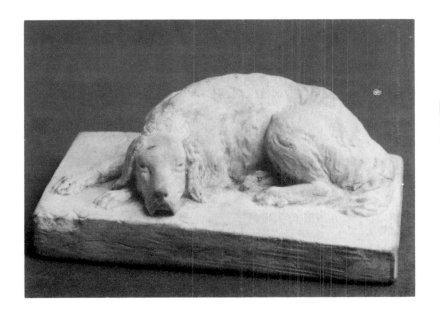

42   43   42a

44. THE PEEP SHOW   c.1815

A small girl to the left bends forward to peep into a magic lantern,
which consists of a rectangular box supported on a wooden tressle.
The lantern's proprietor, a small boy, leans up against it to the
right, operating the machine. On irregular shaped mound base.
Painted in enamel colours.
Mark: Incised 'No.94' and 'D' surmounted by Crown, printed in red.
    12.7 cm.   Private Collection.

        Note: This group is more usually found with a third child who
              stands behind the small girl. It is after a model by Falconet
              'La Lanterne Magique' made for Sèvres 1760 (Troude, 1874,
              op. cit., Pl.24) from a composition La Foire de Campagne
              by François Boucher engraved by Cochin fils. The Sèvres
              model was copied at Derby by 1778 (Fitzwilliam Museum,
              Cambridge; C.1-1965). The palette of No.44 shows that it
              dates from the Bloor period and the inscriptions from in
              or after 1815. The inscriptions read: 'ONLY one/Ha'penny...
              THIS WAY ... Gome sic see only / one / Ha'penny and JOHN
              ROBINS / the only / ORIGINAL SHOW / MAN of the GREAT /
              BATTLE / between / DUKE of WELLINGTON and / NAPOLEON
              Bonaparte on / the field at Waterloo'.

45. FURY GROUP, THE BROKEN CHAIR   c.1820-48

Man lying on a broken chair to the right, above him to the left
stands a furious woman, who pulls at his wig.
On mound base with bocage support.
Painted in enamel colours and gilt.
Mark: 'No.89' in fired ink.
    14.3 cm.   Victoria & Albert Museum.
                                        (3016-1901).

        Note: Originally issued at Derby as No.83 (not 89 as marked)
              and in production in the 1770's.
              The subject is taken from K.G.Lück's 'Disharmony' made
              at Frankenthal, c.1765-70 (Schlossmuseum, Berlin; G.W.Ware,
              1961, German and Austrian Porcelain, Frankfurt-am-Main,
              Fig.126). This is a good example of high quality Bloor
              period decoration.

46. SEATED TURK   c.1830

Moustached Turk, wearing a turban, fur trimmed kaftan, tunic and
striped pantaloons. He sits cross-legged on a tasselled cushion
smoking a hooka. On tall base moulded with satyr masks and leafy
scroll feet.
Painted in enamel colours and gilt.
Mark: 'BLOOR DERBY' surmounted by a Crown in red enamel.
    14 cm.   Private Collection.

        Note: The modeller for this figure is unrecorded but may have
              been George Cocker (1794-1868) who worked at Derby and
              also at Coalport and Worcester. In 1853 Cocker left his
              own small factory situated in Friar Gate Derby, and
              joined Minton at Stoke-on-Trent.
              For the base, the Derby factory adapted an old Chelsea-
              Derby mould for vase plinth (F.S.Mackenna, 1952, Chelsea
              Porcelain, the Gold Anchor Wares, Leigh-on-Sea, Pl.39,
              Fig.74).

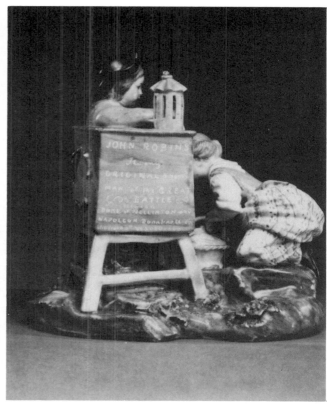

44   45   44a   46

N O T E S

- 44 -

PRE-1756 DERBY ORNAMENTAL AND DOMESTIC WARES

The large Derby centre-pieces of the 'patch-mark' periods, about
1756 to about 1770, are, for the most part, formed as one or more
tiers of scallop shells heavily encrusted with smaller sea shells,
coral and weed. The effect is as if a local grotto had provided
not only the romantic inspiration, but also some actual objects
from which direct castings were taken. The same, somewhat haphazard,
festooned effect can be seen in a rare group of wares which appear
to be their immediate precursors and, as such, some of the first
Derby porcelain.[1] In the earlier group, the shells are generally
deeper and rarely scallop-shaped, forming not only centre-pieces
but also salts and sauceboats. The coral branches cut more boldly
to form arched handles or to encircle a lumpy base. A crayfish,
seeming camouflaged by the marine concretions, may spread its
spidery claws from under arched coral halfway along the deeply
ribbed shell sides of a sauce boat. These pieces lack the precision
of Sprimont's early Chelsea, 1745 to 1750, and they show a certain
clumsiness not observable in designs which were closely related to
silver.

Even the strawberry-moulded cream jugs, (one in the British Museum,
inscribed 'D', a second, 'Derby' at Colonial Williamsburg, and a
third in the Victoria and Albert Museum, 'D 1750') lack the elegance
and style of the 'triangle period' of Chelsea versions, and they
exhibit a certain hesitancy and provincialism when compared side
by side. The Derby strawberry jugs have a distinctive spray of
flowers branching out, for example, to the right and left of a
rudimentary crabstock handle. The flowers recur on the base of
probably the least attractive early Derby figure, the non-phosphatic
'Kitty Clive', and occasionally on other Derby 'dry-edge' figures,
for example that of a pug scratching its ear.

In the early 1750's the Derby factory seems to have had difficulty
in obtaining the services of satisfactory enamellers. The 'dry-
edge' figures were apparently either London decorated or else
mostly left in the white. The earliest domestic wares, however,
sometimes have crude flower sprays which are only very occasionally
found on the early figures.

The early Derby glassy paste, which is somewhat akin to the 'triangle
period' Chelsea, was doubtless not an easy one to work, but nonethe-
less their figure modeller did wonders with it. In comparison, the
earliest Derby domestic wares lag far behind and they were obviously
not considered suitable for sending to London for decoration and for
sale, but were daubed locally with semi-matt pigments. Only the
highly rococo wall-brackets and possibly small cabbage tureens come
anywhere near the quality of the figures; these were, fortunately,
left in the white.

Bernard M. Watney, F.S.A.

[1] B.M.Watney, 1967, Pre-1756 Derby Domestic Wares, Contemporary
with 'Dry-Edge Figures', The Burlington, 109, No.766, January.

47.   TEAPOT AND COVER   c.1756

Four lobed, globular shape with flat scroll handle and fluted
S-shaped spout with leaf moulding at tip, lobed, domed cover with
spinning top knop.
Painted in purple, orange, yellow, green, blue and black enamels,
with some gilding. On one side a chinese scene, with a man standing
and a woman seated beside a table laid with fruit and flowers,
and on the other side, a man reaching towards a flying insect,
surrounded by vases and other objects. The moulding on the spout
picked out in purple, the cover painted with similar motifs and
around the rim a gilt with red loop and dot design.

    14 cm.   Castle Museum, Norwich
                                        (Bulwer Collection 677).

    See. No.48 for similar teapot.

48.   TEAPOT   dated 1756

Shape and decoration similar to No.47.

Mark: '1756' incised on the base.

    10.2 cm. (without cover)   Cecil Higgins Art Gallery,
                                        Bedford. (C.364).

    Lit. F. Hurlbutt, 1926, Chelsea, Bow and Derby Porcelain,
          London, Pl.16.
          J.L. Dixon, 1952, English Porcelain of the 18th Century,
          London, Pl.32a.

49.   TEAPOT AND COVER   c.1756

Four lobed globular shape, with flat scroll handle and fluted
S-shaped spout with leaf moulding at tip, a lobed domed cover
with spinning top knop.
Painted in green, yellow, puce and brown enamels, with a shrike,
vulture and bullfinch perching on the branches of a tree.

    14 cm.   Derby Museum & Art Gallery
                                        (927-1-59).

    Lit. Barrett & Thorpe, 1971, op. cit., Pl.36.

47   48   49

50. TEAPOT AND COVER   c.1756-58

Globular fluted shape with flat scroll handle, S-shaped spout with
leaf moulding at tip, a low domed cover with acorn knop.
Painted on the body and cover in purple, puce, orange, yellow and
green enamels, with sprays and sprigs of flowers, the leaf motifs
at the junction of the spout and the handle to the body in puce
and the rim of the cover and spout outlined in brown enamel.

    13.5 cm.   Castle Museum, Norwich.
                                              (Bulwer Collection 284).

Lit. Barrett & Thorpe, 1971, op. cit., p.16, Pl.35.

51. TEAPOT AND COVER   c.1756-58

Shaped as No.50 with applied leaves on the cover surmounted by a
flower knop.
Painted in enamel colours with a spray of flowers on either side
in the manner of the 'cotton-stalk' painter and three small sprays
on the cover.

    12.5 cm.   National Museum of Wales.
                                         (D.W.2244).

52. TEAPOT AND COVER   c.1765-68

Globular shape with loop handle, slightly domed cover and conical
finial.
Painted in enamel colours with an elaborate bouquet of flowers,
the rim of the pot, cover and spout outlined in brown.

    14.5 cm.   Private Collection.

53. SMALL TEAPOT AND COVER   c.1770

Globular shape with loop handle, S-shaped spout and low domed
cover with onion knop.
Painted in purple, red, orange, yellow, blue, green and brown
enamels, with sprays and sprigs of flowers, brown enamel dashes
on the knop and the rim of the pot cover and spout outlined in
brown.

    8.5 cm.   Castle Museum, Norwich.
                                         (Bulwer Collection 63).

53

51

52

50

54. COFFEE POT AND COVER   c.1758-60

Baluster shape, on a pedestal foot, domed cover with unglazed flange and acorn shaped finial, leaf moulding on the spout and double scroll handle.
Painted in enamel colours with a spray of flowers and insects with a chain loop border around the pot and cover, the rim of the spout outlined in brown.

Mark: Three patches on base.

22.5 cm.   Private Collection.

See. No.136 for similar shape in blue and white.

55. COFFEE POT AND COVER   c.1758-60

Shaped as No.54.
Painted in enamel colours with a spray of flowers on either side, in the manner of the 'cotton-stalk' painter, the rim of the cover and spout outlined in brown.
Foot rim ground.

Mark: Three patches on base.

22.5 cm.   National Museum of Wales.
                                            (D.W. 1450).

56. COFFEE POT AND COVER   c.1758-60

Shaped as No.54.
Painted on enamel colours with, on one side, birds in a landscape and on the other side, a bouquet of flowers, the leaf moulding on the spout picked out in turquoise with traces of gilding.

Mark: Three patches on base.

21.5 cm.   Private Collection.

54   56   55   56

57. COFFEE POT AND COVER   c.1758-60

Shaped as No.54.
Painted in enamel colours with Chinese ladies standing beside a
large jar.

Finial missing.

   19.5 cm.   Derby Museum & Art Gallery.
                                               (404/3-59).

        Lit.   Barrett & Thorpe, 1971, op. cit., Pl.39 (for reverse).

58. COFFEE POT AND COVER   c.1760-62

Shaped as No.54.
Painted in enamel colours with, on one side, an exotic bird
standing between low growing plants, with a roller bird perched
on a bamboo, and on the other side, two jays perched on a branch.

   23 cm.   Private Collection.

58   57   58

59. COFFEE POT AND COVER   c.1760-62

Conical shape, on a flat base, the handle with turned-up thumb
piece terminal, and domed cover surmounted by conical finial.
Painted in enamel colours with sprays of flowers on either side
and on the cover, the handle and knop picked out in puce, the
rim of the spout and cover outlined in brown.

    23.5 cm.   National Museum of Wales.
                                                          (D.W. 1445).

     See.   Nos. 137, 138 & 139 for similar shape in blue
          and white.

60. COFFEE POT AND COVER   c.1760-62

Shaped as No.59.
Painted with the 'banded hedge' pattern in puce enamel with
traces of gilding.

    20 cm.   Private Collection.

     Note: Pattern adapted from a Japanese Kakiamon design.

61. COFFEE POT AND COVER   c.1765

Baluster shape with vertical fluting, ribbed S-shaped spout and
flat scroll handle, a domed cover and spinning top finial also
fluted.
Painted in enamel colours in the chinese manner with, on one
side, three people on a terrace, and on the other a child holding
a parasol over a lady in a garden.

    24.5 cm.   Derby Museum & Art Gallery.
                                                          (505-61).

     Lit.   Barrett & Thorpe, 1971, op. cit., Pl.38.

62. COFFEE POT AND COVER   c.1765

Shaped as No.61 with an ornate handle.
Painted in enamel colours in the chinese manner.

Mark: Three stilt marks.

    14.5 cm.   Private Collection.

     Exh.   W. Williams, 1973, Early Derby Porcelain.
          Exhibition Catalogue No.73.

59   61   60   62

63. PUNCH POT COVER AND STAND   c.1760-62

Globular shaped pot, with recurving terminal and spurs on the
handle, S-shaped spout with leaf moulding, a slightly domed cover
with applied leaves and surmounted by a lemon-shaped finial. The
stand with everted scalloped rim.
Painted with the 'banded hedge' pattern in puce enamel with traces
of gilding, the lemon knop painted in yellow and green enamel.

Mark: Three patches on base.

    20 cm.   L. 27 cm.   National Museum of Wales.
                                                          (D.W. 2141).

    Lit.   Barrett & Thorpe, 1971, op. cit., p.17.
           Gilhespy, 1965, op. cit., Pl.41 for similar punch pot
           (without stand).

64. CREAM JUG   c.1760-62   (detail illustrated)

Baluster shaped jug, with wide sparrow beak and double scroll
handle with raised thumb rest.
Painted in enamel colours with chinoiserie figures, standing
beside a table.

    8 cm.   Private Collection.

    See.   Nos. 47, 48 and 72, for similar decoration,
           No. 140 for similar shape.

63 64

65. CUP   c.1756

   Quatre-foil shape, with wish-bone handle.
   Painted in enamel colours with, on one side, a pipit pecking
   the ground and another in flight, and on the other side, wild
   flowers.

      6 cm.   Private Collection.

66. CUP   c.1756

   Shaped as No.65.
   Painted in enamel colours with, on one side, a bittern perched on
   the branch of a tree and another in flight, and on the other side,
   flowers in the manner of the 'cotton-stalk' painter.

      6 cm.   Private Collection.

67. CUP   c.1756

   Shaped as No.65.
   Painted in enamel colours with, on one side, two bitterns, and
   on the other side, butterflies and insects.

      6 cm.   Private Collection.

68. CUP   c.1758-60

   Shaped as No.65.
   Painted in enamel colours with a spray of wild flowers, in a
   shaped reserve outlined in black, on a yellow ground.

      6 cm.   Private Collection.

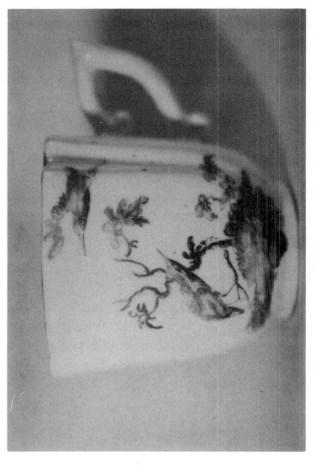

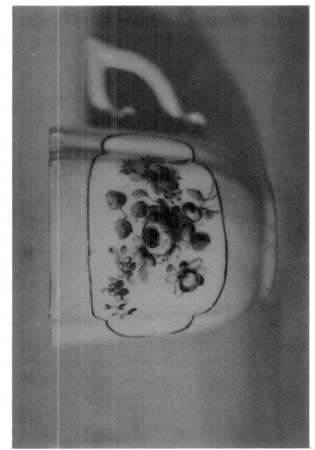

68

66

67

65

69. CUP   c.1756-58

Faceted octagonal shape with wish-bone handle.
Painted in enamel colours with a spray of flowers in the manner
of the 'cotton-stalk' painter: the rim outlined in brown.

   6 cm.   Private Collection.

70. CUP   c.1760

Bell-shaped with undulating rim and flat handle with four
irregular shaped pierced holes.
Painted in enamel colours with a design derived from the Chinese
famille verte.

   8.3 cm.   Victoria & Albert Museum.
                                           (C.1054-1924).

      See. C.H.R.Marshall, 1954, Coloured Worcester Porcelain of
            First Period, 1751-1783. Newport, for similar example.

71. CUP   c.1760

Cup with applied moulded sprigged decoration and wish-bone handle
(restored).
Painted in iron-red enamel with scattered flowers and elaborate
border around the inside of the cup.

   6 cm.   Victoria & Albert Museum.
                                           (C.19-1959).

72. CUP   c.1762

Cup with wish-bone handle.
Painted in enamel colours with, on one side two orientals in a
domestic scene and on the other side, a cock fighting scene, a
loop chain border around the inside of the cup.

   6 cm.   Private Collection.

      See. No.64 for similar pattern of two orientals.
            No.455 for cockfighting scene on Worcester cup.
      Lit. Trans. E.C.C., Vol 4, Pt.1, 1957, Pl. 1A and p.1
            for analysis of paste of octagonal shaped cup with
            similar decoration.

73. CUP   c.1770-72

Cup with broad strap handle.
Painted in enamel colours with scattered flowers, the rim
outlined in brown.

   4 cm.   Private Collection.

74. CUP AND SAUCER   c.1768-72

Cup of cylindrical form with grooved loop handle.
Painted with stylised flowers and leaves in monochrome green
enamel and gilt.

   6.2 cm. Saucer, D. 12.3 cm.   Private Collection.

      Note: Possibly a replacement for Worcester service.

70   (72,73,69)   71   74

75   SALT   c.1758-60

Globular pot on high domed foot with narrow cylindrical neck and
wish-bone handle.
Painted in enamel colours with, on one side, a gallant and a lady
in a landscape, and on the other side, scattered flowers.

    4.5 cm.   Private Collection.

      Note: Design probably taken from a print source.

76. SALT AND COVER   c.1758-60

Globular form on high domed foot, small loop handles forming the
curved horns to the satyr masks with pointed ears, the moulded
cover terminating in an open flower finial with applied leaves.
Painted in enamel colours with, on one side, exotic birds in a
landscape and on the other side, a bouquet of flowers in a
naturalistic palette, on the cover, scattered flower sprays and
gilt geometric design around the rim. Flower finial restored.

    9.8 cm.   Private Collection.

77. SALT   c.1758-60

Shaped as No.76.
Painted in enamel colours with scattered flowers, the mask handles
painted in a naturalistic manner.

    6.5 cm.   Private Collection.

78. SALT   c.1758-60

Shaped as No.76.
Painted in enamel colours with scattered flowers.

Mark: Three patches on base.

    4.6 cm.   Private Collection.

79. SALTS AND COVERS (Pair) c.1760

Shaped as No.76.
Painted in enamel colours and gilt, with rural landscapes and
buildings, the masks picked out in naturalistic colours, the foot
and covers adorned with insects and decorated border around the rim.

    9.2 cm.   Private Collection.

    Lit. Gilhespy, 1965, op. cit., Pl.42, for similar shape.

80. SALT   c.1775

Shallow cup form with applied schneeballen (may flowers) standing
on three lion paw feet.
Painted in turquoise enamel colours.

    5 cm.   Victoria & Albert Museum.
                               (2001-1901).

75   79,78,76,77,79.   80

81. BUTTER POT   c.1758-60

Rectangular form with champhered corners and slightly flaring sides.
Decorated in enamel colours with flowers, in a naturalistic palette,
the rim outlined in brown.

  6.6 cm. L. 13 cm. W. 9.2 cm.   Private Collection.

   See. No.175 for blue and white example.
   Note: The glaze has a very blue tint.
   Lit. Barrett & Thorpe, 1971, op. cit., Pl.83.

82. HONEY POT   c.1760-62

Rounded shape with applied single stemmed branch rising spirally
around the pot.
Decorated with butterflies and other insects painted in naturalistic
colours, the applied leaves and flowers also painted in enamel
colours.
Cover missing.

  9 cm.   Private Collection.

83. BOX AND COVER   c.1760

Moulded in the form of a peach with a loop handle, an applied
spray of leaves and an open flower on the cover.
Painted in naturalistic colours.

  7.5 cm. D. 8 cm.   Victoria & Albert Museum.
               (C.703+A - 1925).

   Note: Similar example in the Derby Museum.
   Lit. Barrett & Thorpe, 1971, op. cit., Pl.40, for similar
     example.

84. MUSTARD POT AND COVER   c.1758-60

Pot and cover with shallow ribbed body, plain shoulder and silver
shaped scroll handle, the cover with cut-out space for a spoon,
and surmounted by applied leaves and a flower finial.
Painted in enamel colours with sprays of garden flowers, the rim
of both pot and cover outlined in brown.

  9 cm.   Private Collection.

   See. No.193 for similar shape handle.
   Lit. S. Spero, 1970, Price Guide to 18th Cent. English
     Porcelain, Woodbridge, p.192.

81   83   82   84

85. SAUCEBOAT   c.1760-62

Moulded in relief with fruit and a rococo reserve.
Decorated in enamel colours, with the moulding picked out in
turquoise, the reserves painted with flowers in the manner of
the 'cotton-stalk' painter, the moulded gadroon rim outlined in
brown.
Foot rim ground.

        L.19.5 cm.   Private Collection.

86. CREAMBOAT   c.1760-62

Moulded in the form of overlapping leaves, the handle formed by
a curved stem.
Painted with stylised flowers en camaieu and gilt.
Foot rim ground.

        L. 16.7 cm.   Private Collection.

        See. No.90 for similar shape in larger size.
        Lit. Gilhespy, 1965, op. cit., Pl.31.

87. SAUCEBOAT   c.1765

Fluted body with thick loop handle, wide lip and scalloped rim.
Decorated in enamel colours with a chinoiserie scene.
Foot rim ground.

        L. 13.6 cm.   Private Collection.

88. SAUCEBOAT   c.1765-68   (not illustrated)

Shaped as No.86.
Painted in polychrome enamel colours with floral sprays, the
rim outlined in green enamel.

        L. 13.3 cm.   Private Collection.

        Lit. Gilhespy, 1965, op. cit., Pl.31 for similar shape.
              Spero, 1970, op. cit., p.182.

85   86   87

89. SAUCEBOAT   1768-72

Lightly fluted sides with scalloped rim, set on a raised foot, moulded in relief with leaves and sprays of flowers, a shaped handle with turned up thumb piece.
Painted in underglaze blue, clobbered with red enamel and gilding, depicting a house and trees, in the chinese style, the moulded relief sprays painted in enamel colours, green, turquoise, yellow, iron-red magenta, brown, blue and black, floral sprays painted on the inside, the foot rim picked out in magenta shading and the rim outlined in gilt.

Mark: '1768', painted in magenta enamel beneath the handle.
     (See 89a).

   L. 15.3 cm.   Holburne of Menstrie Museum,
                                    Bath.   (P.168).

     Note: There is an element of doubt over the authenticity of this date. Mid 19th century clobbering may have occurred.

           Dr. Bernard Watney reported that a similar sauceboat was tested by the British Museum laboratory, and contained phosphate.

     See. No.201 for similar shape and moulded decoration.

90. SAUCEBOAT   c.1768-70

Shaped as No.86.
Painted and decorated similar to No.88.

   L. 18 cm.   Private Collection.

91. LADLE   c.1762-65

Handle of serpentine shape with upturned end.
Painted in enamel colours with a curlew, butterflies and insects.
Traces of gilding on the handle and on the inside of the bowl.

   L. 17 cm.   Private Collection.

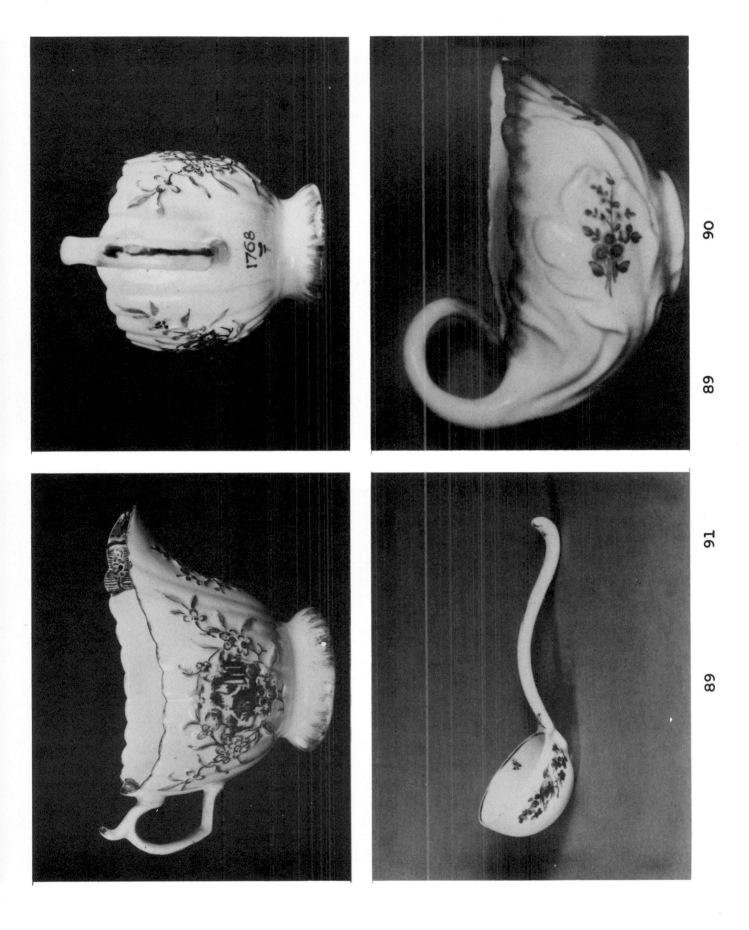

90

89

91

89

92. BROTH BOWL AND COVER   c.1758-60

The bowl of ogee shape and two scroll shaped handles, a slightly
domed cover with moulded leaves and flower finial.
Painted in enamel colours with, on one side, a gallant holding
a flute, lying on the ground in front of a seated lady, and on
the other side a teacher holding a violin and a young pupil;
the cover painted with birds set in a stylised landscape with
interspersed sprays of flowers, the rim outlined in brown.

    13.5 cm. D. 21.5 cm.   Private Collection.

      See. Colour Plate p.45 for other side.
      Note: Designs after Watteau.

93. BOWL AND COVER   c.1762-65

Bowl with basket moulding and applied flowers, the cover pierced
and decorated with applied flowers and rope twist finial (restored).
Painted in enamel colours with an oriental scene on the inside of
the bowl, the flowers on the outside picked out in naturalistic
colours and the base of the bowl and rim of the cover outlined in
brown.

    16.5 cm.   Derby Museum & Art Gallery.

      See. No.208 for similar shape in blue and white.
      Lit. Barrett & Thorpe, 1971, op. cit., Pl.74.

94. TURTLE DOVE TUREENS (pair) c.1775-80

Pair of tureens moulded in the form of two turtle doves, nesting
on a base encrusted with moss and leaves.
Painted in naturalistic enamel colours.
Foot rims ground.

Mark: '5' painted in puce.

    12 cm. L. 18.3 cm. W. 8.3 cm.   Private Collection.

      Lit. Barrett & Thorpe, 1971, op. cit., Pl.55 for
            similar style.

95. STAND   c.1758-60

Plate with a scallop shaped rim, the border with moulded decoration
of circles and a zig-zag line, with florets at the intersection.
Painted in naturalistic enamel colours with day-lilies and other
flowers in the manner of the 'cotton-stalk' painter, the rim
outlined in brown.

    D. 18 cm.   Private Collection.

95

93

94

92

96. STAND   c.1760-62

Plate moulded with overlapping leaves, a pierced border and applied
florets at the intersection of the circular piercing.
Painted in green and yellow enamel colours, the veins of the leaves
picked out in puce, and the edge outlined in brown.

    D. 18 cm.   Private Collection.

      Exh. Williams, 1973, op. cit., No.18
      Lit. Barrett & Thorpe, 1971, op. cit., Pl.31 for similar
           example.

97. LEAF DISH   c.1760

Moulded in the form of five overlapping leaves, the stem forming
the handle.
Painted in enamel colours with five sprays of flowers, the leaves
picked out in yellow and green and the handle in pink.
Foot rim ground.

    L. 21 cm.   Private Collection.

98. VINE LEAF DISH   c.1762-65

Dish with undulating rim and moulded with leaves and grapes.
Painted in enamel colours with fruit and insects in the centre
and the leaves and grapes in naturalistic colours, the rim
outlined in brown.
Foot rim ground.

    L. 22.3 cm.   Private Collection.

      Lit. Barrett & Thorpe, 1971, op. cit., Pl.45 for similar
           example.
           Spero, 1970, op. cit., p.188.

99. OVAL DISH   c.1762-65

Flat oval dish with elaborate moulding around the rim.
Painted in enamel colours with trees and pagodas in an oriental
landscape, the moulding around the edge picked out in turquoise
and gilt.

    L. 24 cm.   Derby Museum & Art Gallery.

      Lit. Barrett & Thorpe, 1971, op. cit., Pl.79.

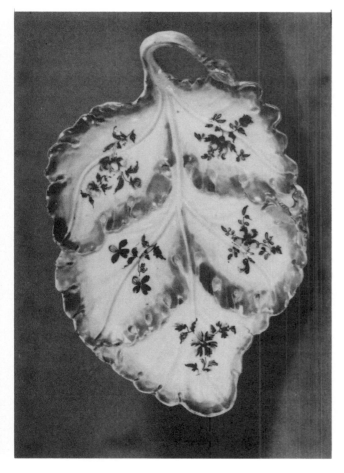

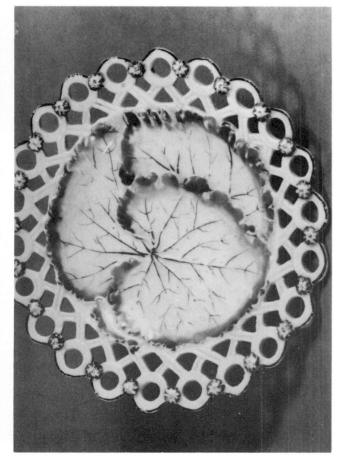

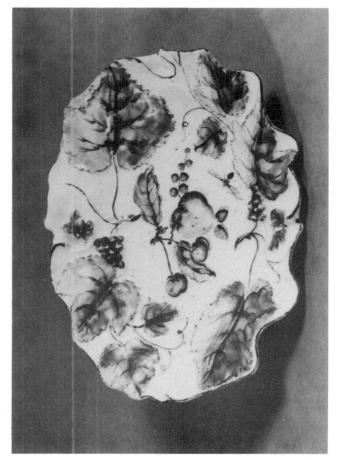

99

97

98

96

100. OVAL BASKET   c.1758-62

Basket of shallow form, the exterior moulded with loosely interwoven
straps, moulded florets on the intervening section, a rope twist
moulded foot, floral handle terminals to single rope twist loop
handle (missing).
Painted in enamel colours with a blue-tit set in an elaborate
cartouche of flower scrolls and insects, the exterior picked out
in yellow enamels, the florets outlined in red, the centre painted
in naturalistic colours and gilt.

    L. 28 cm. W. 24 cm.   Private Collection.

101. BASKET   c.1758

Of oval shape with single loop handles, moulded on the exterior
in the form of a woven basket.
Painted in enamel colours with a meadow pipit and lark in a
landscape, surrounded by scattered flowers in naturalistic colours,
the rim outlined in brown.

    L. 14 cm.   Private Collection.

      Note: The enamel colour round the florets on the inside,
           where the handles join the body, has run.
      Exh. Williams, 1973, op. cit., No.16.

102. BASKET   c.1760-62

Of oval shape similar to No.101 with single rope twist handles,
moulded on the outside with double crossed lines and applied
florets at the intersections.
Painted on the inside in naturalistic colours with a cuckoo and
another bird perching on branches and surrounded by scattered
flowers, on the outside the sepals of the florets painted blue
and yellow, the rope twist around the base painted yellow and the
rim outlined in brown.

    L. 23 cm.   Private Collection.

     Lit. Gilhespy, 1965, op. cit., Pl.44 for similar shape.

103 BASKET   c.1760-62

Small basket with flaring fluted sides and applied florets around
the top rim, single loop handles terminating in flowers and
leaves.
Painted with stylised flowers en camaieu and gilt.

    L.9 cm.   Private Collection.

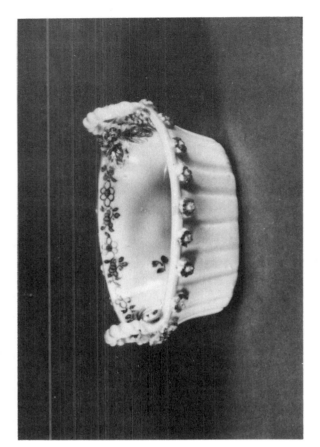

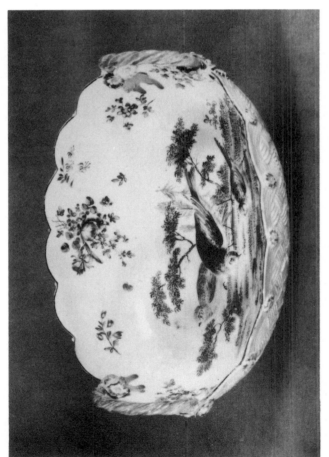

103

100

102

101

104. PIERCED BASKET   c.1760

'Spectacle basket' of small form with cut-out sides, rope twist
handles terminating in flower finials, moulded on the exterior
with double crossed lines and applied florets at the intersections
and rope moulded base.
Painted on the inside with a heron and a golden oriel in polychrome enamel colours, the rope moulding in yellow enamel and the
rim outlined in brown.

    D. 12 cm.   Private Collection.

      Lit. L. Jewitt, 1878 The Ceramic Art of Great Britain, Vol.1
           pp. 68-9. 1763 Shipment of china to London, Box No. 11..
           '12 open-work Spectacle Baskets'.

105. PIERCED BASKET   c.1760

Circular open-work pierced basket of flaring form, moulded on the
outside as No.104, with single loop handles.
Painted in enamel colours with flower sprays on the inside, the
florets on the outside picked out in yellow, the handles turquoise
and the rim outlined in brown.

    D. 17 cm.   Private Collection.

      Exh. Williams, 1973. Op. cit., No.19.
      Lit. Gilhespy, 1965, op. cit., Pl.32 for similar shape.

106 OVAL PIERCED BASKET   c.1760

Pierced 'spectacle basket' of oval form with double rope twist
handles, moulded on the outside as No.104.
Painted in enamel colours on the inside with a pear attached to a
leafy twig surrounded by a caterpillar and flying insects, the
handles picked out in turquoise and yellow and the rim outlined
in brown.

    L. 20.5 cm.   Private Collection.

      See. No. 210 for similar shape in blue and white.
      Exh. Williams, 1973, op. cit., No.46.
      Lit. Spero, 1970, op. cit., P.187.

107 PIERCED BASKET   c.1760

Oval open-work pierced basket with single rope twist handles,
moulded on the outside as No.104. (Flower finials broken off.)
Painted in enamel colours on the inside with a gooseberry spray
surrounded by insects, the handles picked out in green, the sepals
of the florets painted in yellow and the rim outlined in brown.

Mark: Four patches on base.

    L. 8.8 cm.   National Museum of Wales.
                                        (D.W. 1468).

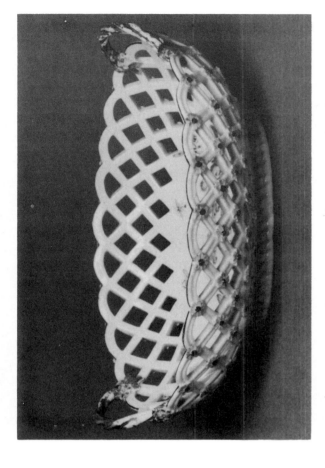

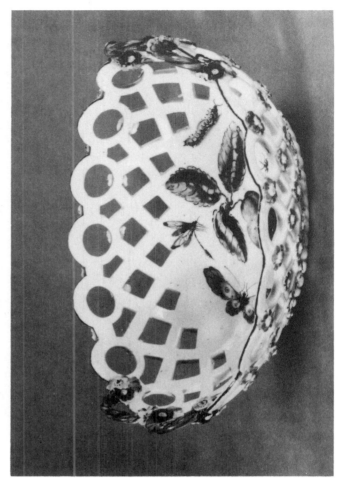

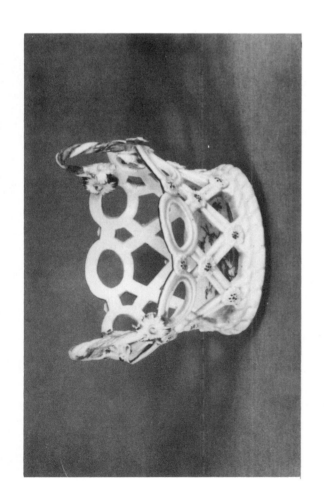

106

107

105

104

108. ICE PAIL   c.1760

Four-lobed shape with circular rim set on raised circular foot and
two elaborate scroll handles set just below the rim.
Painted in enamel colours, on both sides with moorhens and other
exotic birds amidst foliage with scattered fruit and various
insects, the handles and rim outlined in gilt.

Mark: Three patches on foot rim.

    12.4 cm.   City of Manchester Art Galleries.
                                                           (1947-678).

      See. Colour Plate p.46,   for other side.
      Note: Similar example, with turquoise ground, in Victoria
          & Albert Museum. (C 1072-1924).

109. MUG   c.1756-58

Barrel-shaped, with scroll handle and three bands of turned
decoration at the top and the base.
Painted in enamel colours with, on one side, a blue-tit and a
dipper perched on the branches of a tree stump and on the other
side, a cock bullfinch perched on a branch, the handle painted
with rococo ornament in dark red and the rim outlined in the same
enamel colour.

Marks: Three stilt marks on the foot rim.

    12 cm.   City of Manchester Art Galleries.
                                                           (1947-595)

      See. No.216 for similar shape in blue and white.

110. MUG   c.1756-58

Shaped as No.109.
Painted in enamel colours with, on one side, three flower groups,
and on the other side a spray of wild pansies, in the manner of
the 'cotton-stalk' painter, the rim outlined in brown.

    14.5 cm.   Private Collection.

      Exh. Williams, 1973, op. cit., No.70.
      See. No.216 for similar shape in blue and white.

111. MUG   c.1760-62

Bell-shaped with S-scroll handle.
Painted in naturalistic enamel colours with a cluster and sprig
of flowers and two ears of barley, the rim outlined in brown.

    4.5 cm.   Private Collection.

      Lit. Spero, 1970, op. cit., p.185.

108   110   109   111

112. HARVEST JUG   c.1758-60

Ovoid shape with wide lip and S-scroll handle.
Painted in a naturalistic palette with, on one side, a shepherd
boy holding a pitch fork, a shepherdess pouring liquid from a
bottle into a glass, a dog at their feet, and on the other side,
a bouquet of flowers.
The rim outlined in brown.

    17.2 cm.   Private Collection.

      Lit. Gilhespy, 1965, op. cit., Pl.49. for similar shape.

113. JUG   c.1760-62

Baluster shape with a sharp uptilted spout.
Painted in enamel colours with a loose bunch of wild flowers and
an ear of wheat, the rim outlined in brown.
Foot rim ground.

    14.5 cm.   Private Collection.

      Lit. Barrett & Thorpe, 1971, op. cit., Pl.46 for similar shape.
          Spero, 1970, op. cit., p.184.

114. MASK JUG   c.1762-65

Ovoid shape with mask spout and S-scroll handle.
Painted in enamel colours with, on one wide, exotic birds in a
landscape, and on the other side, two roller birds perched on a
branch.
The mask face depicted with a ruff beneath the chin, is painted in
naturalistic colours, with dark brown hair.

    18.5 cm.   Private Collection.

      Exh. E.C.C. 1948, op. cit., No.290, Pl.69.
      Lit. Barrett & Thorpe, 1971, op. cit., Pl.81 for similar
          mask jug.

115. PUNCH JUG   c.1780

Baluster shape with mask lip in the form of a man wearing a tricorn
hat.
Painted in naturalistic enamel colours with bouquets of flowers,
the edge of the handle, the rim and around the foot outlined in
dark red.

    24 cm.   Private Collection.

      See. No.220 for similar shaped jug, but slightly different
          mask lip.
      Note: The excellent flower painting shows stylistic affinities
          with decoration on Strasbourg and Sceaux faience.

112   114   113   115

116. 'PARFUM' VASES AND COVERS (pair)   c.1760

The body of both vases is pear-shaped, with pierced and moulded
decoration, set on high pedestal foot, high domed covers also
with pierced and moulded decoration, surmounted by moulded leaves
and open flower finial.
Painted in enamel colours with reserves showing long-legged exotic
birds, scattered flowers around the base and birds in flight on
the covers.

    23 cm.   Private Collection.

117. VASES   (pair)   c.1760

Pear-shaped with rococo style moulded decoration with applied
floral decoration, set on a high pedestal base with flaring foot.
Painted in enamel colours with reserves showing exotic birds, the
flowers picked out in naturalistic colours and scattered flowers
around the base.
Unglazed foot.

    11.5 cm.   Private Collection.

        Exh. Williams, 1973, op. cit., Nos. 29.31.
        Lit. Barrett & Thorpe, 1971, op. cit., Pl.29 for similar
              example.

118. VASE   dated 1764

Baluster shape pot-pourri vase with pierced shoulders and a
frill of leaves at the waisted foot, two applied masks at the
centre and applied flowers.
Painted in enamel colours with winged insects, the flowers
picked out in naturalistic colours.

Marks: Incised 'Jonathan Boot 1764' on the base. (See 118a).

    18 cm.   Victoria & Albert Museum.
                                              (C.17 - 1973).

        Exh. Williams, 1973, op. cit., No.45.
        Lit. Barrett & Thorpe, 1971, op. cit., p.28.

118a

118

117

116

119. VASE   c.1760-65

Tall vase of baluster shape with four rectangular panelled sides
set on a small square foot with flared base, rectangular shaped
shoulder panels and flared trumpet shaped neck with square shaped
vertical rim.
Painted in enamel colours on all four sides with sprays of
flowers, willow trees and prunus branch.

    25.5 cm.   City Art Gallery, Bristol
                                          (G.1814)

    Note: Copied exactly from a chinese original.

120. VASE   c.1765-70

The body of the vase baluster shape with ornate scroll handles, a
flared neck with pierced holes and serrated edge, decorated with
applied flower sprays, supported on a flared foot beneath a frilled
flange.

Mark: Three patches on base.

    19.5 cm.   Private Collection.

121. MAYFLOWER VASE   c.1770-75

Square baluster form with applied <u>schneeballen</u> (mayflowers) and
twigs.
Painted in enamel colours of green and red and gilt.

    8 cm.   Private Collection.

122. GUGLET   c.1758

Bulbous shape with a long neck and a swelling below the flared
rim.
Painted in enamel colours with flower sprays and sprigs, the
rim round the top of the bottle outlined in gilt.

    23 cm.   Derby Museum & Art Gallery.
                                          (267-1-75)

    See. No.227 for a blue and white example.
    Lit. Gilhespy, 1965, <u>op. cit.</u>, Pl.29 for similar shape.

119   121   120   122

123. FLOWER POT   c.1765

The pot moulded with horizontal bands, of slightly flaring form,
filled with a moulded display of flowers and leaves arranged in
pyramidal form.
Painted in enamel colours, the leaves green, the flowers with
yellow centres, butterflies on the pot and the bands outlined
in gilt.

    13.2 cm.   Private Collection.

      Lit. Gilhespy, 1965, op. cit., Pl.149 for other shapes.

124. INKSTAND   c.1765

Comprising a pen tray with three depressions for the inkpot,
pounce pot and wafer box (all missing), the cover for the tray
moulded with two children playing with a lamb.
Painted in enamel colours with winged insects, caterpillars and
on the cover, two landscapes enclosed in rococo cartouches.

    9.5 cm. L. 24.7 cm.   Victoria & Albert Museum.
                                  (1148-1924).

    Note: The finial mould was also used on a set of dressing
           table boxes. (Victoria & Albert Museum, Sch.1. 441).
    Lit. Barrett & Thorpe, 1971, op. cit., Pl.80 for slightly
           different style.

125. POUNCE POT   c.1760-62

Squat bellied body with flat pierced top.
Painted in naturalistic enamel colours with flowers and sprigs.

    4.5 cm.   Private Collection.

126. TOILET POT AND COVER   c.1762-65

The pot of plain cylindrical form with low domed cover surmounted
by a flower finial with moulded leaves.
Painted in enamel colours with sprays and sprigs of flowers and
gilt dentil border round the rim of the cover.

    7.5 cm.   Private Collection.

124   123   125   126

127. CHAMBER CANDLESTICK   c.1760

On circular base with slightly up turned quatre-foil rim, with
raised centre surmounted by shaped candle nozzle, moulded
decoration around the base of applied leaves and scattered florets.
Painted in enamel colours with scattered flowers. Handle missing.

    8 cm.   Private Collection.

128. CHAMBER CANDLESTICK   c.1768-70

Shaped as No.127 with twisted snake-like handle and a floral
rosette for the thumb rest.
Painted in enamel colours with scattered flowers, the leaves and
handle green, the border around the base and the moulding on the
nozzle dark blue with a gilt dentil border.

    8 cm.   Derby Museum & Art Gallery.

129. PIPE STOPPER   c.1775

A fluted column on a flared circular base and moulded with head
and shoulders of a child dressed as a Turk wearing a shirt, shawl
and headdress.
Painted in enamel colours and gilt.

    6.8 cm.   Private Collection.

130. SEAL   c.1770

Moulded in the form of a milk maid wearing a wide brimmed hat,
laced bodice and overshirt with full petticoat, carrying a yolk
supporting two pails, standing on a mound base.
Painted in enamel colours.
The base mounted with an agate set in gold.

    3.5 cm.   Private Collection

131. SEAL   c.1770

Moulded in the form of harlequin wearing a jacket, pantaloons,
ruff, and hooded cloak, sitting on a grassy mound base and playing
a hurdy gurdy.
Painted in enamel colours with a gilt line round the base.

    2.2 cm.   Private Collection.

    Lit. Barrett & Thorpe, 1971, op. cit., Pl.116 for a group
        of toys.

132. BUTTONS   c.1790

Two buttons of stud form each consisting of two discs, the upper
circular the lower crescent shaped, joined together at the centre
by a shank. The upper surface of the white buttons gilded with a
motif of a central star within concentric circles of dots and beading.
The underside of the bases left in the biscuit.

    1.2 cm. D (upper side) 2.2 cm.   Private Collection.

    Note: Many small utilitarian items like buckles, thimbles
         and bell-pulls were also made at Derby.

130, 131, 129

132

127

128

ONGLAZE TRANSFER PRINTING IN BLACK AND PUCE RED

Much research still remains to be done on this subject. D. Towner[1] in his paper, argues most convincingly that the pieces which are marked 'Derby Pot Works', and 'Pot Works in Derby' were both made and printed at the Pot Works on Cockpit Hill, but it is not certain if the pieces with the 'anchor' rebus and the word 'Derby' were confined to this one factory.

It is possible that the Coronation Mug[2] (No.133) was produced at the St. Mary's Bridge, Nottingham Road Factory, whereas the mug[3] of similar shape, in the British Museum, printed in underglaze blue with 'Derby' and an 'anchor' rebus and a 'sun-face' is considered to have been produced at Cockpit Hill. Another mug, in the Museum and Art Gallery, Derby, with the 'anchor' rebus and 'Derby' has a transfer print in black of Sutton Hall[4]. This print was used at Worcester[6] and was subsequently found at Caughley, according to Jewitt[4].

A fuller example of the use of designs used at both Derby and Worcester is the 'Marine Society' print, designed by Samual Wale, which Cyril Cook[7] attributes to Hancock. It was used on a Worcester bowl and inscribed 'Marine Society' with patriotic exhortations, and was later used on the barrel shaped mug, now in the Derby Museum and Art Gallery, where it is called 'Distressed Family', with electioneering slogans for the 1768 Election (see p.235).

Perhaps even more surprising is the use of the King of Purssia print, seen on Mug No.134. This print, together with the subsidiary prints, of a floral spray and a butterfly, have been taken from a copper etching, as was usual when coppers were used for onglaze printing (see Sandon[8]), and the design shows signs of having been strengthened by a graver, which was done after the etching had been sufficiently bitten into by the acid. The pink enamel colour used for the onglaze printing has not been recorded on any other Derby or Worcester porcelain, but is similar in colour to printing done by Sadler of Liverpool.

At a Sotheby (London) Sale on January 25th, 1977, Lot 121 included a sucrier and cover in the Worcester section and judging from the paste and glaze only, this attribution was probably correct; however the black transfer prints (see No.173) of 'the six storey pagoda' and 'the house surrounded by a fence' pattern had only previously been recorded on Derby wares. These prints are different from those produced at Worcester and may indicate that wares were purchased 'in white' from Worcester and printed either at Cockpit Hill or some other Derbyshire factory.

If Holdship used onglaze transfer printing in black whilst at Worcester then there is no reason to doubt that a similar process could not have been used at Derby, albeit on a smaller scale. Holdship's agreement with the Derby factory (see p.235) no mention is made of transfer printing. It may be significant that the 'King of Prussia' mug c.1765 is printed in onglaze pink, which may have been one of the Holdship ideas following his move.

H. Gilbert Bradley.

References:

1. D. Towner, 1967, Trans. E.C.C. Vol.6, part 3.

2. B. Watney, 1964, Trans. E.C.C. Vol.5, part 5, Pls.268A & B, 270C.

3. Towner, 1967, op. cit., Vol.6, part 3, Pl. 188A.

4. Jewitt, op. cit.,

5. A. Toppin, 1957, Trans. E.C.C. Vol.3, Pl.1, p.68.

6. Toppin, 1951, op. cit., Pl. 28B.

7. C. Cook, 1955, The Life and Work of Robert Hancock, London.

8. H. Sandon, 1969, Illustrated Guide to Worcester Porcelain, London, p.40.

133. MUG   Dated 1761

Bell-shaped with everted rim and grooved loop handle.
Transfer-printed in black with portraits of Busts of King George III
and Queen Charlotte, both busts terminating in crossed branches of
myrtle and palm, symbols of peace. The centre printed with a seated
figure of Britannia looking towards a standing figure of Minerva.
Above the head of George III, a flying angel blowing a trumpet held
in her right hand and a crown in her left, representing Fame. Above
the head of Queen Charlotte, a putto holding in his right hand a
crown and in his left, a trailing ribbon bearing the inscription,
'Crown'd Sept. 22^d 1761'. An anchor and 'Derby' printed below the
handle.

        13 cm.   Royal Crown Derby Museum.
                                   Ex. Dyson Perrins Museum, Worcester.

        See. Nos. 218 & 219 for similar shape.
        Note:Marked with the rebus of an anchor, it is probably the
             work of Richard Holdship.
        Lit. J. Toppin, 1946, Battersea, Ceramic and Kindred Associations,
             Trans. E.C.C., Vol.2, No.9, Pl.63a.
             B.M. Watney, 1964, Derby Transfer Prints, Trans. E.C.C.,
             Vol.5, Pt.5, p.297.

134. MUG   c.1765

Bell-shaped with everted rim and grooved loop handle.
Onglaze transfer-printed in pink enamel with a portrait of the
'King of Prussia', a floral spray and a butterfly.

        8.5 cm.   Private Collection.

        Note: The print of the King of Prussia, b.1712, d.1786,
              is taken from a copper plate engraved by R. Hancock,
              after a painting by Antoine Pesne. It was used
              extensively on black printed Worcester. It has not
              been previously recorded on Derby. See Introduction,
              p. 92.
        Lit. C. Cook, 1955, Life and Work of Robert Hancock, London,
              (Supplement. Item No.56).

133

134

BLUE AND WHITE

For many years it was thought that very little blue and white porcelain was produced at Derby and when compared with the quantity produced at other eighteenth century factories which has survived, it must be admitted that it is small, but this is also true of the polychrome wares when compared, for instance, with Worcester. From a glance at the pieces illustrated it can be seen that the output was very uneven; there is a predominance of sauce-boats, leaf dishes and small pickle dishes, but very few teapots, coffee pots and other tea ware. This, however, may have been due to a technical fault in the manufacture and not necessarily due to William Duesbury's dislike of cobalt, as has been frequently suggested. Even as late as 1788 there is mention in one of the Joseph Lygo/Duesbury letters, in the Derby Archives complaining of the difficulties still being experienced in the manufacture of soup tureens and teapots which it is stated both 'flew' when hot liquids were suddenly introduced.

Writing in 1878, Jewitt[1], lists several articles decorated in blue and white which were sent from Derby to London in 1763. 'Box No.11 contined 12 blue, round fourth-sized, open-worked Baskets and the list included blue fluted boats, blue strawberry pots, blue guglets and basins to ditto.' The Duesbury (Derby) Account Book as quoted by Barrett and Thorpe[2] lists for the year 1787: Egg Spoons and Egg Cups, Hartichoke Cups, Pint and Half Pint Basins, and Toy Cream Jugs all in blue and white; also Small jugs and a Slop basin enamelled fine blue and white.

There is no mention in these lists of transfer printing, but we know from the Agreement signed in 1764 by Duesbury, Heath, and Richard Holdship, one of the original partners of the Worcester Porcelain Co., that Holdship agreed to sell his 'secret process' for making china using soapstone and to teach enamelling 'in blew' and blue-printing, but again, judging from the few examples of transfer printing that have survived, either it was not a full-time job and Holdship did complain about the lack of work in the printing line, or he failed to teach the art. About a dozen transfer prints have been identified, but apart from the 'stag at lodge' on the jug (No.220), none seem peculiar to Derby. It is generally considered that transfer printing in blue did not start until the mid 1760's, probably following the arrival of Richard Holdship, but the coronation mug (No.133) transfer printed in black must be earlier, though the same shape was later used for the blue transfer mugs (Nos.218 & 219).

Recently it has been realised that 'powder blue' was a form of decoration used at Derby. The bowl and cover (No.170) and the leaf dish (No.180) are examples of this style of decoration and although the designs closely follow patterns painted at Bow, the reserves are not bordered by a line, which Dr. Redstone has pointed out was a practice usually carried out at Bow. Franklin Barrett has kindly brought to my notice an undated letter amongst the Duesbury manuscripts in the Derby Public Library, which, when attempting to classify them in 1950, he numbered No.508, which refers to 'powder blue'.

'Mrs. Balm's compliments to Mr. Duesbury and informs him that
Hull is the best market for Powder Blue. If agreeable to
Mr. Duesbury she will write to a merchant and enquire the
price. There are three or four sorts, some light and some
dark. Mr. Duesbury will be kind enough to let Mrs. Balm
know whether he will wish her to order the P.Blue immediately
or enquire the Prices first'.

Dated pieces are extremely rare. The earliest date so far recorded,
August 1762, is on the underside of a perforated cover of a bowl
(see foot note to No.208) in Mr. Geoffrey Godden's collection. A
salt (No.181) in the Castle Museum, Norwich, formerly attributed
to Lowestoft, is dated 1772, and a mug (No.463) also in the G.
Godden Reference Collection is dated 1779. However there is some
doubt about a Derby attribution to this mug.

None of the early pieces are marked, apart from the three cream
jugs mentioned earlier. The factory mark of a crown over a cursive
'D' was introduced from the early 1770's. Sometimes a painted or
incised 'N' was used on a few items, although recently a bowl
(No.172) with a crescent mark has also been attributed to Derby.

Very little blue and white has been attributed to Cockpit Hill, one
of the other factories in Derby, which was also owned by John Heath.
The pair of leaf dishes (No.381) and the soup tureen and cover
(No.382) are now attributed to this factory as is the lobe shaped
dish (No.380). It should also be noted that the style of tree
painting on the tea bowl and saucer (No.153) and on the miniature
tea ware (Nos. 161, 162 & 163) also occurs on the Cockpit Hill
Mug (No.400) thus proving the close links between the two factories.

H. Gilbert Bradley.

1. L. Jewitt, 1878, The Ceramic Art of Great Britain, London,
2. Barrett & Thorpe, 1971, op. cit., pp. 154-5.

135. TEAPOT AND COVER   c.1768-72

Globular shape, S-shaped spout with five perforated holes at the junction with the body, plain loop handle with broad outer rib, shallow domed cover with stylised acorn knop.
Painted in underglaze blue with two houses having fanciful projections to the roof, set beneath a willow tree on an island; floral sprays above and below the spout and a double line border on the shoulder and round the rim of the cover.
Foot rim ground.

    12.8 cm.   Private Collection.

        Note: Several fire cracks in the pot and around the handle.

136. COFFEE POT AND COVER   c.1758-60

Pear shape, with broad strap handle and moulded spout.
Painted in underglaze blue with a group of houses beneath a spreading willow tree and shading two bushy-top trees, a floral spray beneath the spout and a lattice border around the rim.
Replacement cover.

Mark: Three patches on foot.

    21 cm.   Private Collection.

        See. No.54 for similar shape.

137. COFFEE POT AND COVER   c.1760

Of tapering cylindrical form with spreading base, S-shaped spout and domed cover.
Painted in underglaze blue with, on one side, a Chinese lady holding a bowl, standing beneath a willow tree and on the other side, a Chinese lady and a small child holding a stock; a floral spray on the spout and an elaborate border around the top of the pot and on the cover.

Mark: Three patches on foot.

    24 cm.   Private Collection.

        See. No.59 & 60 for similar shape.
        Note: This pattern also occurs on early Worcester and Liverpool
              (Gilbody).
        Lit. Gilhespy, 1965, op. cit., Pl.66.

138. COFFEE POT AND COVER   c.1760

Shaped as No.137.
Painted in underglaze blue with, on one side, a Chinese lady standing beside a small child holding a toy and on the other side, two Chinese ladies standing beside the branch of a tree; a floral spray on the spout and an elaborate border around the top of the pot and on the cover.

Mark: Three patches on foot.
    20.5 cm.   City of Birmingham Museum.
        See. Note No.137.
        Lit. B.M.Watney, 1973, English Blue & White Porcelain.
              (2nd Edition) London, Pl.69a.

135   138   136   137

139. COFFEE POT   c.1765

Shaped as No.137.
Transfer-printed in underglaze blue with, on one side, the 'boy on
the buffalo' and on the other side, the 'spinning maiden' pattern,
with a painted lattice border around the top of the pot and the edge
of the cover.

Mark: Three patches on foot.

    21 cm.   Private Collection.

      Note: The patterns are probably inspired by the story of the
           oxherd 'Shien Niu' and the spinning maiden 'Chih Nu'.
      Lit. Gilhespy, 1965, op. cit., Pl.2.
           B.Watney, 1972, Notes on Bow Transfer-Printing, Trans.E.C.C.
           Vol.8, Pt.2, Pl.176a for print used on a Bow mug.

140. CREAM JUG   c.1768-70

Pear shape, with sparrow-beak lip and grooved loop handle.
Transfer-printed in underglaze blue with, on one side, the 'boy on
the buffalo' and on the other side, 'buffalo beside a river with a
chinese sailing junk', with a painted lattice border on the inside rim.

    8.5 cm.   Castle Museum, Norwich.
                                            (102-933).

      See. No.150, for similar pattern.
           No.64, for similar shape.
      Note: Registered as Worcester, re-attributed to Chelsea/Derby
           by Dr. Watney in late 1950's.

141. CREAM JUG   c.1770-72

Bucket shape, moulded in the form of a quilt or lozenge pattern,
with a shaped rim and loop handle.
Painted in underglaze blue with stylised flower heads set in the
centre of each lozenge and a lattice border on the inside rim.

    7.6 cm. L. 12.7 cm.   Victoria & Albert Museum.
                                          (C.447-1924).

      Lit. B.M.Watney, 1973, op. cit., Pl.65c, for similar shape.

142. JUG   c.1775-85

Baluster shape, with strap handle.
Transfer-printed in bright underglaze blue with flower sprays and
winged insects, the rim outlined in blue.

    6.2 cm.   Private Collection.

      Note: This small-size jug also occurs with the 'open zig-zag
           fence' pattern.

139   142   140   141

143. TEA BOWL   c.1756-58

Small size, with moulded leaf decoration on the outside of the bowl.
Painted in underglaze blue with floral sprays on the alternate
leaves and a painted roll border on the inside of the bowl.

    4 cm.   Derby Museum & Art Gallery.
                                                    (1168-1).

144. COFFEE CUPS (Pair)   c.1756-58

Squat shape, with vertical fluting and wide grooved handle.
Painted in underglaze blue with a stylised bunch of leaves and
trailing flowers, the rim outlined in blue.

    5 cm.   Derby Museum & Art Gallery.
                                                    (1168-2, 3).

145. COFFEE CUP   c.1760   (not illustrated).

Bell shape, with pointed wish-bone handle.
Painted in underglaze blue with a ruined arch beneath a willow
tree and a sailing ship.
Foot rim ground.

    6.5 cm.   Private Collection.

    Lit. Watney, 1973, op. cit., Pl.67a.

146. COFFEE CUP   c.1768-70

Cup with 'spurs' and scroll handle.
Transfer-printed as No.140 with painted lattice border on the inside
rim.
    6.3 cm.   Victoria & Albert Museum.
                                                    (C. 836-1925).

147. TEA BOWL, COFFEE CUP AND SAUCER   c.1770
Transfer-printed on one side of the bowl and cup as No.140 and on
the other side with a sailing junk; combined patterns on the saucer.

    Coffee cup 6.5 cm., Saucer D. 12 cm.   Private Collection.

148. COFFEE CUP   c.1770   (not illustrated).
Transfer-printed as No.140.

    6 cm.   National Museum of Wales.
                                                    (D.W.3312).

149. TEA BOWL AND SAUCER   c.1770

Transfer printed with three oriental figures minding oxen, in a
landscape, with a lattice border round the rim of the saucer and
inside of the bowl.

    Bowl, 4.5 cm. Saucer D. 12 cm.   Private Collection.

    Note: Slight marks of the border pattern on the underside of
          the saucer, from another stacked beneath before firing.
    Lit. Gilhespy, 1965, op. cit., Pl.67.

150. TEA BOWL AND TWO SAUCERS   c.1770-72

Transfer-printed as No.149 with double line border and minor
variations in the transfer pattern.

    Bowl, 4.5 cm. Saucer D. 12 cm.   Private Collection

147

146

150,149

144,143

151. CUP   c.1770-75   (not illustrated).
     Tall cylindrical shape with wish-bone handle.
     Transfer-printed in underglaze blue with the 'house on an island
     surrounded by a fence' pattern.
     Mark: Patches.
         6.5 cm.   Private Collection.
           Lit. Watney, 1973, op. cit., Pl.67a.
           Note: This print is also found on Bow porcelain.

152. TEA BOWL   c.1770-72
     Painted in a dark underglaze blue with the 'peg top and ramp' pattern.
     Mark: Three stilt marks.
         7.7 cm.   Private Collection.

153. TEA BOWL AND SAUCER   c.1770-72
     Transfer-printed in underglaze blue with the 'house on an island
     set beside a stylised tree' pattern, with a double line border
     round the rim of the saucer and the inside rim of the bowl.
         Bowl 7 cm. Saucer D. 7.5 cm.   Private Collection.
           See. No.400.
           Note: Similar stylised trees also found on Cockpit Hill creamware.

154. TEA BOWL   c.1775
     Painted in underglaze blue, on the exterior of the bowl with the
     'Mansfield' pattern and on the interior, with a single sprig and
     diaper border round the rim.
         4.2 cm.   Private Collection.
           See. No.168 for similar pattern.
           Lit. H.Sandon, 1969, Illustrated Guide to Worcester Porcelain,
                 London, Pl.108, for 'Mansfield' pattern on Worcester
                 porcelain.

155. COFFEE CAN   c.1775-78
     Cylindrical form with grooved handle and broad foot rim.
     Painted in underglaze blue as No.152, with a lattice border round
     the inside rim.
         5.7 cm.   Private Collection.
           See. No.225 for similar broad foot rim.

156. COFFEE CUP   c.1775-78
     Spirally fluted with moulded acanthus leaves rising from the foot rim.
     Painted in underglaze blue with the peony spray pattern, the inside
     of the rim outlined in blue.
         7 cm.   Private Collection.
           See. No.244 for similar style moulded decoration.

157. TEA BOWL AND SAUCER   c.1775-80
     Transfer-printed in dark underglaze blue with an oriental landscape
     and diaper cell border round the rim of the saucer and the inside
     of the bowl. Traces of gilding.
         Bowl 4.5 cm. Saucer D. 12.5 cm.   Derby Museum and Art Gallery.
                                                      (568-4-62).

158. COFFEE CUP   c.1775-80   (not illustrated).
     Transfer-printed as No.157, with traces of gilding.
         6.5 cm.   Private Collection.

157,211

154,156

153

152,155

159. SAUCER   c.1770-72

Transfer-printed in underglaze blue with an 'open zig-zag fence'
trailing plants, two flying birds and a pavilion on an island with
a double line border painted round the rim.

   D. 11.7 cm.   Private Collection.

      See. No.167 for nearly similar transfer pattern.
            Also No.382 for use of transfer in the reverse 'mirror'
            position on the inside of the tureen.

160. MINIATURE TEAPOT AND COVER   c.1768-72

Globular body with loop handle and low domed cover with onion finial.
Painted in underglaze blue with a pagoda on an island and stylised
tree.

Mark: Patches on foot.

   7.5 cm.   Private Collection.
      See. No.153 for transfer of this pattern.
            Also No.161.

161. MINIATURE TEA BOWL AND SAUCER c. 1768-72.

En suite to No.160 painted in underglaze blue.

   Bowl 4.2 cm. Saucer D. 6.4 cm.   Private Collection.

162. MINIATURE SAUCER   c.1768-72

Transfer-printed in underglaze blue as No.160.

   D. 7 cm.   Private Collection.

163. MINIATURE TEA BOWL AND SAUCER c.1770-72

Painted in underglaze blue as No.160.

   Bowl 2.3 cm. Saucer D. 6 cm.   Derby Museum & Art Gallery.
                                              (584-63).

      Note: Decoration on bowl badly blurred.

164. CAUDLE CUP AND COVER   c.1765-1770

Double-handled vessel, on a low dome-shaped foot and high domed
cover with a naturalistically moulded cherry as knop.
Painted in underglaze blue with bamboos and stylised plants and
rocks, the cherry knop painted bright blue.

Mark: Patches on base.

   15.2 cm.   Private Collection.

      Note: Pronounced ridge down the centre of the handles
            similar to shards found on the site at Melbourne.
      Lit. Watney, 1973, op. cit., Pl.66c.

164

160,161,162

163

159

165. TEAPOY   c.1768-70

Ovoid shape with narrow cylindrical neck and flared foot.
Transfer-printed in underglaze blue with, on one side, the
'boy on the buffalo' and on the other side, a 'river scene
with a house surrounded by a fence and a six storey pagoda'
pattern, a diaper border round the neck.

    14.8 cm.   National Museum of Wales.
                                   (D.W.3311).

      See. No.166 for 'boy on the buffalo' transfer print.

166. TEAPOY   c.1768-70

Shaped as No.165.
Transfer-printed in underglaze blue with the 'boy on the buffalo
and chinese sailing junk' pattern, floral border round the neck.

    14.6 cm.   Victoria & Albert Museum.
                                 (C. 364-1924).

      See. No.147 for similar transfer.
             Also No.165, with a different transfer border round
             the neck.

167. SPOON TRAY   c.1765-68

Hexagonal shape with fluted sides and flat base.
Transfer-printed in underglaze blue with the 'open zig-zag fence'
pattern.

    L. 14 cm.   W. 7.3 cm.   Victoria & Albert Museum
                                   (C. 436-1940).

      See. No.159 for nearly similar transfer pattern.
      Note: Steatitic (soapstone) porcelain.
      Lit. Watney, 1973, op. cit., Pl.67c.

165   167   166

168. SUCRIER AND COVER   c.1765-70

Deep bowl and low domed cover with applied moulded leaf and open
flower knop.
Painted in underglaze blue with the 'Mansfield' pattern and a scroll
border round the rim of the bowl and the edge of the cover.
Ground foot rim.

    9.5 cm.   Private Collection.

      See. No.154 for similar pattern.

169. SUCRIER AND COVER   c.1775-80

Fluted circular form with fluted domed cover and finely moulded
unglazed flower finial.
Transfer-printed in underglaze blue with pagodas in a woodland
scene set on an island; similar transfer pattern on the cover, and
a painted double line border round the rim of the cover and the
inside rim of the bowl.

    13 cm.   Private Collection.

      See. No.264 for similar shaped finial.

170. BOWL AND COVER   c.1770-75   Colour Plate p.98

The bowl of bulbous form, supported on a flared foot, the cover
with a scalloped flange and surmounted by a flower finial.
Painted in underglaze blue in an oriental style with fan and
circular-shaped panels with landscapes, reserved on a powder blue
ground.

    15.2 cm.   Private Collection.

      See. Introduction to Blue and White, p.96.
      Lit. S. Spero, 1977, Auction Report, Antique Collecting,
          Vol.12, No.2, Fig.2.

171. BOWL   c.1770

Painted in underglaze dark blue with the 'Mansfield' pattern on
the outside and a scroll and diaper border round the inside of the
bowl.

    D. 15 cm.   Private Collection.

172. BOWL   c.1770-72

Painted in underglaze blue as No.171.
Mark: Open crescent in underglaze blue.

    D. 13.2 cm.   Private Collection.

      Note: Previously, crescent marks have not been recorded on
          Derby porcelain.

173. BOWL   c.1775-78

Transfer-printed in pale underglaze blue with, on one side, the
'house surrounded by a fence' pattern and on the other side, the
'six storey pagoda' pattern, on the inside of the bowl, a small
transfer of a weeping willow tree and a painted lattice border.

    D. 15.5 cm.   Private Collection.

173

169

171,172

168

174. BUTTER TUB STAND   c.1758-60.

Circular shape with upturned scallop rim.
Painted in underglaze blue with floral reserves in cloud-shaped panels,
on a solid blue diaper ground and a cell border round the rim.

  D. 14 cm.   Private Collection.

   Lit. Watney, 1973, op. cit., Pl.66d, for the stand together
     with butter tub and cover.

175. BUTTER TUB   c.1760

Rectangular form, with canted corners and tapering sides.
Painted in underglaze blue with pagodas on islands and flower
sprays, divided by diaper reserves on a wash-blue ground, the rim
outlined in brown.

  L. 11 cm. W. 8 cm.   Private Collection.

   See. No.81 for polychrome example.
   Lit. Watney, 1973, op. cit., Pl.65b.
     Barrett & Thorpe, 1971, op. cit., Pl.83, for an example
     shown with a cover.

176. BUTTER TUB AND COVER   c.1768

Oval shape on a spreading base with feather moulded handles, the
sides moulded with fluted decoration and plain reserves, a flat
domed cover with similar moulded decoration, surmounted by applied
moulded leaves and flower knop with insets to locate the upright
handles.
Painted in underglaze blue in the reserves with Chinamen seated
beside a table on which is placed a bowl of flowers and another
pot of flowers, a cell diaper border round the rim and base,
similar style of painting and cell border on the cover.

  11.5 cm. D. 13 cm.   Private Collection.

177. BUTTER TUB COVER AND STAND   c.1768-70

The tub of cylindrical form with upright feathered handles, decorated
with raised concentric moulded rings, the cover moulded with similar
decoration, surmounted by a foliate ring finial with insets to locate
the upright handles, the stand also decorated with moulded rings
and upturned scallop rim.
Painted in dark tones of underglaze blue with sprays of cornflowers
and winged insects with a cobweb style border round the rim of the
tub, cover and stand.

  10.7 cm. Stand D. 15.5 cm.   Private Collection.

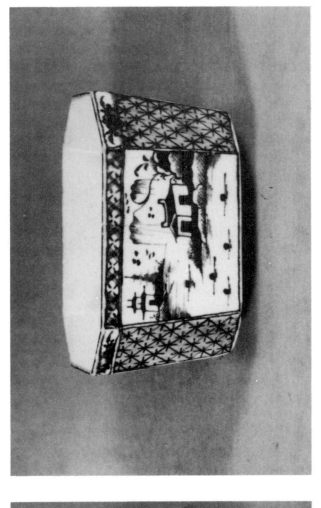

177

175

176

174

178. KINGFISHER CENTRE PIECE c.1758-60

Six open scallop shells set on a coral and shell encrusted base and surmounted by a kingfisher perched on a branch.
Painted in underglaze blue with stylised peonies on each shell and surrounded by a lattice border, the moulding on the shell encrusted base picked out in blue, the kingfisher painted blue with the head, wings and tail picked out in turquoise.

Mark: Patches on base.

 5.5 cm.   Private Collection.

  Lit. Watney, 1973, op. cit., Pl.65a.

179. SHELL SALT   c.1762-65

Three deep scallop shells set on a coral and shell encrusted base with a conch shell finial.
Painted in underglaze blue with flowers and winged insects and surrounded by a diaper border, the moulding on the conch shell and the shell encrusted base picked out in dark blue.

 10.5 cm. D. 16.5 cm.   Private Collection.

  Lit. Spero, 1970, op. cit., p.202.

180. LEAF DISH   c.1768

Moulded in the form of a vine leaf with serrated edge, the stem forming the handle, with veins of the leaf moulded on the underside and set on a heart-shaped foot rim.
Painted in underglaze blue in an oriental style with a large circular-shaped panel in the centre and surrounded by three fan and three small circular-shaped panels with alternate chinese river scenes and flower sprigs, reserved on a powder-blue ground.

 L. 10.4 cm.   Private Collection.

  Note: The blue has become fused with the glaze causing it to 'run' and obscure some of the panels and also spread to the underside.
  Lit. Spero, 1977, op. cit., p.26.

181. SALT   Dated 1772

Oval shape with flaring foot and moulded on the sides with four lobed panels.
Painted in underglaze blue with alternate chinese river scenes and flower sprigs.

Mark: Inscribed on the base 'M x S 1772'.

 4.2 cm.   Castle Museum, Norwich.
                 (48-941).

  Lit. B.M.Watney, 1963, English Blue & White, (1st Ed.) p.104 (as Lowestoft).
     Watney, 1973, op. cit., Pl.69c, (as Derby).
     G.A.Godden, 1969, The Illustrated Guide to Lowestoft Porcelain, p.70 (as doubtful Lowestoft).

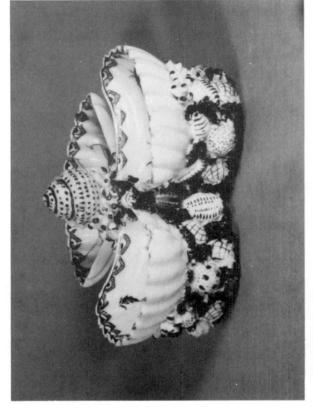

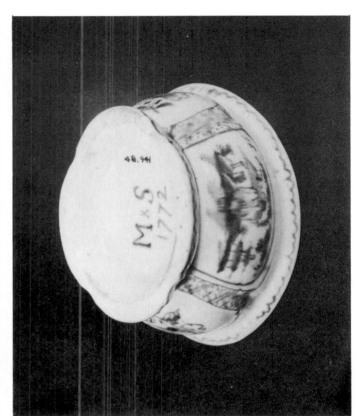

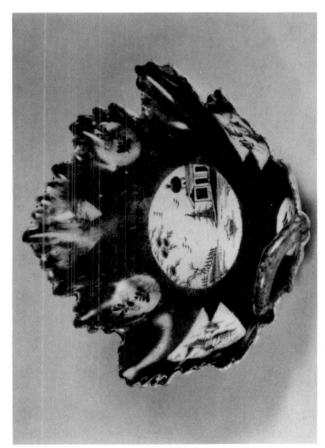

181

179

180

178

182. SHELL DISH   c.1772-75
    Moulded as a scallop shell.
    Painted in underglaze blue with flower sprays and a winged insect,
    with a roll scroll border round the scalloped edge and a lattice
    border at the hinge end.
    Mark: '3' incised on the base.
        L. 10 cm.   Castle Museum, Norwich.
                                                        (45-932).

        Note: The mark is possibly intended to denote the size.
              Registered as Lowestoft in 1932, re-attributed to Derby
              by Dr.Watney in 1958. This shape also occurs with a slightly
              different border pattern.

183. PICKLE LEAF   c.1770
    Moulded in the form of a vine leaf with serrated edge and triangular
    shape stalk handle.
    Painted in underglaze blue with a floral spray. The serrated edge
    and handle picked out in dark blue.
    Mark: Indistinct stilt marks.
        D. 12 cm.   Private Collection.

184. PICKLE LEAF   c.1770-72
    Shaped as No.183.
    Painted in underglaze blue with a floral spray, the serrated edge
    and handle in dark blue.
    Mark: Indistinct stilt marks.
        D. 8.5 cm.   Private Collection.
          Note: Blue has 'run' extensively.

185. PICKLE LEAF   c.1770-72
    Shaped as No.183.
    Transfer-printed in underglaze blue with a floral spray, the
    serrated edge and handle painted in dark blue.
        D. 8.5 cm.   Private Collection.

186. PICKLE DISH   c.1768-70
    Moulded in the form of overlapping geranium leaves with a rustic
    loop handle.
    Painted in underglaze blue, on the interior, with flower sprays and
    winged insects.
        D. 8.3 cm.   Private Collection.
        Note: This was also done earlier in a slightly smaller size using
              a different paste and glaze and a more clearly defined
              leaf moulding.
        Lit. Spero, 1970, op. cit., p.151. for similar form made at
              Worcester.

187. ASPARAGUS BUTTER BOAT   c.1768-70
    Moulded in the shape of a leaf, on trefoil feet, with rustic handle.
    Painted in underglaze blue, on the interior, with a pagoda on an
    island and a solid blue tufted border design round the edge.
        L. 7.3 cm.   Private Collection.
        Lit. Watney, 1973, op. cit., Pl.66b.
              Spero, 1970, op.cit., p.203.

188. ASPARAGUS BUTTER BOAT   c.1768-70
    Shaped as No.187.
    Transfer-printed in underglaze blue, on the interior with a man
    standing on a boat punting and a rocky island. The border painted
    as No.187.

        L. 7 cm.   - 118 -   Private Collection.

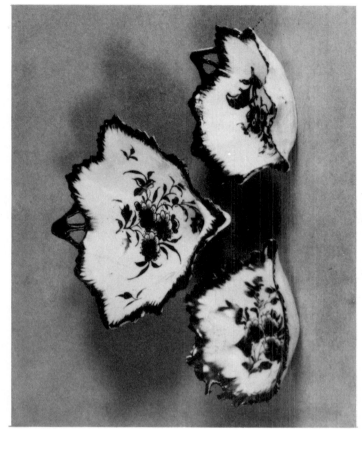

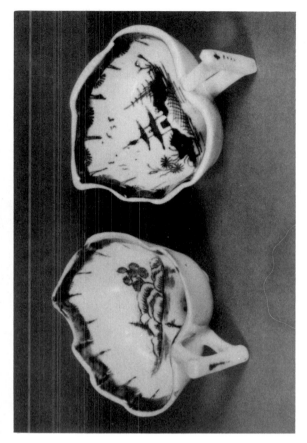

184,183,185

188,187

186

182

189. ASPARAGUS SERVER   c.1775-78
     Tapering fan-shaped body with upright sides.
     Painted in underglaze blue with a stylised daffodil, floral sprays
     on the side walls and a cell diaper border at the outer edge.
          L. 7.3 cm.   Private Collection.

190. ASPARAGUS SERVER   c.1778-82
     Shaped as No.189.
     Painted in underglaze blue with a pagoda beside an estuary.
     Mark: 'N' in underglaze blue.
          L. 7.5 cm.   Private Collection.
            Lit. Spero, 1970, op. cit., p.205.

191. ASPARAGUS SERVER   c.1778-82
     En suite with No.190.
     Mark: 'N' in underglaze blue.
          L. 7.5 cm.   Private Collection.

192. ASPARAGUS SERVER   c.1780-85
     Shaped as No.189.
     Painted in overglaze 'dry' blue enamel with scattered flowers,
     the wide rim outlined in blue.
          L. 7.7 cm.   Private Collection.

193. BUTTER BOAT   c.1760-65
     Reeded body moulded with flowers and a fruiting vine, and silver
     shape scroll handle.
     Painted in underglaze blue on the inside, with a floral spray, winged
     insect and cell diaper border on the lip, and the handle decorated
     with a scroll.
          L. 11.5 cm.   Private Collection.
            See. No.84 for similar shape handle.
            Note: Pattern taken from a salt-glaze mould.
            Lit. Spero, 1970, op. cit., p.195.

194. BUTTER BOAT   c.1765
     Fluted shell moulded body with a high scroll handle.
     Painted in underglaze blue with a pagoda and stylised tree on an island.
          L. 10.5 cm.   Private Collection.
            See. No.400 for similar stylised tree painting.

195. BUTTER BOAT   c.1768
     Shell-moulded body, with feather moulded edge surrounding a scalloped
     rim, supported on a flaring foot and S-shaped handle.
     Painted in underglaze blue in a manner similar to No.194.
          L. 10 cm.   Private Collection.
            Note: Moulded feather edge bears some resemblance to Derby
                  Creamware.

196. BUTTER BOAT   c.1768
     Crisply moulded helmet-shaped body with addorsed dolphins beneath
     the spout, and high scroll handle.
     Painted in dark underglaze blue on the outside picking out the
     lines of the moulding and on the inside, with a flower and lattice
     border.
          L. 9 cm.   Private Collection.
            See. No.198 for same shape in larger size.
            Lit. Spero, 1970, op. cit., p.195.

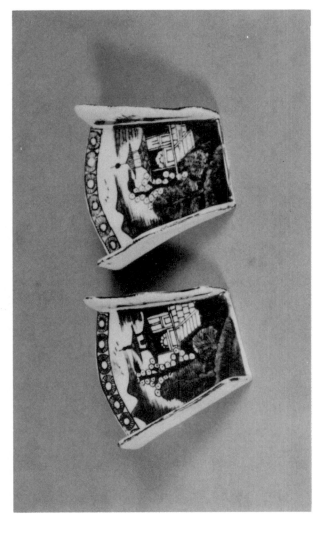

194,193,195,196

190,191

192

189

197. SAUCE-BOAT   c.1756-58

Lobed form with a double line moulded round the rim and grooved
scroll handle.
Painted in underglaze blue with, on the outside, a landscape and
on the inside, a peony and a trellis pattern border round the
lip.

    L. 23.2 cm.   Victoria & Albert Museum.
                                                    (C. 23-1964).

198. SAUCE-BOAT   c.1762-65

Helmet shape with shell-moulded sides and intertwined dolphins,
a paddle and a trident under the lip, set on a raised foot with
a high scroll handle.
Painted in dark underglaze blue, on the outside, picking out the
lines of the moulding, and on the inside, with a flower and a
trellis pattern border round the lip.

    L. 14.2 cm.   Private Collection.
     See. No.196 for smaller size.

199. SAUCE-BOAT   c.1768

Moulded in panels on each side and beneath the spout, the body
finely ribbed.
Transfer-printed in underglaze blue with, on the outside, a
chinoiserie scene and a cell diaper border round the rim and on
the inside, with floral sprays and a flower spray beneath the lip.

    L. 20.5 cm.   Private Collection.
     See. Nos. 200, 212 & 382, for same floral transfer.

200. SAUCE-BOAT   c.1768

Shaped as No.199.
Transfer-printed in underglaze blue with a chinoiserie scene
and floral sprays as No.199.

    L. 17.5 cm.   Private Collection.
     See. Nos. 199, 212 & 382 for same floral transfer.
     Lit. Watney, 1973, op. cit., Pl.67d.

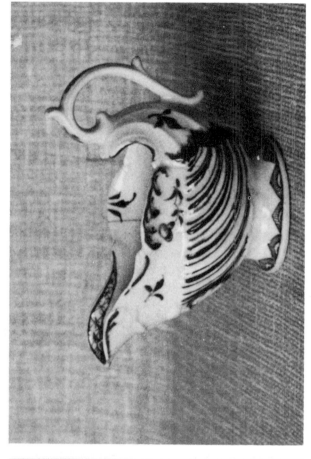

197

198

199

200

201. SAUCE-BOAT   c.1768-72

Lightly fluted sides with scalloped rim, set on a raised foot,
moulded in relief with leaves and sprays of flowers, a shaped
handle with turned up thumb piece.
Painted in underglaze blue with, on the outside, an oriental
fishing scene, and on the inside, a peony spray.
Foot rim ground.

    L. 15.1 cm.   Private Collection.

     See. No.89 for similar shape with 'clobbered' decoration.
     Note: Possibly under fired.

202. SAUCE-BOAT   c.1768-72

Moulded on both sides with rococo cartouches on a ground of
flower heads, set on a raised foot with a shaped handle and turned
up thumb piece (broken off).
Painted in underglaze blue with, on the outside, flower sprays set
within the cartouches and a cell diaper border on the scalloped
rim, and on the inside, a floral bouquet and a trellis pattern
border round the lip.

    L. 18.5 cm.   Private Collection.

203. SAUCE-BOAT   c.1768-72

Elaborately moulded sides with overlapping scales and three plain
reserves with scroll borders, set on a raised foot, a very small
handle with thumb rest and kick terminal.
Painted in underglaze blue with fishing scenes in the side
cartouches and a floral spray beneath the lip.

    L. 13.8 cm.   Private Collection.

     Note: Phosphatic paste.

204. SAUCE-BOAT   c.1770-72

Fluted form with high scroll handle.
Painted in underglaze blue with, on the outside, trailing flower
sprays beneath a formal border, and on the inside, a transfer print
of a chinese river scene, with washed-in colour, and a printed cell
diaper border.

Mark: Workman's mark 'X' on the handle.

    L. 23.5 cm.   Private Collection.

     Note: This pattern was also used on Worcester (see No.462),
           Caughley and Lowestoft, in a variety of sizes.
     Lit. S.W. Fisher, 1947, English Blue & White Porcelain of
           the 18th Century, London, Pl.15.

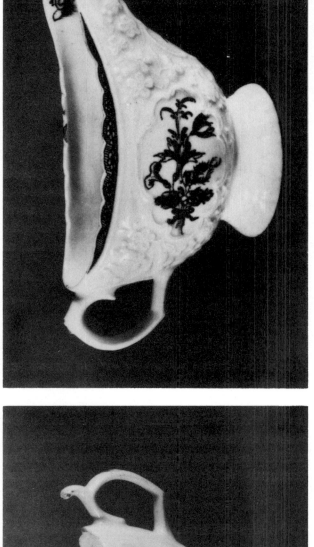

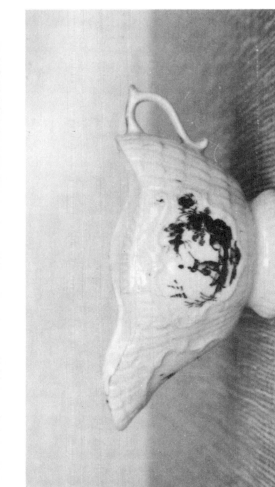

202   462,204

203

201

205. TUREEN, COVER AND STAND   c.1768

Quatrefoil shape with rounded sides, slightly domed cover with
applied moulded leaf and cherry knop (cover a Bow replacement),
and stand also quatrefoil shape.
Painted in underglaze blue with pagodas on islands, divided by
peony sprays and amusing looking phoenixes. The stand also
painted with floral sprays and a cell diaper border round the rim
of the tureen and the stand.

    14 cm. L. 22 cm.   Private Collection.

      Note: On a Derby cover the sides rise more steeply than
           on other English porcelain factories, while the
           cut-out leaves are shaped slightly differently and
           lie almost flat, the cherry knop, placed centrally
           is usually larger and painted.

206. LADLE   c.1758-60

The bowl moulded in the form of a scallop shell, with a long
straight handle terminating in rococo scrolls with plain ribbing
on the under side.
Painted in underglaze blue with stylised flowers in the centre of
the bowl and on the handle, the moulding on the handle picked out
in blue and an uneven dentil border round the rim of the bowl.

    L. 18.5 cm.   Private Collection.

    See. No.229 for similar dentil border.

205   206

207. LOBED DISH   c.1758   (Not illustrated)

Twelve-lobed flat dish.
Painted in underglaze blue with pagodas on islands, with pine
and 'telegraph' trees and a man standing punting, the scallops
round the rim picked out with a decorative design and the whole
surrounded by a lattice border.

Mark: Stilt marks on foot.

   L. 23 cm.   Private Collection.

     Note: Many air bubbles in the paste.
     Lit. Watney, 1973, op. cit., Pl.63d.

208. BOWL, COVER AND STAND   c.1762

The bowl with double line basket moulding with applied floral
decoration, the cover pierced between the bands of the moulding
and decorated with applied floral designs and surmounted by a
rope twist handle, the rim of the stand moulded with inset
cartouches on a ground of double line basket moulding, with
applied florets at the intersections.
Painted in underglaze blue picking out the floral decoration
on the outside of the bowl, and on the inside, painted with a
pagoda and trees on an island and an elaborate border round the
rim; the floral decoration on the cover and the rope twist
handle also picked out in blue with a similar elaborate border
round the rim.
The stand painted with an island in the centre surrounded by a
similar border painted in the cavetto, winged insects in the
cartouches and the florets picked out in blue with a double line
round the rim.

Mark: Patches on the foot of the bowl.

   20.5 cm.   Bowl D. 17.7 cm.   Private Collection.

     See.   No.93 for bowl and cover with polychrome decoration.
     Lit.   Watney, 1973, op. cit., Pl.64a, for similar bowl.
          Barrett & Thorpe, 1971, op. cit., Pl.74, for similar bowl.
          Gilhespy, 1965, op. cit., Pl.137, for similar bowl.
          Spero, 1977, op. cit., Fig.3&4 for bowl cover dated
          August 1762 in G. Godden Reference Collection.

209. STAND FOR BOWL   c.1762

Moulded on the rim with inset cartouches on a ground of double
line basket moulding with applied florets at the intersections and
cut-out sections.
Painted in underglaze blue as No.208, the island the same as on
the inside of the bowl.

   D. 21.7 cm.   Leeds Art Galleries.
                                  (EP.2.10.150/38)

208   209

210. BASKET   c.1760

The oval body with pierced sides and applied florets at the
intersections and double rope twist handles.
Painted in underglaze blue with an oriental landscape set in a
central reserve and a small cell diaper border round the 'spectacle'
rim, the handles and the florets on the outside picked out in blue.

    D. 19.5 cm.   Private Collection.

      See. No.106 for similar shape.
      Lit. B. Watney, 1973, op. cit., Pl.64c.

211. SAUCER DISH   c.1775-80

Transfer-printed in dark underglaze blue with a river scene, a
house on an island and a cell diaper border.
Traces of gilding round the rim.

    D. 19.5 cm.   Derby Museum & Art Gallery.
                                                 (235).

      See. Nos. 157 & 158 for similar pattern.
      Lit. Gilhespy, 1965, op. cit., Pl.67.

212. PLATE   c.1770

Transfer-printed in thick underglaze blue with, in the centre, the
'plantation' pattern and on the everted rim, meandering flower sprays.

    D. 23 cm.   Private Collection.

      See. No.199, 200 and 382 for similar floral transfer pattern.
      Lit. B. Watney, 1973, op. cit., Pl.68c.

213. PLATE   c.1770-75

A shallow spirally fluted rim with a scalloped edge.
Transfer-printed in underglaze blue with, in the centre, a jardiniere
containing a flowering peony, chrysanthemum and seed pods and painted
round the rim with a formal border.

    D. 22.5 cm.   Private Collection.

214. SAUCER DISH   c.1770-75   (Not illustrated)

Shaped as No.213.
Transfer-printed in underglaze blue en suite.

    D. 20.5 cm.   Private Collection.

      Exh. 'China Choice & Venners Antiques, 1976, Caughley
            Exhibition Catalogue, saucer of similar pattern.

215. PLATE   c.1780-85

Painted in underglaze blue with, in the centre, a sun-flower head
surrounded by two alternate sprays of stylised flowers with
trailing floral sprays round the rim and enclosed in a double
line border, the rim outlined in brown.

    D. 22 cm.   Private Collection.

 213

210

215

212

216. MUG   c.1758-60

Barrel shape with three moulded bands equally spaced around the
top and bottom of the mug, with S-scroll handle.
Painted in underglaze blue with pagodas and trees on a mountainous
island.

    17 cm.   Private Collection.

      See. Introduction to Cockpit Hill, p.235.
          No.109 & 110 for similar shape.
      Lit. Gilhespy, 1965, op. cit., Pl.7, for similar shape.

217. MUG   c.1760-62

Cylindrical shape, with S-scroll strap handle and tapering foot.
Painted in bright tones of underglaze blue with an oriental
landscape.

Mark: Stilt marks on base.

    10 cm.   Private Collection.

      See. Nos. 99, 209, 210, for similar design.
      Note: This shape has not been recorded previously.

218. MUG   c.1765

Bell shape with a grooved handle.
Transfer-printed in underglaze blue with, on one side, the 'boy on
the buffalo' and on the other side, the 'six storey pagoda' pattern,
scattered butterflies and a trailing floral band beneath the lip.

    13 cm.   Derby Museum & Art Gallery.
                                      (610-63).

      See. Nos. 133 & 219 for similar shape.
          Nos. 140, 146, 147 and 166 for 'boy on the buffalo' pattern.
          Nos. 165 & 173 for 'six storey pagoda' pattern.
          Introduction to onglaze Black Transfer Printing, p. 92.

219. MUG   c.1765

Shaped as No.218.
Transfer-printed in underglaze blue as No.218.

    13 cm.   Private Collection.

      See. Foot-notes to No.218.
      Note: The position of the transfer prints have been reversed
             and the floral border and the butterflies omitted from
             this mug.
      Lit. Spero, 1970, op. cit., p.199.

216   218   217   219

220. MASK JUG   c.1765

Tall baluster shape with a moulded mask face beneath the lip.
Transfer-printed in underglaze blue with, on either side,
hunting trophies and beneath the mask lip, a buck at lodge,
encircled in a chaplet.

Mark: Patches on base.

   19 cm.   Derby Museum & Art Gallery.
                                                (349-58).

    Prov. Duke of Rutland Collection.
    See. No. 115, for slight variation of the mask.
          P.XVI, Map of Derby published Apr. 1st, 1806, showing
          the Seal of the Town.
    Lit. Barrett & Thorpe, 1971, op. cit., Pl.81.
    Note: The old crest of the Town of Derby, and known locally
          as the 'Buck in the Park'. It was also printed as a
          crest under the heading of Drewry's Derby Mercury.

221. WINE TASTER   c.1768

Moulded externally with sixteen lobes, an everted rim and a cut-
out shaped handle.
Painted in underglaze blue with a floral spray in the centre and
dog-tooth border round the rim.

   L. 7.3 cm.   Private Collection.

    Lit. B. Watney, 1973, op. cit., Pl.66b.
          Spero, 1970, op. cit., p.204.
          Trans. E.C.C., Vol.2, Pt.9, 1946, Pl.71b (as Lowestoft).

222. WINE TASTER   c.1768-70

Shallow fluted circular body with a shaped lug handle.
Painted in underglaze blue with a central floret and dog tooth
border round the rim.

Mark: Evidence of stilt marks.

   L. 8 cm.   Private Collection.

221 222 220

223. VASE   c.1765   Colour Plate p.99.

Baluster form with a flared neck and supported on a splayed foot.
Painted in underglaze blue with two European landscapes in
reserves, beneath two smaller panels, each containing a winged
insect, on a sponged blue ground.

Mark: Three patches.

Foot rim ground.

    12.5 cm.   Private Collection.

      Note: Sponged blue decoration is more commonly found on
            tin-glazed earthenware. Similar European landscapes
            have also been noted on a 'powder blue' plate.

224. VASE   c.1765-68

Inverted pear-shaped body with a spreading mouth and foot, the
body moulded in relief with spiral gadrooning and leaves springing
from the base.
Painted in underglaze blue with, on one side, a Chinaman standing
between rocks, and a willow tree, and on the other side, a Chinese
fisherman seated under a tree.

    14.5 cm.   Private Collection.

      Exh. E.C.C., 1948, op. cit., (Exhib. Cat.) Pl.113 (Described
           as Liverpool).

225. INKWELL   c.1775-80

Straight sided cylindrical shape with a central well for the ink
and four holes in the shoulder for quill pens, on a broad foot
rim.
Transfer-printed in underglaze blue with scattered sprigs of
gillyflowers.

    4.5 cm.   G.Godden Collection.

      See. No.155 for similar foot rim.
      Note: Transfers of a similar style were also used at
           Worcester and Caughley.
      Lit. Watney, 1973, op. cit., Pl.70a.

226. FEEDING CUP   c.1775-78

Semi-circular form and partially covered over, with a slender
S-shaped spout and upright shell moulded handles.
Transfer-printed in underglaze blue with scattered sprigs of
gillyflowers.

    9 cm. L. 17.7 cm.   Private Collection.

      See. No.225 for similar transfer pattern.
      Note: The transfer pattern on the sides has run extensively.

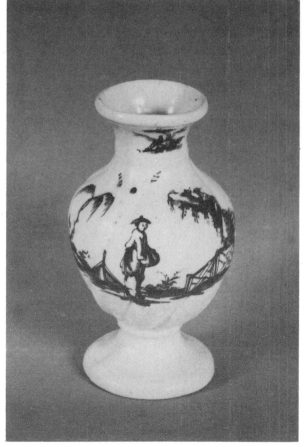

224   225   226

227. GUGLET   c.1760

Bulbous shape with a long neck and a swelling below the flared rim.
Painted in underglaze blue with two oriental landscapes of rocks,
buildings and trees, floral sprays round the neck with a stylised
border round the swelling on the neck and foot rim and a cell
diaper border round the mouth.

   23.5 cm.   Leeds Art Galleries.
                                                (EP2. 1901 - 116).

      See. No.122 for similar shape.

228. BASIN   c.1760

En suite with No.227. Circular form with everted lip and set on
a flared foot.
Painted in underglaze blue with, on the interior, a chinoiserie
scene with pagodas and pine trees on an island, within a band of
flower sprays, a cell diaper border round the lip and on the
exterior further 'Shan-Shui'.

Mark: Patches on base.

   D. 23 cm.   Private Collection.

229. CHAMBER CANDLESTICK   c.1758-60

Lozenge shape with a wavy upturned edge and raised candle holder
in the centre.
Painted in underglaze blue with stylised flowers on the base,
scattered flowers on the candle holder and an uneven dentil border
round the upturned edge.

Mark: Patches on base.

   L. 13 cm.   Private Collection.

      See. No.206 for similar dentil border.
      Lit. Watney, 1973, op. cit., Pl.63b.

230. CHAMBER CANDLESTICK   c.1768-70.

Circular quarter-lobed base with a raised dome centre, surmounted
by a shaped candle nozzle, moulded decoration round the base with
applied leaves and scattered florets, with a twisted snake-like
handle and a floral rosette thumb rest.
Painted in underglaze blue with scattered flower sprays, winged
insects, the moulding round the candle nozzle and the rosette on
the handle all picked out in blue and the rim of the base outlined
with a dog-tooth border.

   6.5 cm.   D. 13.5 cm.   Private Collection.

      See. No.127 for polychrome example.
      Lit. R. Blunt, 1924, op. cit., No.66, Pl.20, identified
           as Chelsea.
      Exh. E.C.C., 1977, op. cit., (Exhib. Cat.) No.145.

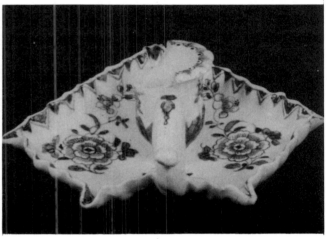

227   230   228   229

- 140 -

THE NOTTINGHAM ROAD FACTORY 1770-1848

At this period of the factory's history production had increased and the takeover of the Chelsea works had enabled William Duesbury to make further improvements in his factories, and to add many new shapes and figures to his already growing list.

The neo-classical style was very much in vogue throughout Western Europe and Derby followed the current fashion with the production of useful wares in this style. Predominant at this time was the use of the celebrated blue on-glaze colour known as 'Smith's blue'; the colour being a variation of royal blue, but lighter, and the name taken from the head colour man at the factory.

By 1773 Duesbury had found it provident to open a London showroom at No.1, Bedford Street, Covent Garden. It is stated, by his agent Joseph Lygo, that 'Duesbury had the Royal Appointment first in 1775'. This is an important statement by Lygo which many subsequent ceramic historians appear to have missed.

Prior to the period under consideration, the factory did not use a mark. However, after the Chelsea merger, the first mark used on wares was a painted or incised N. It is sometimes accompanied by a gold anchor, a reference to the Chelsea works. The usual Duesbury-Chelsea (Chelsea-Derby) mark was an anchor and the letter 'D', sometimes separate but more usually intertwined. The mark at Derby was a crown over 'D' in blue or puce. Shortly after 1782 the crossed batons and six dots were introduced between the crown and 'D'. Normally the colour of the mark was puce, but, where a description was written on the ware, it would appear in blue. This mark, it is important to record, was continued for over forty years, although varying in colour.

With the death of his father in 1786, William Duesbury II was set to raise the standards, both artistically and commercially to perhaps the peak of the factory's history. For it was this Duesbury who gathered round him possibly the finest group of painters in the history of ceramic decoration. The figure painting by Richard Askew and James Banford; the fine water colour style of painting of Zachariah Boreman who specialised in landscapes to be joined later by John Brewer. The cylindrical coffee cans with finely painted groups of fruit and birds by George Complin who went to Derby from Chelsea in 1789. Complin had earlier worked on enamels at Battersea; the flower painting of Edward Withers, Billingsley and later the shipping subjects by George Robertson and fine landscapes by Jockey Hill; all these and others beside amounted to a great wealth of talent.

Billingsley was important because of his connections with the porcelain works at Pinxton, Worcester, Swansea and Nantgarw and his decorating establishments at Mansfield and Torksey. It was his style of painting that made him the most copied of all flower painters giving the ceramic world a style of painting that gave a more natural

appearance to the flowers. This method of painting was to
become increasingly popular during the nineteenth century.

It is fairly obvious, but has sometimes in the past been missed
by writers, that the shape, designs and pattern books are the basis
of any porcelain works. It is from the pattern books that we have
gleaned information about the painters and dates at the factory.
Commenced originally about the time of the merger, only a few
fragments remain from this period as the surviving books date
from about 1780 and would have been completed about 1810.

1797 marked the death of William Duesbury II, but the family
managed to retain control until 1811 when Robert Bloor leased the
Nottingham Road factory.

Much criticism has been launched at Bloor but the good points of
this man's connection with our subject factory should not be
treated lightly. Before his unfortunate illness left the running
of the works in the hands of people unfitted to try to continue
the famous old porcelain traditions of Derby, Bloor had engaged
many new and fine painters such as Thomas Steel, Richard Dodson,
Moses Webster, Daniel Lucas and to re-engage perhaps the best
flower painter of all, William Pegg the Quaker.

Many new figures were added to the lists; these were principally
modelled by Edward Keys and John Whitaker, who had followed the
Duesbury modellers such as Pierre Stephan, Coffee and Spängler.

The mark of the period was the traditional crown, crossed batons
and dots over the letter 'D', until 1825 when it was decided that
it took too long for the gilder to execute the mark by hand. The
first printed Bloor mark was used and these marks were used until
the close of the factory. After a long illness Robert Bloor died
in 1846 and by 1848 it was decided by Alderman Clarke, the husband
of Bloor's grand-daughter, to close the works.

John Twitchett, F.R.S.A.

231. TEAPOT, COVER AND STAND   c.1773-82

Baluster shape, moulded with spiral flutes with leaf moulding within
each flute, with ribbed loop handle and facetted spout, a fluted
domed cover surmounted by a pine-apple knop. The stand, a four lobed
oval shape with flared rim and unglazed base.
Painted in enamel colours with swags of flowers suspended from a
gilt line below a band of turquoise and a dentillate gold band,
the edge of the handle and tip of the spout outlined in gilt, the
cover and stand painted with swags of flowers with a turquoise and
gilt border round the rim.

    15.8 cm.   Stand, L. 13.7 cm.   Castle Museum, Norwich.
                                             (Bulwer 680).

232. TEAPOT AND COVER   c.1775-82

Cylindrical shape, tapering towards the foot, with sloping shoulders
and a pierced gallery round the rim, a flat angled handle with
pierced moulding at the upper terminal, a curved spout with basket
and leaf moulding round the lower part, a low domed cover with a
sphinx terminal.
Painted in enamel colours with a cartouche of flowers enclosing the
initials 'M B', swags of flowers hanging from a band of reticulated
gilding below the shoulder, the edge of the handle, tip of the
spout and rim of the gallery outlined in gilt and details of the
sphinx picked out in gilt.

Mark: Crown & 'D' in blue enamel on base.

    10.5 cm.   Castle Museum, Norwich.
                                            (Bulwer 484).

233. TEAPOT AND COVER   c.1775-80

Shaped as No.232 with a fluted cover.
Painted with scattered sprays of flowers and the sphinx painted
in gilt.

Mark: 'D' intersected by an Anchor in gold.

    10.8 cm.   Victoria & Albert Museum.
                                      (C. 254+A - 1922).

234. TEAPOT AND COVER   c.1775-80

Fluted globular shape, with S-shaped spout and wish-bone handle,
a low domed cover with onion finial.
Painted in green and lilac enamel colours with neo-classical
arabesques hanging from a band of gilding and scattered insects,
the cover painted with similar arabesques and a gilt dentil
border.

Mark: 'D' intersected by Anchor in gold.

    18 cm.   Private Collection.

232

231

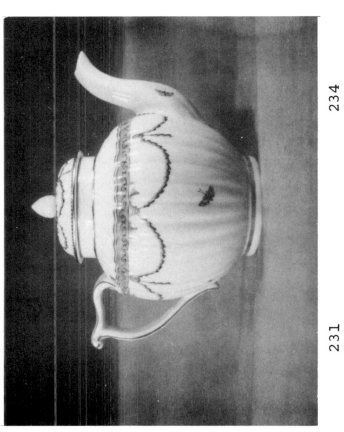

234

233

235. TEAPOT AND COVER   c.1775

Globular shape with wish-bone handle and crabstock spout, a low
domed cover with a carefully moulded biscuit flower terminal.
Painted en camaieu with cupids and a quiver of arrows, resting on
clouds, surrounded by a gilt border on a striped blue and gilt
ground, the cover also painted in like manner.

    10.5 cm.   Private Collection.

      See. Nos. 169 & 264 for biscuit finials.
      Note: Cupids possibly painted by Richard Askew.
            Foot note to Nos. 31-35 for references to Richard Askew.
      Lit. W.A. Tapp, 1934, Richard Askew, Painter of Ceramics,
            Connoisseur, 93, June, pp. 359-363.
            J.C. Austin, 1977, Chelsea Porcelain at Williamsburg,
            Williamsburg, Virginia, No.91 for references to
            Richard Askew's work.

236. VEILLEUSE   c.1835-40

Squat shaped teapot with a large ring handle, curved spout and an
almost flat cover surmounted by an 'onion' knop. The stand of
cylindrical form with pierced vents, a castellated rim and
spreading foot.
Painted in enamel colours with, on the pot, an open-sided building
set in a landscape beside a river with a bridge and mountains in
the distance, and painted on the stand with a continuous shipping
and harbour scene.

Mark: 'Bloor Derby' and Crown painted on the base in red enamel.

    21.5 cm.   Private Collection.

237. CHOCOLATE POT   c.1785

Pear shape with a curved spout and shaped handle, a low domed cover
with an onion finial.
Painted in enamel colours with scattered floral sprigs and a gold
band entwined with stylised leaves below a gilt dentil band round
the centre of the pot, the rim of pot, the edge of the handle and
the tip of the spout outlined in gilt, the cover also painted in
like manner.

    22.5 cm.   Private Collection.

      See. No.242 for bowl, cup & saucer with same pattern.
      Lit. Pattern No.85 in the Derby Pattern Book.

236   235   237

238. TEA BOWL   c.1770

   Painted in enamel colours with a rose and another floral spray,
   the rim outlined in brown.

      2.3 cm.   Private Collection.

239. TEA BOWL AND SAUCER   c.1775-80

   The bowl of ogee shape.
   Painted in overglaze blue enamel with neo-classical arabesques
   hanging from a blue band painted with dots, the centre of the
   saucer painted with a floral spray set in a circle of elongated
   arrow heads.

   Mark: Crown, crossed batons, six dots and 'D' painted in blue
         enamel. '18' in blue enamel.

      5.4 cm.   Saucer D. 13.3 cm.   Victoria & Albert Museum.
                                              (3009+A - 1901).

240. TEACUP AND SAUCER   c.1775-80

   The cup of fluted form with serrated edge, a double scroll handle
   with a pronounced thumb rest and terminal kick, the saucer of
   similar form.
   Painted in enamel colours in the Jabberwocky pattern.

   Mark: Crown, crossed batons, six dots and 'D' painted in red enamel.
         '20' in red enamel.

      5.1 cm.   Saucer D. 14 cm.   Private Collection.

      Lit.   Pattern No.20 in Derby Pattern Book.

241. COFFEE CUP   c.1770-75

   Of standard Derby form, with a grooved loop handle.
   Painted in enamel colours with, on one side, a truncated oval
   reserve containing two oriental figures standing beside a table,
   the ground covered with enamel foliate sprays surrounding an
   irregular shaped reserve set between two circular ones.

      6.7 cm.   Private Collection.

240

239

241

238

242. TEA BOWL, COFFEE CUP AND SAUCER   c.1780

All pieces shaped with shallow ribbed moulding and serrated edge.
Painted in enamel colours as No.237.

Mark: Crown, crossed batons, six dots and 'D' painted in puce enamel.

  Bowl, 5.4 cm. Cup 6.3 cm. Saucer D.13 cm.   Private Collection.

243. TEA BOWL, COFFEE CUP AND SAUCER   c.1775-80

Of standard Derby shape, the cup with a simple ear-shaped handle.
Painted in enamel colours with rural landscapes in the centre of
the saucer, the interior of the tea bowl and the coffee cup and
set within a circular border, an overglaze blue line intertwined
with a gilt foliate leaf motif, set between two chain and band
borders, the rim of each piece outlined with a gilt dentil border.

Mark: Crown, crossed batons, six dots and 'D' painted in puce enamel.
      'N 86' on the tea bowl and coffee cup.
      '86' on the saucer.
      '3' on the tea bowl and saucer painted in puce enamel.
      Impressed 'D' on the tea bowl, 'F' on the saucer.

  Bowl, 4.9 cm. Cup 6.7 cm. Saucer D.12.9 cm. Private Collection.

    Lit. Pattern No.86 in the Derby Pattern Book.

244. COFFEE CUP AND SAUCER   c.1775

Moulded with shallow spiral flutes and elongated acanthus leaves,
with a simple loop handle on the cup.
Painted in enamel colours with a floral chain, the edge of the
handle outlined in gilt and a gold dentil border round the rim
of the cup and saucer.

Mark: 'D' intersected by Anchor in gilt.

    6.3 cm. Saucer D. 12.7 cm.   Private Collection.
      See. No.156 for similar style moulded decoration.

245. TEA BOWL AND SAUCER   c.1780

Shaped as No.244.
Painted with an overglaze blue line intertwined with a gilt
foliate motif, repeated in a smaller manner in the centre of the
saucer, the rim of the bowl and saucer outlined with a gilt dentil
border.

Mark: Crown, crossed batons, six dots and 'D'; '110' painted in
      puce enamel. '8' impressed on the bowl.

    5.4 cm. Saucer D. 13 cm.   Private Collection.

      Lit. Pattern No.110 in the Derby Pattern Book.

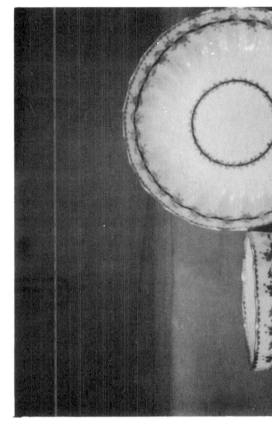

245

243

244

242

246. TEACUP AND SAUCER   c.1775

Tall shaped cup with plain loop handle and deep shaped saucer.
Painted in enamel colours with puce and pink ribbons suspended
from a gilt band forming festoons with ears of wheat, set between
a puce and pink band entwined with wheat stalks and green leaves,
the edge of the handle and the rim of both the cup and the saucer
outlined in gilt.

> 7.1 cm.   Saucer D. 13.2 cm.   City of Bristol Museum & Art
>   Gallery.   (N 8150).

> Exh.   Bristol Museum & Art Gallery, 1970, Bicentenary Porcelain
>   Exhibition, Catalogue No.98.
>   Made as a replacement for a Bristol service (Butts
>   service).

247. TEA BOWL AND SAUCER   c.1775

Tea bowl and saucer of shallow fluted form with serrated edge.
Painted in enamel colours with festoons of flowers suspended
from gilt rings with leaves in two shades of green outlined in
black, a gilt dentil border round the rim of the bowl and saucer.

Mark: Crown over 'D' painted in overglaze blue, on both the bowl
      and saucer.

> 4.3 cm.   Saucer D. 12.3 cm.   City of Bristol Museum & Art
>   Gallery.   (N 4030 a, b.).

248. TEACUP   c.1780

Deep shaped cup with entwined loop handle terminating in leaves.
Painted en camaieu with a draped cupid reclining on soft clouds,
on one side and on the other side, a trophy composed of a violin,
trumpet, an open book, with a quill pen and inkwell, a bow and
arrow and a quiver, all resting on soft clouds, set below sprays
of green leaves picked out in gilt, the handle and terminals also
picked out in gilt.

Mark: 'D' intersected by Anchor in gold.

> 4.8 cm.   City of Bristol Museum & Art
>   Gallery.   (4041a).

249. TEACUP AND SAUCER   c.1805

Wide ogee-shaped bowl with fluted rim and plain loop handle,
the saucer similarly profiled and fluted.
Painted with a band of interlaced ovals and dots above a gold
band of stylised gold leaves, and in the centre of the saucer
and inside the cup, a gilt 'Chantilly' sprig.

Mark: Crown and crossed batons painted in puce enamel on both
      the cup and saucer.
      '8' painted in puce enamel inside the foot rim of the cup.

> 4.6 cm.   Saucer D. 12 cm.   City of Bristol Museum & Art
>   Gallery.   (N4031 a, b.).

> Note: Possibly made as a replacement for an Anstice, Horton
>   & Rose service.

246,247   249,248

250. TEACUP AND SAUCER   c.1785-90

The cup of slightly flaring form with a simple loop handle.
Painted in enamel colours with a rural landscape inside the cup
and the centre of the saucer, a flesh pink ground terminating
mid-way with a gilt zig-zag line and enclosing a broad band of
gilt pendant droplets, and a gilt dentil border round the rim of
the cup and saucer.

Mark: Crown, crossed batons, six dots and 'D'; '118' painted in
      puce enamel.
        '2' on the cup, '11' on the saucer painted in puce enamel.
        '7' impressed on the cup, '5' impressed on the saucer.

    6.2 cm.   Saucer D. 13.9 cm.   Private Collection.

        See. No.262 for cream jug with same decoration.
        Lit. Pattern No.118 in Derby Pattern Book.

251. COFFEE CAN AND SAUCER   c.1790

The can of cylindrical form, with a loop and spur handle and a
deep shaped saucer.
Painted in enamel colours with, on the can, two birds perched on
a basket containing grapes, peaches and white currants, with the
basket set on a slab, enclosed by a gilt ropework border, the sides
decorated with reserves containing bands of roses set on a yellow
ground, and inside the can, a leaf motif border, the saucer
decorated with alternate oblong and irregular shaped reserves
containing roses painted in naturalistic colours outlined in gilt
and set on a yellow ground with a similar leaf motif border in the
centre.

Mark: Crown, crossed batons and 'D'; '236' painted in puce enamel.
        'G' impressed on the can, 'H' impressed on the saucer.

    6.2 cm.   Saucer D. 13.3 cm.   Private Collection.

        Note: The source of the decoration is taken from Jean Pillemont,
              1760, The Ladies Amusement, London.
        Lit. Pattern No.236 in Derby Pattern Book, 'Fruit with Birds
              by Complin'.
              C. Cook, 1948, The Life and Work of Robert Hancock,
              London, item No.13.

252. TEACUP AND SAUCER   c.1795-1800

Shaped as No.250.
Painted in enamel colours with swags of flowers supported by gilt
rosettes and intersected by branches painted in pale blue and
purple with gilt dots and tied at the base with ribbons tied in
bows, surrounding a central reserve containing a rural landscape
painted in naturalistic colours and a gilt border round the rim.

Mark: Crown, crossed batons, six dots and 'D'; '320' and '3'
      painted in puce enamel.
        '5' impressed on the saucer.

    6.2 cm.   Saucer D. 14 cm.   Private Collection.

        Lit. Pattern No.320 in Derby Pattern Book.
              Haslem, 1876, op. cit., p.190, painted by John Moscrop.

250

251

252

253. TEACUP AND SAUCER   c.1795-1800   (Cup not illustrated)

Cup with double crossed handle.
Painted in naturalistic enamel colours with a river flowing through
a valley, set in a central reserve, surrounded by a bead moulding
border and a gilt pendant of vine leaves round the rim.

Mark: Crown and crossed batons painted in blue enamel.
      Inscribed 'View in Dovedale, Derbyshire'.

    6.5 cm.   Saucer D. 13.5 cm.   Private Collection.

       Note: Possibly painted by Zachariah Boreman.

254. CUP   c.1798

Shaped as No.253.
Painted in naturalistic enamel colours with trees growing on the
banks of a river which flows under a bridge with a town in the
distance, surrounded by a gilt octagonal border and a gilt border
round the rim.

Mark: Crown, crossed batons and 'D' painted in blue enamel.
      Inscribed 'Near Coupar, in Angus, Scotland'.

    6.5 cm.   Private Collection.

       Note: Possibly painted by George Robertson.

255. CUP AND SAUCER   c.1795-1800

Cup and saucer of standard Derby shape.
Painted in green monochrome and a pale flesh wash, edged with a
gilt line, with landscape views on the cup and in the centre of
the saucer.

Mark: Crown, crossed batons and 'D'; '409' painted in blue enamel.
      Inscribed 'In Dovedale, Derbyshire' on the cup.
      'Near Breadsall, Derbyshire' on the saucer.

    6.5 cm. Saucer D. 14 cm.   Private Collection.

      Lit. Pattern No.409, 410 in Derby Pattern Book.
            Inscribed 'Tinted with Olive and soft Flesh'.

256. TEA BOWL   c.1795-1800

Of standard Derby cup shape.
Painted in naturalistic enamel colours with a river flowing through
a steep valley, set in a reserve, surrounded by a gilt line with
pendant vine leaves round the rim.

Mark: Crown, crossed batons and 'D' painted in blue enamel.
      Inscribed 'View on the Derwent, Derbyshire'.

    6.5 cm.   Private Collection.

254

253

255

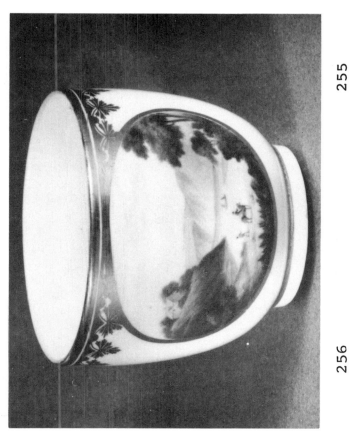

256

257. COFFEE CAN AND SAUCER   c.1790

Shaped as No.251.
Painted in enamel colours within a circular gilt reserve, on the
can, with a riverside landscape of a cottage on a bank overlooking
the river, and on the saucer, within a circular gilt reserve a
woodland scene, a claret coloured border with a gilt line round the
rim of the can and the saucer.

Mark: Crown, crossed batons, six dots and 'D' painted in puce enamel.

   6.4 cm.   Saucer D. 14.1 cm.   Private Collection.

258. TEACUP AND SAUCER   c.1785

Shaped as No.255.
Painted in enamel colours on the front of the cup and within a
circular gilt reserve on the saucer, a crest comprising a talbot
couchant collared, and the initials 'E.C.', a gilt line border
with a chain of buds and dots round the rim of the cup and the
saucer.

Mark: Crown, crossed batons, six dots and 'D' painted in puce enamel.

   6.3 cm.   Saucer D. 13.8 cm.   Private Collection.

     Note: The crest and initials are thought to belong to the
           Coleridge family.

259. CUSTARD CUP   c.1775

Cup of baluster shape, with wish-bone handle.
Painted in enamel colours with a rose and floral spray.

   7 cm.   Private Collection.

260. CHOCOLATE CUP AND STAND   c.1830

The cup of inverted-bell shape on a low domed foot and two applied
C-scroll handles, the saucer of deep form with an everted rim.
Painted with excentric figures, including animals, birds and trees,
in gilt, on a dark ground, a trailing border of leaves painted
round the inside of the cup.

   8 cm.   Saucer D. 13 cm.   Private Collection.

     Note: Possibly painted by William Watson.

257   259   258   260

261. CREAM JUG   c.1780

Pear-shaped form with sparrow beak lip and grooved loop handle.
Painted in enamel colours with an overglaze iron-red and gilt
decoration superimposed on an elaborate underglaze blue border,
with stylised chrysanthemum heads in red and blue enamel painted
round the widest part of the jug.

    8.6 cm.   Private Collection.

      Note: Possibly made as a replacement for a Worcester service.

262. CREAM JUG   c.1785-90

Shallow jug, moulded with shallow vertical flutes, small sparrow
beak lip and applied wish-bone handle.
Painted in enamel colours as No.250 with a rural landscape on
the inside of the jug depicting a farmhouse surrounded by trees
near the edge of a pond, with two small figures in the near
foreground at the waters edge.

    7 cm.   Private Collection.

      See. A similar example in the Derby Museum & Art Gallery.
           No.250 for teacup & saucer with same decoration.
      Lit. Pattern No.118 in Derby Pattern Book.

263. CREAM JUG   c.1790-95

Of baluster form, with a wide flaring lip and simple loop handle.
Painted in enamel colours on the front of the jug with a rural
landscape and two figures walking with a dog, set in an oval gilt
frame, with a gilt line and a chain of flower buds round the rim.

Mark: Crown, crossed batons, six dots and 'D'; '230', 'IV' painted
      in blue enamel.
      Inscribed 'Near Burton, Staffordshire' painted in blue enamel.

    8.5 cm.   Private Collection.

      Lit. Pattern No.230 in Derby Pattern Book.

264. SUCRIER AND COVER   c.1780

The bowl moulded with spiral flutes and elongated acanthus leaves,
a domed fluted cover with serrated edge and terminating in a
flattened section surmounted by an unglazed flower finial.
Painted on the alternate flutes in underglaze blue and iron-red
enamel outlined in gilt.

Mark: 'D' intersected by Anchor in gold.

    13 cm.   Derby Museum & Art Gallery.
                                 (1407-1).

      See. No. 169 and 235 for similar unglazed finials.
      Lit. Barrett & Thorpe, 1971, op. cit., Pl.109.

261   264   262   263

265. SORBET CUP   c.1790

The cup of inverted-bell shape set on a low domed foot, with an
elaborately moulded C and S-scroll handle.
Painted in enamel colours with drapes and tassels above a band of
foliate scrolls and flower buds with scattered roses below a gilt
line, a gilt dentil border round the rim and the edge of the handle
picked out in gilt.

    6.7 cm.   Private Collection.

      Note: The shape is derived from French examples, which occur
            in sets of six, set out on a tray.

266. EGG CUP   c.1825-35

The shaped egg cup and stand moulded in one piece.
Painted in enamel colours with full blown roses and _Myosotis_
(forget-me-not) the leaves painted in gilt and a gilt line border
round the rim of the cup and stand.

Mark: 'Bloor Derby' encircling Crown printed in red enamel.

    6 cm.   Private Collection.

267. PATTY PANS (Three)   c.1790-95

Each patty pan of shallow flaring form with flanged rim.
Painted in overglaze blue enamel with scattered flower sprays
and a blue line and dot border round the flange.

Mark: Crown, crossed batons, six dots and 'D' painted in blue enamel.

    D. 9.5 cm.   Private Collection.

268. BUTTER TUB, COVER AND STAND   c.1810

The tub of oval shape with slightly flaring sides and small upright
handles, a slightly domed cover with cut-out sections to accomodate
the handles and surmounted by an oval ring handle. The stand
lozenge shape.
Painted in enamel colours with a blue band border and a bouquet of
flowers on either side of the tub and in the centre of the stand,
the edge of the ring handle, the rim of the tub, the cover and the
stand outlined in gilt.

    Tub L.15.2 cm. Stand L.20.3 cm., W.15.2 cm.   Private Collection.

269. BUTTER TUB AND COVER   c.1820   Colour Plate p.141

The tub of cylindrical form with two small upright handles, a
slightly domed cover with cut-out sections to accommodate the
upright handles and surmounted by an angular shaped handle.
Painted in enamel colours with pattern in imitation of Japanese
'Imari'.

    9 cm. D. 22.6 cm.   Royal Crown Derby Museum.

265   266   268   267

270.   PLATE   c.1790

Fluted rim with scalloped edge.
Painted in enamel colours with a broad blue band, overpainted with
gilt and white enamel, containing six irregular shaped reserves with
full blown roses in naturalistic colours, the centre painted with a
circular reserve enclosing a rural landscape, bordered by a blue
line and gilt foliate chain.

Mark: Crown, crossed batons, six dots and 'D'; '35' painted in blue
      enamel. Inscribed 'View Kedleston Park, Derbyshire' painted
      in blue enamel.
   D. 23 cm.   Private Collection.
      Lit.   Pattern No.35 in Derby Pattern Book.

271.   PLATE   c.1790

Shallow moulded slightly spiral fluting with scalloped edge.
Painted in enamel colours on the flange with a wreath of alternate
pink and green leaves with gilt tendrills, the centre painted with
a circular reserve enclosing a view of a river valley, bordered by
an elaborate design of interlocking ovals painted in gilt.

Mark: Crown, crossed batons, six dots and 'D'; '148' painted in blue
      enamel. Inscribed 'On the Dove, Derbyshire' painted in blue
      enamel.
   D. 22.4 cm.   Private Collection.

272.   PLATE   c.1790

Shaped as No.271.
Painted in enamel colours on the flange with a broad band of blue,
adorned with arcaded gilt lines shadowed in black with shorter
lines of black and gilt, set between a chain motif of leaves and
tendrils. The reserve in the centre painted with 'Palemon and
Lavinia' standing in a rural landscape, set within a double gilt
border.

Mark: Crown, crossed batons, six dots and 'D'; '181' painted in
      blue enamel.
   D. 22.7 cm.   Private Collection.
      Note: The subject is taken from 'The Seasons - Autumn' by
            Thomson, and was probably copied from the engraving
            by C.Knight after the original painting by Angelica
            Kauffmann.
      Lit. Pattern No.181 in Derby Pattern Book and marked
            'Palemon and Lavinia by Askew in colour'.
            E.C.C., 1973, Miscellany, Trans. E.C.C., Vol.10, Pt.1,
            Pl.37.
            Herculaneum pearlware jug transfer printed in mauve-
            pink, bears the same subject.

273.   PLATE   c.1790

Shaped as No.270.
Painted in enamel colours on the flange with a broad band of pale
pink bordered by gilt lines and a gilt dentil edge, the centre
painted with a circular reserve enclosing a rural landscape,
bordered by a gilt line.

Mark: Crown, crossed batons, six dots and 'D'; '205' painted in
      blue enamel.
   D. 21 cm.   Private Collection.
      Lit.   Pattern No.205 in Derby Pattern Book.

273

272

271

270

274. PLATE   c.1785   (Not illustrated)

Plate of deep form with a scalloped edge.
Painted in underglaze blue and overglaze enamel colours in imitation
of a Japanese 'Imari' design.
Mark: A pseudo-Chinese square seal.

    D. 20.7 cm.   Private Collection.
      Lit.   Pattern No.3 in Derby Pattern Book.
           Barrett & Thorpe, 1971, op. cit., Pl.111 for similar plate.

275. PLATE   c.1790

Circular form with a slightly indented six-lobed edge.
Painted in enamel colours with a broad band of dark red on the flange,
the ground colour of the plate apple green and the centre painted
with a circular reserve enclosing a river waterfall in a landscape.

Mark: Crown, crossed batons, six dots and 'D'; '321' painted in
      red enamel. Inscribed 'Ruins of Bridge at Pandupenmaihno,
      Wales' painted in red enamel.
    D. 22.5 cm.   Private Collection.

276. PLATE   c.1805

Shaped as No.275.
Painted in enamel colours on the flange, on a black background,
scattered playing cards, three dice symetrically placed in the well
of the plate and painted in the reserve in the centre, additional
scattered playing cards, placed round a centre card, painted en
grisaille with a coat-of-arms, a coronet surmounting a garter ribbon,
inscribed Honi soit qui mal y pense, a wreath of laurel leaves and a
ribbon inscribed Dieu et mon droit, to either side at the top 'G III
REX' and below, 'No.XXIV' with the name 'Hardy' painted below.

Mark: Crown, crossed batons, six dots and 'D' painted in red enamel.

    D. 21.9 cm.   Private Collection.
      Note: Possibly made as a replacement for a Coalport service.
          An example of this service was at Messrs.Jellinek &
          Sampson in 1976.
      Lit.   Gilhespy, 1965, op. cit., Pl.169, for another 'Hardy'
          card plate.

277. PLATE   c.1815

Painted in naturalistic enamel colours with butterflies and moths,
on a white and grey marbled ground, an elaborate border pattern of
stylised flowers and tendrils, in gilt, round the well, and the rim
outlined in gilt.
Mark: Crown, crossed batons, six dots and 'D' painted in red enamel.
    D. 22.9 cm.   Private Collection.

278. PLATE   c.1815

Painted in naturalistic enamel colours with a grayling fish surrounded
by aquatic plants in the centre of the plate and decorated round the
flange with an elaborate gilt border.
Mark: Crown, crossed batons, six dots and 'D' painted in red enamel.
    Inscribed 'A Grayling' painted in red enamel.
    D. 23 cm.   Private Collection.
      Lit.   Gilhespy, 1965, op. cit., Pl.170, where it is stated
          that the fish was possibly painted by Thomas Tatlow.

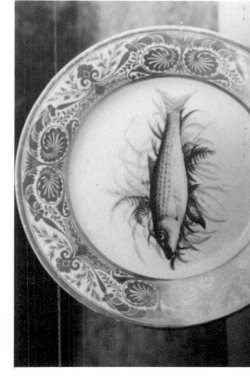

278

276

277

275

279. SAUCER DISH   c.1810

Painted in naturalistic enamel colours with a gothic ruin set in a
rural landscape, surrounded by an elaborate C-scroll border with a
gilt line round the rim.
Mark: Crown, crossed batons, six dots and 'D' painted in red enamel.

   D. 20.9 cm.   Private Collection.

280. DISH   c.1780

Of square form, with canted and fluted corners,
Painted in naturalistic enamel colours with a chain border of
sixteen roses and in a central reserve, a spray of full-blown
roses, on a white ground surrounded by a gilt line, the well of
the dish painted in a sea-green overglaze enamel colour, with a
gilt line and dentil border round the rim.
Mark: Crown, crossed batons, six dots and 'D'; '185' painted in
     red enamel.

   D. 22.2 cm.   Private Collection.
     Lit.   Pattern No.185 in Derby Pattern Book.
           Pattern for plate is marked '14 roses in border'.

281. DISH   c.1790-1800   (Not illustrated)

Lozenge shape, with flared sides giving an irregular scalloped edge.
Painted in underglaze blue, overglaze enamel colours and gilt, in
imitation of a Japanese brocade design.

   L. 26.5 cm.   Private Collection.
     Note: This was probably made as a replacement for a Worcester
          service.

282. CENTRE DISH   c.1785

Lozenge shape, with fluted and flared sides, giving an irregular
scalloped edge, set on an oval domed foot.
Painted in enamel colours as No.274.
Mark: A pseudo-Chinese square seal in underglaze blue.
     An incised script 'N'.

   9.5 cm. L. 31.5 cm. W. 24 cm.   National Museum of
                                         Wales (D.W.2327).

     Lit.   Pattern No.3 in Derby Pattern Book.
           Haslem, 1876, op. cit., p.186.

283. DESSERT DISH   c.1830   Colour Plate p. 142

Shell shape, with raised scroll moulding for a handle and
gadroon edging round the rim.
Decorated with a bouquet of flowers, painted in naturalistic
enamel colours, in a central reserve, surrounded by a gilt dentil
border, the well of the dish painted in underglaze blue with a
stylised gilt decoration. Four irregularly shaped reserves, three
filled with sprays of flowers and the fourth painted with a full
coat-of-arms; the gadrooned edge picked out in gilt.
Mark: 'Bloor' in a circle printed in red enamel.

   D. 24.5 cm.   Royal Crown Derby Museum.

     Note: This service was specially commissioned by Earl Ferrers
          The painting is attributed to John Hancock, Jnr.

279 282 280

284. DISH   c.1805

Lozenge shape, with fluted and flared sides giving an irregular
scalloped edge.
Painted in naturalistic enamel colours with an old building in a
rural landscape set in a central oval reserve and surrounded by
a broad and elaborately stylised foliate gilt border.

Mark: Crown, crossed batons, six dots and 'D' painted in black
      enamel. Inscribed 'Near Bredsall, Derbyshire' painted in
      black enamel.

   L. 27.7 cm. W. 21.1 cm.   Private Collection.

285. MUG   c.1815

Of cylindrical form, with two moulded bands and a D-shaped handle.
Painted in naturalistic enamel colours with a 'Man-o-War' and other
shipping enduring a 'fresh gale', with figures on a promontory,
in the foreground, and in the distance, a castle built above a
range of white cliffs, set below a broad and elaborately stylised
foliate gilt border.

Mark: Crown, crossed batons, six dots and 'D' painted in red enamel.
      Inscribed 'Fresh Gale' painted in red enamel, on the base.

   12.5 cm.   Private Collection.

286. MUG   c.1825-35

Shaped as No.285 with a scroll handle, with a pronounced thumb
rest and kick terminal.
Painted in naturalistic enamel colours with a coastal harbour
scene and workmen standing beside blocks of granite, constructing
a breakwater, set in a central rectangular reserve surrounded by
a gilt frame, below a stylised leaf border in gilt.

Mark: 'Bloor Derby' in a circle, and Crown transfer-printed in red
      enamel. Inscribed 'Plymouth Breakwater from the West' painted
      in red enamel.

   12.8 cm.   Private Collection.

287. MUG   c.1825-35

Shaped as No.285.
Painted in naturalistic colours with a gold crest and a grey
wagtail, in a waterside landscape, set in a central rectangular
reserve with canted corners, on a cobalt blue ground ornamented
with stylised gilt motifs, with a broad stylised gilt design
round the rim.

Mark: 'Bloor Derby' in a circle and Crown transfer-printed in
      red enamel.

   12.8 cm.   Private Collection.

286

287

285

284

288. ICE PAIL AND COVER   c.1785   Colour Plate p. 143

Circular form, set on a low domed foot, with scroll handles, the flat cover surrounded by a deep flange rim and surmounted by a twisted ring finial.

Painted on either side of the pail with rural landscapes, in brown monochrome, set in an oval reserve, surrounded by a gilt line border, a stylised floral border round the rim of the pail and the upright flange of the cover, the handles and the ring finial picked out in gilt and a gilt line round the rim of the pail and the cover.

Mark: Crown, crossed batons, six dots and 'D'; '74' and a small 'S' in the foot rim painted in blue enamel. Impressed 'B'.
      Inscribed 'Farm House, Bredsall, Derbyshire'.
      'View near Leek, Staffordshire', painted in blue enamel.

      22.9 cm.   Private Collection.

289. TUREEN, COVER AND STAND c.1795

Neo-classical oval form, with exaggerated loop handles, slightly domed cover, with entwined scroll finial and a shallow oval stand with ring handles at each end.

Painted in enamel colours with a rural landscape on either side of the tureen, on the cover and on the stand, each set in an oval frame, a broad pale pink band round the upper half of the tureen, the edge of the cover and the rim of the stand, the ring finial and the handles picked out in gilt and a gilt dentil border round the rim.

Mark: Crown, crossed batons, six dots and 'D'; '205' painted in blue enamel.
      Inscribed 'Thoyer Cloud, Derbyshire' and
      'Near Ingleby, Derbyshire' on the tureen.
      'On the Dove, Derbyshire' on the cover.
      'Near Burrowash, Derbyshire' on the stand, painted in blue enamel.

      15.5 cm. L. 24 cm.   Private Collection.
      Lit. Pattern No.205 in Derby Pattern Book.

290. TUREEN BASE   c.1790

Four-lobed oval shape, with elaborate scroll handles.
Painted in enamel colours with a coat-of-arms surmounted by a coronet and surrounded by an ermine mantle, the rim of the tureen and the moulding on the handles picked out in gilt.
Mark: 'Duesbury, London' in a square, painted in black enamel.

      7 cm. L. 18.4 cm.   Private Collection.
      Note: The arms belong to James, 8th Duke of Hamilton &
            5th Duke of Brandon, (b. 1756, d. 1799).
      Lit. Gilhespy, 1965, op. cit., Pl.72, showing the arms of
            the 5th Duke of Hamilton with Spencer in pretence.

291. BOUGH POT   c.1795

Semi-circular form, set on a stepped foot, with angular shaped handles and fitted with a drop-in cover, pierced with holes, for flowers.
Painted in enamel colours with a central oval reserve, depicting a rural landscape with a high tower and buildings set above a waterfall, enclosed in a gilt zig-zag line border and surrounded by flowers painted in naturalistic colours, on an orange and gilt ground.
Mark: Crown, crossed batons, six dots and 'D' painted in blue enamel.
      Inscribed 'Villa of Mecenas, Italy' painted in blue enamel.

      15.2 cm.
                          - 174 -   Private Collection.

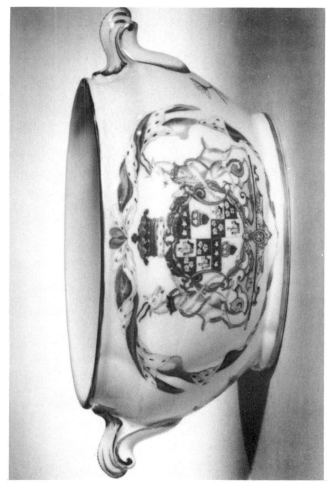

290

288

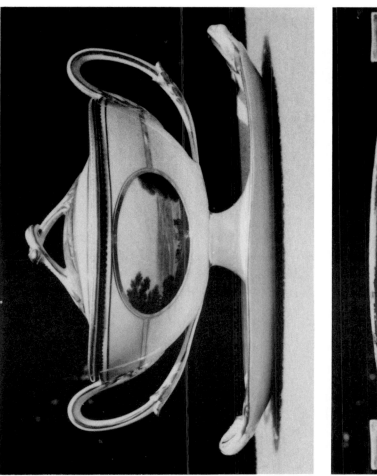

291

289

292. VASE   c.1815

The vase of flaring trumpet form, with diamond shaped piercing and
a scalloped rim, supported on three seated cats, on a triangular
plinth set on three shell feet.
Painted in gilt.

Mark: Crown, crossed batons, and 'D' painted in red enamel.

      11.5 cm.   Private Collection.

         See. Schreiber Collection, Victoria & Albert Museum. (Sch.1.460).
         Ref. Similar examples are found with owls instead of cats.

293. INKSTAND   c.1815

An ornate stand with two depressions for pens, with two loop handles
and set on four paw feet, fitted with a raised inkwell and cover,
set between two candle holders.
Painted in enamel colours with Italianate views set in oval gilt
reserve placed in the pentray depressions, the remainder decorated
with an elaborate gilt floral motif.

Mark: Crown, crossed batons, and 'D'; '44' painted in red enamel.

      13.3 cm. L. 29.2 cm.   Private Collection.

294. INKWELL   c.1815-20

Cylindrical form, with an elaborate ring handle, the top depressed
and pierced with four holes, for quill pens, and a central well
for the ink.
Painted in enamel colours with scattered flowers, the rim and the
edge of the handle outlined in gilt.

Mark: Crown, crossed batons and 'D' painted in red enamel.

      7.3 cm. L. 14.5 cm.   Private Collection.

295. CHAMBER CANDLESTICK   c.1835

Saucer shaped form, with inverted bell shaped nozzle, ovoid
handle with a pronounced thumb rest.
Painted in naturalistic enamel colours with butterflies, moths
and insects, including small tortoise-shell, meadow green, meadow
blue, and speckled wood butterflies, garden tiger moth, click
beetle, green-bottle fly and a ladybird.

Mark: Crown over a gothic 'D' printed in red enamel.

      5.8 cm. D. 13 cm. L. 14.6 cm.   Private Collection.

         Lit. Gilhespy, 1965, op. cit., Pl.130.
               where it is stated that it is painted by W.Salter, Senr.

295

293

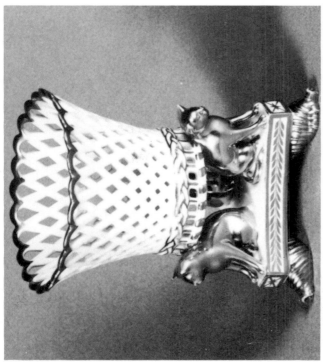

294

292

Marks

Extracted from J. Twitchett, 1976, The Story of Royal Crown Derby China, with an additional entry for the Planché Period.
(Reproduced by kind permission of J. Twitchett.)

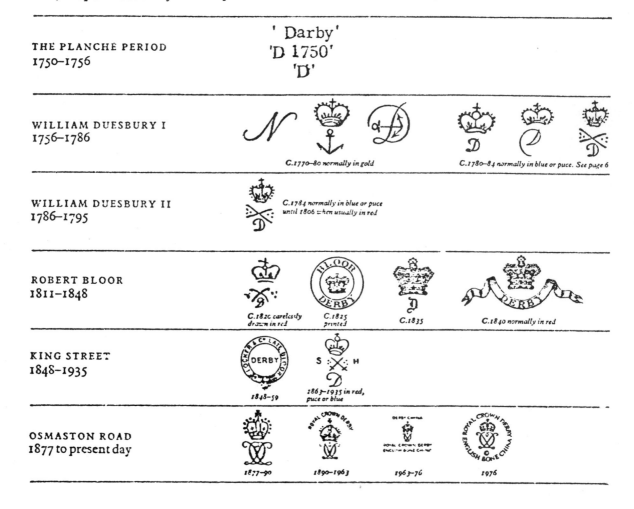

THE PLANCHE PERIOD 1750–1756	' Darby' 'D 1750' 'D'

WILLIAM DUESBURY I 1756–1786

C.1770–80 normally in gold   C.1780–84 normally in blue or puce. See page 6

WILLIAM DUESBURY II 1786–1795

C.1784 normally in blue or puce until 1806 when usually in red

ROBERT BLOOR 1811–1848

C.1820 carelessly drawn in red   C.1825 printed   C.1835   C.1840 normally in red

KING STREET 1848–1935

1848–59   1861–1935 in red, puce or blue

OSMASTON ROAD 1877 to present day

1877–90   1890–1963   1963–76   1976

Derby Year Cyphers

The V mark of 1904 is accompanied by the word 'England' and that of 1942 with the words 'Made in England'. The same applies to the 'X' marks of 1901 and 1947.

1880	1881	1882	1883	1884	1885	1886	1887	1888	1889	1890	1891	1892	1893
1894	1895	1896	1897	1898	1899	1900	1901	1902	1903	1904	1905	1906	1907
1908	1909	1910	1911	1912	1913	1914	1915	1916	1917	1918	1919	1920	1921
1922	1923	1924	1925	1926	1927	1928	1929	1930	1931	1932	1933	1934	1935
1936	1937	1938	1939	1940	1941	1942	1943	1944	1945	1946	1947	1948	1949
1950	1951	1952	1953	1954	1955	1956	1957	1958	1959	1960	1961	1962	1963
1964	1965	1966	1967	1968	1969	1970	1971	1972	1973	1974	1975		

KING STREET AND OSMASTON ROAD 1848-1975

Subsequent to Robert Bloor's mental illness the Nottingham Road factory had been managed by John Haslem's uncle, James Thompson and regrettably by 1848 the standards were so low and the artistic level so declined that, as previously stated, Alderman Clarke closed the works.

This of course was a sad blow to the prestige of the ancient town of Derby and to the workpeople. Samuel Keys, a fine gilder stated in his account of the old works "...and how it has since been conducted and by who, with the history of them, would be distressing to my own feelings and unpleasant to others." The reference to Thompson's mismanagement and Bloor's unfortunate mental incapacity illustrate the two unfortunate features which brought about the closure of an old established and famous porcelain works.

William Locker, who had been the chief clerk, was joined by five other old hands, Sampson Hancock, James Hill, Samuel Fearn, Samuel Sharpe and John Henson in setting up the King Street factory. This small but admirable concern flourished, making good quality wares which, although mostly traditional, brought credit and Royal patronage. The works bravely competed during the last quarter of the nineteenth century and the first thirty years of the present century before trade recession and the fame of its more illustrious neighbour on the Osmaston Road made the merger inevitable, and actually taking place in 1935.

The story at Osmaston Road is different. Although many traditional figures, such as the 'Elements', 'Seasons' and 'Dwarfs' were in current production from the beginning, many new figures were introduced, mostly modelled by Herbert Warrington Hogg and William Stephan. Many painters were to come to Derby from the continent of Europe; Count Holtzendorf, a fine figure and landscape painter, G. Landgraf who came to Derby after having been the chief painter at the Royal factory in Berlin, Déseré Leroy originally hailing from the Sèvres works and of course, P. Taillandier whose figure painting is so much sought after today.

In the early days the influences were very varied coming from France and from the Islamic countries as well as the Orient. In 1890 Queen Victoria granted the use of Royal as a prefix, and since that time Royal Crown Derby has continued to hold the prestige of its ancient town high, throughout all the countries of the world.

As a conclusion it is interesting to note that the 'Imari' type patterns, which were originally inspired by the richly decorated porcelain of the Arita province of Japan, have been made continuously at Derby since the last quarter of the eighteenth century and especially interesting to note that 'Old Japan' is still produced today, known less romantically, as '383'.

John Twitchett, F.R.S.A.

296. COFFEE CAN AND STAND   1884

The can of wedge shape with applied pierced fan shaped handle,
known as 'Duchess' shape, made in egg-shell porcelain.
Painted in enamel colours with an Islamic design, on a pink and
yellow ground.
Painted by George Lambert.
Mark: Derby Crown (printed).

    5 cm. D. 10 cm.   Private Collection.

    Note: Pattern No.1294.
    Lit. J. Twitchett & B. Bailey, 1976, Royal Crown Derby,
         London, p. 18 for similar shape.

297. TEACUP AND SAUCER   1886   (Not illustrated)

Transfer-printed in underglaze blue with the 'Osborne' design.
Mark: Derby Crown (printed).

    4.5 cm. D. 12.5 cm.   Private Collection.

    Note: Reg. of Design No.33644.

298. TEACUP, SAUCER AND PLATE   1912   (Not illustrated)

Painted in enamel colours with a spray of roses in naturalistic
colours, a blue border round the rim and in the centre, a crest
and coronet, in gilt.
Probably painted by Cuthbert Gresley, but not signed.
Mark: Royal Crown Derby.

    6 cm. Saucer D. 13.3 cm. Plate D.18 cm.   Private Collection.

    Lit. Twitchett & Bailey, 1976, op. cit., pps. 56 & 66.

299. TEAPOT STAND   1903

Of oval shape.
Painted in enamel colours with a floral spray in the centre and a
chain of flowers in naturalistic colours round the well of the
stand and a decorative gilt border round thr rim.
Signed: G. Rowley, on a stem in the centre.
Mark: Royal Crown Derby.

    D. 18 cm.   Private Collection.

    Lit. Twitchett & Bailey, 1976, op. cit., p.79 for work by
        George Rowley.

300. PLATE   1880

Decorated with a floral bouquet in the centre and an elaborate
design round the flange, all done in raised gilding.
Mark: Crown, crossed swords, six dots and 'D', flanked by 'S & H'
painted in red enamel. 'J.W.' on the foot rim.

    D. 25.5 cm.   Private Collection.

    Note: This gilder's initials J.W. are found on many of the
        signed pieces, left by Edward Prince.
        Similar marks were used during successive partnerships
        at King Street, see Twitchett & Bailey, 1976, op. cit.
        p.14.

296   299   300

301. PLATE   1884

Of standard shape with shallow moulded lines radiating from the
centre, round the flange and the well, the flange pierced with
six leaf designs and the rim pierced with a chain loop design.
The pierced shape known as 'Victoria'.
Painted in the centre, in naturalistic colours, with a running
Cupid, wearing a quiver tied round his waist and holding a bow in
his left hand and a blazing torch in his right hand, the moulding
round the flange and well picked out in gilt.
Signed with initials by Count George Holtzendorf.
Mark: Derby Crown, (printed).

    D. 21.5 cm.   Private Collection.

     Lit. Twitchett & Bailey, 1976, op. cit., pp. 48 & 85.

302. PLATE   c.1885   (Not illustrated)
Of standard shape.
Painted in enamel colours with harebells and other flowers, in
naturalistic colours on a pale pink ground.
Mark: Derby Crown (printed).
    D. 23.2 cm.   Private Collection.

303. PLATE   1889   (Not illustrated)

Of standard shape.
Transfer-printed in underglaze blue with the 'Wilmot' design.
Mark: Derby Crown (printed).
        Register of Design.
    D. 16.5 cm.   Private Collection.

304. PLATE   1890

Of standard shape, with shallow fluting round the flange and the
well, known as 'Harrow' shape.
Painted in the centre, in naturalistic colours, with a terraced
garden and buildings, the flange of the plate painted in dark blue
enamel with an elaborate gilt border.
Painted by Ellis Clarke.
Mark: Royal Crown Derby.
        Inscribed on base 'View of Haddon Hall'.

    D. 21.5 cm.   Private Collection.
     Lit. Twitchett & Bailey, 1976, op. cit., p.199.

305. PLATE   1904   Colour Plate   p. 179

Of standard shape, with a raised gadroon edge, known as 'Royal
Gadroon' shape.
Painted in naturalistic enamel colours with a full floral bouquet
in the centre, a cobalt blue border round the flange with solid
gold decoration and raised enamel round the edge.
Signed A. Gregory.
Mark: Royal Crown Derby.

    D. 21.5 cm.   Royal Crown Derby Museum.

     Lit. Twitchett & Bailey, 1976, op. cit., p.169.

301 304

306. PLATE   1907   Colour Plate P. 180

Shaped as No.305.
Painted in naturalistic enamel colours with roses, an acorn and a
bunch of black grapes, a cobalt blue border round the flange, divided
into sections, three large and three small, by rows of raised
jewelling, with floral sprays in the alternate large sections.
Signed Désiré Leroy.

Mark: Royal Warrant and Royal Crown Derby.

    D. 21.5 cm.   Royal Crown Derby Museum.

        Lit. Twitchett & Baïley, 1976, op. cit., p.65.
              for plate of similar shape, but slightly different
              decoration.

307. PLATE   1911

Of standard shape, with raised ribbon and shell motifs round the
flange and a 'banded rods' design round the rim.
Decorated lavishly with raised and chased gilding, on a white ground
and embossed with the initials 'J.D.' on one of the shell motifs.
Mark: Royal Warrant, Royal Crown Derby and Tiffany.

    D. 25.5 cm.   Private Collection.

        Note: This service was specially commissioned by Mr. James
              Deering through Tiffany's for use at Viscaya, Miami, Florida.
        Lit. Twitchett & Bailey, 1976, op. cit., p.53 for a cup &
              saucer of this service.

308. PLATE   1920

Of standard form, with a shaped edge and slight gadrooning round
the rim.
Painted in naturalistic enamel colours with a view of Derby, in the
centre, and a gilt scroll border on a white ground round the flange.
Signed. H.S. Hancock.

Mark: Crown, crossed swords, six dots and 'D', flanked by 'S & H'
      painted in puce enamel.
      Inscribed 'Derby from the meadows'- 'H.S.Hancock'.
    D. 21.5 cm.   Private Collection.

        See. Note to No.300.
        Lit. Twitchett & Bailey, 1976, op. cit., p.27, No.36 & p.116
              for other views of Derby on plates made at King Street.

309. PLATE   1926

Of 'Talbot' shape, with a 'Princess' scroll border.
Painted in naturalistic enamel colours with a view of Loch Katrine,
Scotland, in a central reserve and a purple scroll border on a
white ground round the flange.
Signed. C. Gresley.

Mark: Royal Crown Derby.
    D. 21.5 cm.   Private Collection.

        Lit. Twitchett & Bailey, 1976, op. cit., p.40 for 'Talbot'
              shape with a view of Chatsworth by Cuthbert Gresley.
              F.B.Gilhespy & D.M.Budd, 1964, Royal Crown Derby China,
              London, Fig 51, for another Scottish view in this service,
              painted by C. Gresley.

307   308   309

310. **PLATE**   1939

    Of standard form, with a slightly scalloped rim and shallow
fluting round the flange.
Painted in naturalistic enamel colours with a full rigged clipper
and fishing barques at sea, in a central reserve, on a white
ground and a pale pink border round the well and flange.
Signed. W.E.J.Dean.

Mark: Royal Crown Derby.

     D. 21.5 cm.   Private Collection.

311. **PLATE**   1975

    Shaped as No.309.
Painted in the Japanese 'Imari' style.
Pattern No.1128.

Mark: Royal Crown Derby.

     D. 17.5 cm.   Private Collection.

       Note: This pattern was first designed at Osmaston Road; it
             is not one of the traditional patterns carried forward
             from Nottingham Road or King Street.

312. **PLATE**   1975

    Of standard form, with shallow fluting round the flange, known as
'Burford' shape.
Painted in naturalistic colours with a floral spray, the 'Derby
Posie' pattern, in a central reserve, on a white ground.

Mark: Royal Crown Derby.

     D. 25.5 cm.   Private Collection.

       Note: The 'Derby Posie' design was originally introduced c.1930.
       Lit. Twitchett & Bailey, 1976, op. cit., p.94 for 'Derby
             Posie' design on a cup and saucer and a plate.

310   311   312

313. DESSERT DISH   c.1865   (Detail)

A rectangular shaped dessert dish, with a scalloped edge and twisted
loop handles.
Painted in naturalistic enamel colours with a view of the Old Silk
Mill at Derby, in a central oval medallion and the sides decorated
with an elaborate design of raised and plain gilt.
Signed. E. Price.

Mark: Crown, crossed batons, six dots and 'D', flanked by 'S & H'
      painted in red enamel. 'J.W.' painted in red enamel.
      Inscribed 'The Old Silk Mill'.

    L. 28 cm. W. 21.5 cm.   Private Collection.

      See. No.300 for reference to the gilder J.W. and list of
            partnerships at King Street.
      Note: J.W. always used 'crossed batons' - not the King Street
            mark of 'crossed swords'.

314. DISH   1904

Of rectangular shape, known as 'Talbot' shape, with applied pierced
leaves forming the handles.
Transfer-printed in underglaze blue with the 'Mikado' pattern.

Mark: Royal Crown Derby.

    D. 21.5 cm.   Private Collection.

      Lit. Twitchett & Bailey, 1976, op. cit., p.76 for 'Talbot'
            shape, also p.167 for print on part of a tea service.
            Gilhespy & Budd, 1964, op. cit., Pl.9, for the same
            design on a plate.

315. DISH   1920

A scalloped edge dessert dish, with a cut-out loop handle.
Painted in naturalistic enamel colours with a view of Derby in a
circular reserve and surrounded by a looped border of gilding.
Signed. H.S. Hancock.

Mark: Crown, crossed swords, six dots and 'D', flanked by 'S & H'
      painted in puce enamel.

    D. 21.5 cm.   Private Collection.

      See. No.308 for a plate painted by H.S. Hancock.

316. SQUARE DISH   1926

A square shaped dish, with moulded loop handles.
Decorated with an elaborate design known as 'Old Japan'.

Mark: 'Royal Crown Derby'.

    D. 26.5 cm.   Private Collection.

      Note: Pattern No.383.
      Lit. Twitchett & Bailey, 1976, op. cit., p.42 for reference
            to the pattern.

314

313

316

315

317. VASE   1888

Ovoid shape with a high capstan shaped neck, two serpentine shaped
pierced handles and a pierced dome shaped cover, surmounted by an
onion shaped finial. The body coloured maroon and pale yellow and
decorated in the 'Islamic' manner with raised gilt motifs.

Mark: Derby Crown (printed).

   35 cm.   Private Collection.

     Note: Shape No.322.   Pattern No.689.

318. VASE   1900

Ovoid shape with a trumpet shaped neck and flared mouth with
serrated rim, set on a high domed foot and two elaborate scroll
handles.
Painted with a stylised floral pattern, known as 'Witches'.

Mark: Crown, crossed swords, six dots and 'D', flanked by
      'S & H' painted in red enamel.

   11.5 cm.   Private Collection.

     Lit. Twitchett & Bailey, 1976, op. cit., p. 30 & 31,
       for examples of 'Witches' pattern on other items.

319. VASE   1912

Inverted bell shape, set on a high domed foot and square plinth
with two applied S-shaped handles.
Painted in naturalistic colours with a small landscape set in an
oval panel, on a reserved ground of alternate blue and white
stripes, the edges of the plinth, the handles and the rim, picked
out in gilt.
Signed W.E. Mosley on the panel.

Mark: Royal Crown Derby.

   12.5 cm.   Private Collection.

     Note: Shape No.1520 known as 'Campana' shape.
     Lit. Twitchett & Bailey, 1976, op. cit., p.93 for 'Campana'
       shape, p.122 for watercolour painting by W.E.Mosley.

320. VASE   1919

Inverted bell shape with flared and serrated rim, a band of
raised jewelling below the rim and round the foot, with applied
scroll handles.
Painted with a reserve of flowers set in a raised gilt panel, on
a cobalt blue ground.
Flowers painted by George Jessop.

Mark: Royal Crown Derby.

   14 cm.   Private Collection.

     Lit. Twitchett & Bailey, 1976, op. cit., p.138.
       for similar style floral painting by George Jessop.

317   319   318   320

321. EWER   c.1884

   Pear-shaped with a tall swan neck, an elongated spout and
   serpentine shaped pierced handle.
   Painted in pale yellow and turquoise enamels and decorated in
   the 'Islamic' manner with raised gilt motifs.

   Mark: Derby Crown (printed).

      34.5 cm.   Private Collection.

         Note: Shape No.385.

322. BELL   1893

   Shaped as a hand bell, with a handle terminating in a pine-apple
   finial.
   Decorated with embossed gilt moulding, on a pale peach and green
   ground.

   Mark: Royal Crown Derby.

      16.5 cm.   Private Collection.

323. MATCH HOLDER AND SNUFFER   1900

   Modelled in the shape of an old lady, wearing a long skirt with a
   bonnet and shawl, placed over a circular base, containing a
   holder for matches.
   The face and hands painted in naturalistic colours, with floral
   sprays scattered over the skirt.

   Mark: Crown, crossed swords, six dots and 'D', flanked by 'S & H'
         painted in underglaze blue.

      10 cm.   Private Collection.

         Note: Pattern No.69, known as 'Mother Gamp'.
         Lit. Twitchett & Bailey, 1976, op. cit., p.33.
               Quoted in Catalogue of 1934-35; price 11s. 9d.

321   323   322

324. DON QUIXOTE   c.1878-80

Standing figure of an old man leaning on a lance, which he holds
in his right hand, holding a shield on his left arm, and resting
on the plinth at his feet, his breastplate and helmet.
Painted in naturalistic colours.

Mark: Derby Crown (printed).

   20 cm.   Private Collection.

      Lit. Twitchett & Bailey, 1976, op. cit., p.111 for similar
            version in white.

325. MORNING   1880

Model of the crouching figure of a young girl resting on a plinth,
made to represent a padded cushion, tying the laces of her right shoe.
Painted in naturalistic colours.

Mark: Crown, crossed swords, six dots and 'D', flanked by 'S & H'
      painted in red enamel.

   7 cm.   Private Collection.
      Note: Pattern No.44 known as 'Morning'.
      Lit. Twitchett & Bailey, 1976, op. cit., p.28.
            Quoted in Catalogue of 1934-35, price 12s. 6d.

326. NIGHT   1880

Model of kneeling figure of a young child praying and kneeling
on a cushion, shaped as No.325.
Painted in naturalistic colours.

Mark: Crown, crossed swords, six dots and 'D', flanked by 'S & H'
      painted in red enamel.

   7 cm.   Private Collection.
      Note: Pattern No. 45, known as 'Night'.
            These figures 'Morning' and 'Night' were originally
            modelled by George Cocker when he had for a short time a
            small establishment in Friar Gate, Derby.
            They were later produced by Minton c.1830-50.
      Lit. E. Aslin & P. Atterbury, 1976, Minton 1798-1910,
            Catalogue of Exhibition at Victoria & Albert Museum.
            Twitchett & Bailey, 1976, op. cit., p.28.

327. FOX   c.1870

Model of a fox sitting on its hind quarters with its head turned
to the right, set on a square plinth.
Painted in naturalistic colours with a trailing leaf decoration
twisted round a continuous gilt line round the side of the plinth.

Mark: Crown, crossed swords, six dots and 'D', flanked by 'S & H'
      painted in red enamel.

   9.5 cm.   Private Collection.

328. KITTENS   c.1910

Model of three kittens playing, two sitting on their hind quarters
with their front paws in the air, with the third kitten placed
between them playing with a ball, set on a rectangular base, in white.

Mark: Crown, crossed swords, six dots and 'D', flanked by 'S & H'
      painted in underglaze blue.

   L. 5 cm. W. 4 cm.   Private Collection.

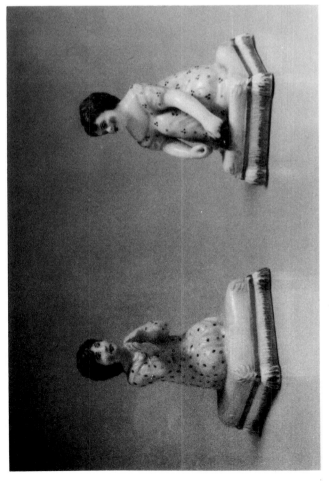

324 326,325 327 328

329. DOCTOR SYNTAX   1934-35

Figure of Dr. Syntax, dressed in a black coat and breeches and
wearing a black tricorn hat, with a scarf tied round his neck,
sitting on a tree stump, holding a pencil in his right hand and an
open sketch book on his knee, with two mallard ducks at his feet,
set on a low mound base.
Painted in naturalistic colours.
Mark: Crown, crossed swords, six dots and 'D', flanked by 'S & H'
      painted in puce enamel.

    13.5 cm.   Private Collection.

      Note: Taken from an episode in W.Coombe 1813, <u>The Tour of Dr.</u>
          <u>Syntax</u>, London. Originally modelled by Edward Keys,
          c.1825, at Nottingham Road, price 5s.
      Lit. Quoted in Catalogue of 1934-35, No.3, price £1.16s.
          Gilhespy & Budd, 1964, <u>op. cit.</u>, p.80.
          Gilhespy, 1965, <u>op. cit.</u>, Fig.169.
          Twitchett & Bailey, 1976, <u>op. cit.</u>, p.20.

330. THE THROWER   1934-35

Figure of a potter dressed in shirt sleeves and striped trousers and
wearing a coloured waistcoat and head scarf, sitting barefoot on a
stool turning a potters wheel, with a model of a pot on the wheel
and two other finished pots placed on a bench beside him, all set
on a mound base.
Mark: Crown, crossed swords, six dots and 'D', flanked by 'S & H'
      painted in puce enamel.

    9 cm.   Private Collection.

      Lit. Quoted in Catalogue of 1934-35, Fig. No.41, price £3.0s.
          Twitchett & Bailey, 1976, <u>op. cit</u>., p.28.

331. THE VIRGINS AWAKENING CUPID   1934-35

Figure of two young women wearing flowing draperies and sandals,
standing under a flowering tree stump, looking at the figure of a
young boy with wings, lying asleep on a bank, all set on a low mound.
Painted in naturalistic colours.
Mark: Crown, crossed swords, six dots and 'D', flanked by 'S & H'
      painted in puce enamel.

    25 cm.   Private Collection.

      Note: Taken from an engraving by Francesco Bartolozzi after
          Angelica Kauffmann and originally modelled c.1780.
      Lit. Quoted in Catalogue of 1934-35, Fig.No.18, price £6.14s.6d.

332. THE TYTHE GROUP   1934-35

Three figures standing below a flowering tree stump, one dressed as
a farmer wearing 18th Cent. clothes holding a staff in his left hand,
a young woman wearing a long dress with a cape and bonnet and
holding in her arms a small baby wrapped in a shawl, with a fully
laden basket of eggs at her feet and a parson wearing clerical garb
and a wig, with his hands clasped together holding a prayer book
and a cross on a long chain, all set on a low mound.
Painted in naturalistic colours.
Mark: Crown, crossed swords, six dots and 'D', flanked by 'S & H'
      painted in puce enamel.

    22 cm. W. 16.5 cm.   Private Collection.

      Note: The group was originally modelled in the 18th Century.
      Lit. Quoted in catalogue of 1934-35, Fig.No.40, price £6.14s.6d.
          Twitchett & Bailey, 1976, <u>op. cit.</u>, p.28.
          Gilhespy, 1965, <u>op. cit.</u>, Fig.152.

329   331   330   332

PINXTON PORCELAIN 1796-1813

It is possible that clay samples sent to William Billingsley prompted him to contact John Coke, June 1795. John Coke had originally sent these samples, which he had obtained from his father's estate at Brookhill Hall on the outskirts of Pinxton, to Billingsley to see if they were suitable for the manufacture of Porcelain. In the following month, the two men met again to discuss the founding of a proposed New China Factory. The Trusley Archives contain a letter from Billingsley to John Coke at Brookhill Hall, giving details of estimates, expenses and profits which could be expected from a China Factory. Following further discussions as to whether Derby or Pinxton should be the site of the factory, Billingsley wrote in October 1795 enclosing plans and layouts for the proposed factory at Pinxton.

Digging out the foundations for the factory began on October 21st, 1795 and the first workmen were paid on October 26th. Records of building costs, materials and wages paid were kept in great detail. On April 15th, 1796 Jacob Spooner and his son with Richard Robins, were paid for one night at the kiln probably for carrying out tests. Also on this date, payments are recorded for the purchase of raw materials used in the manufacture of porcelain.

On April 23rd, 1796 the first kiln was fired and the manufacture of porcelain began at the 'New Pinxton China Factory". The factory was at peak production between December 1797 and January 1798. The total wage bill was £4 per day and amongst the 50 men employed was James Clark, decorator, paid 4s. 0d. per day, and George Mellors, both from the Derby factory.

By April 1799 the pay roll had been reduced to 30 employees, and the last entry in the factory book is dated April 20th, 1799. The partnership between John Coke and William Billingsley was terminated by mutual agreement leaving John Coke as sole proprietor. The London Gazette of June 15th and 18th, 1799 announced the dissolution of the partnership and stated that 'the said business will be carried on by John Coke on his own separate account and that he will pay and receive all debts owing to the said partnership."

To help raise more capital John Coke in September 1801 took into partnership Henry Banks, an Attorney in Lincoln who was in partnership with John Thomas Bell, trading as "Banks and Bell" Attorney at Law. The partnership between John Coke and Henry Banks was signed on September 4th, 1801 and traded as John Coke & Co, but the partnership was dissolved by mutual consent on January 1st, 1803.

John Coke then placed John Cutts in charge of the pottery and William Coffee in charge of the potting. In February 1805, John Coke's brother William, writing to their father, Rev. D'Ewes Coke states: "I find from John that he makes no way yet of withdrawing from one of his concerns, is judicious. I think he had too many irons in the fire for one with so little, I almost say no capital. - I wish he could get rid of the china works with honours by selling or letting them."

In March 1806, the factory was leased to John Cutts, on an annual basis, renewable on Lady Day, and by April 1806, when he had married Susanne Wilmot of Trusley and Spondon, John Coke was residing at Debdale Hall, Mansfield Woodhouse, seven miles from Pinxton. There are recorded receipts for the purchase of porcelain from John Cutts for £18. 1s. 9d. dated June 12th, 1807, (see No.344), and in August 1812, he purchased four jugs and a tea set for £2. 4s. 6d.

The factory finally closed in March 1813 and in a letter written by John Cutts to Josiah Wedgwood, he states that he will be moving from Pinxton on Lady Day (March 25th), after settling his affairs, and will then bring his family in the next fortnight or three weeks. Documentation of the John Coke, John Coke/Henry Banks partnership and of the later John Cutts period, are limited and need to be researched.

The products of the factory during the Coke/Billingsley period are of a fine, thinly potted, translucent, soft paste porcelain, with a warm, well fitting glaze. Marks on Pinxton porcelain are rare. Sometimes the word Pinxton is written in full, either with or without a pattern number; occasionally a 'P.N' followed by a number is used. The highest pattern number, so far recorded is 367. These marks are usually written under the cover of the teapot or sucrier. Other rare marks are the Crescent and Star (see No.368), taken from the Coke family Crest, and one mark, known to collectors as the 'Bow and Arrow' (see No.343).

Writing in 1869, Jewitt[1] stated that the factory had for some time been converted into cottages. The Old Factory was demolished in 1937, and the only building still left standing is the derelict Old Mill House.

C.B. Sheppard.

1. L. Jewitt, 1883, Ceramic Art of Great Britain, London.

333. PORTRAIT OF JOHN COKE by S.H. PLUMB

A three quarter length portrait of John Coke, Esq., by S.H.Plumb,
painted when he was High Sherrif of Nottingham in 1834.
John Coke who was born in 1774, was the youngest son of the Rev.
Mr. D'Ewes Coke of Brookhill Hall, near Mansfield, Notts.
He married Miss Susanne Wilmot, of Trusley in April 1806 and
settled at Debdale Hall where he died aged 66.

> The founder with William Billingsley of the Pinxton
> China Works.
> Prov. Brig. Gen. E.S.D'E. Coke Collection.

334. TOKEN   Dated 1801.

A plain circular china disc.
Painted on one side, 'Let the Bearer have 7 in Goods' (seven
shillings) and on the reverse 'Which place to account with 7,
John Coke Pinxton, Dec. 2, 1801'.

D. 3 cm.   Private Collection.

> Note: China tokens for other values including 10s., 7s.6d.,
>   5s., 3s.6d., 1s.6d., 1s.0d., were also issued as
>   promissary notes and in the locality were called
>   'Mr. Coke Coin' or 'Chaine Money'. China tokens
>   were also produced at Worcester.

334   333   334

335. **TEAPOT, COVER AND STAND**   c.1798

Oval boat shape, with a serrated edge rim to the pot, S-shaped
spout, a high rising moulded handle and a domed cover with an
acorn finial. An oval-shaped stand with fish-tail ends and a
flat base.
Painted in enamel colours with oak leaves and acorns in brown,
set between broad gilt bands, the serrated edge and the rim of
the spout outlined in gilt and the acorn finial painted in gold.

   16.5 cm.   L. 26.7 cm.   Private Collection.

336. **TEAPOT AND COVER**   c.1798

Oval shape with straight spout and angular shaped handle, a low
domed cover surmounted by a ring finial.
Painted in naturalistic colours with a landscape placed on either
side of the pot and enclosed in a square gilt frame, between
swags of roses painted in puce enamel on a ground of gilt seaweed,
a gilt leaf border round the shoulder of the pot between a gilt
line round the rim and the shoulder, and the base of the pot.
The handle, the spout and the ring finial all outlined in gilt.

Mark: 'P No.253' in gilt under the cover.

   14.5 cm.   L. 15 cm.   Private Collection.
                                        Illustration by kind permission
                                        of W.W.Warner (Antiques) Ltd.

337. **COFFEE POT AND COVER**   c.1797

Of flaring form, with concave shoulder, S-shaped spout and angular
handle, set on a low domed foot, a high domed cover surmounted by
a semi-spherical finial.
Painted in naturalistic colours with lake-side landscapes in gilt
oval medallions. A stylised border and scattered gilt sprigs on
the pot and cover and a gilt foliate band round the neck of the pot.

   24 cm.   Private Collection.
                                          (Ex. R.S. Coke Collection).

      Note: Known as 'Brookhill Hall' service.
      Lit. G.A. Godden, 1972, Jewitt's Ceramic Art of Great Britain
            1800-1900, London, p.216, where it is stated that it was
            painted by James Hadfield.
            R.J. Charleston, ed., 1965, English Porcelain, 1745-1850,
            London, Pl.49a.

338. **TEAPOT STAND**   c.1798

Oval shape, with a moulded rim between the well and the steeply
rising flange, on a flat base.
Painted in enamel colours with eight orange poppies and scattered
foliage, between two gilt bands. The rim outlined in gilt.

   L. 17 cm.   W. 12.5 cm.   Private Collection.

      Note: This pattern, known as No.104, is also called 'The Poppy'
            pattern.
            Shards of similar form have been excavated on the site
            of the factory.

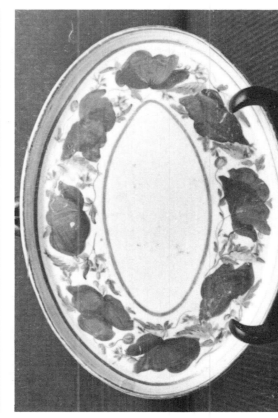

338

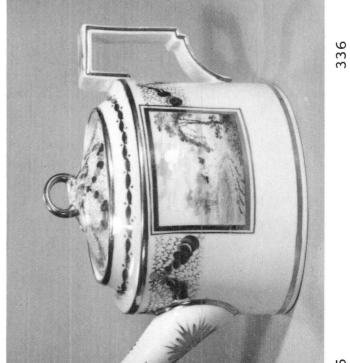

337

336

335

339. TEACUP, COFFEE CAN AND SAUCER   c.1797

The teacup wedge-shaped with a loop handle. The coffee can of
cylindrical form with ear-shaped handle.
Decorated in sepia with a rose spray, and scattered rose buds,
the rim of the cup, can and saucer outlined in brown enamel.

Mark: '12' in sepia, on the base of the can.

Cup 5.7 cm. Can 6.5 cm. D. 14.5 cm.   Private Collection.

340. COFFEE CUP AND SAUCER (Pair)   c.1797

Painted in naturalistic colours on the cup and in the centre of
the saucer with different landscapes surrounded by a chain leaf
band on a pale yellow ground decorated with gilt catherine-wheels
from which are suspended swags of husks, the rim of the cup and
saucer outlined in gilt.

Mark: 'P 157' in red enamel.

7 cm. D. 13.3 cm.   Private Collection.

341. TEACUP AND SAUCER   c.1799

Painted with a broad gilt scroll border, enclosing two oval
landscapes, painted in naturalistic colours, on a yellow ground
and framed with a gilt line border, between two diamond-shaped
motifs painted in purple enamel, enriched in the centre with
four gilt stars and leaves.

5.7 cm. D. 14.5 cm.   Private Collection.

   Note: Teapot marked 'P 345' in the Western Park Museum,
         Sheffield: a cream jug of similar pattern in the
         Victoria & Albert Museum.

342. TEACUP AND SAUCER   c.1800

Cup and saucer moulded with shallow vertical fluting.
Painted in iron-red enamel with scattered debased 'Angoulême'
sprigs, the serrated rim of the cup and saucer outlined in
iron-red enamel.

6.5 cm. D. 14 cm.   Private Collection.

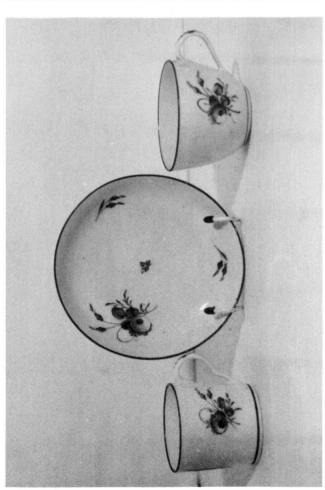

342

340

341

339

343. TEA BOWL   c.1800

Painted in enamel colours with floral sprays and sprigs, the
rim outlined in blue enamel.

Mark: Crossed Arrow and '190' painted in blue enamel.

    5 cm.   Private Collection.

344. TEACUP, COFFEE CAN AND SAUCER   c.1807

Shaped as No.339.
Decorated in the bold 'Imari' style in enamel colours and gilt.

Mark: '342'.

    Cup 6 cm. Can 6.4 cm. D. 14 cm.   Private Collection.

    Note: There still survives a receipted bill, made out by
          John Cutts to John Coke, dated June 12th, 1807, for
          'Over forty pieces of china, decorated 'Pattern 342'
          Price £18. 1s. 9d.

345. COFFEE CAN AND SAUCER   c.1797

The can of straight sided cylindrical form with ear-shaped handle.
Painted round the can with a continuous landscape in naturalistic
enamel colours, an elaborate border comprising a foliate chain
surmounting a scalloped formal design painted in gilt round the
interior. The edge of the handle and the rim of the can outlined
in gilt. The centre of the saucer painted in naturalistic colours
with a hay cart drawn by a team of horses set in a rural landscape,
surrounded by an elaborate gilt border.

Mark: 'P 115'

    6.5 cm. D. 7 cm.   Private Collection.

346. COFFEE CAN

Shaped as No.345.
Painted in naturalistic enamel colours with a river valley and
a cottage beside a single span bridge, enclosed in an oval shaped
reserve, composed of a gilt band, with an outer gilt foliate band.

    6.5 cm.   Private Collection.

345

346

344

343

347. COFFEE CAN   c.1798

Shaped as No.345.
Painted in enamel colours with a broad band of trailing foliage
and butterflies, enclosed by gilt lines, the base of the can
and the edge of the handle picked out in gilt.

Mark: Impressed 'A'.

6 cm.   Private Collection.

348. COFFEE CAN   c.1798

Cylindrical form with simple loop handle.
Painted in enamel colours with three bands, two of diamond shapes
containing three dots and a centre band of foliate scrolls, each
section separated by a gilt line, the handle also outlined in gilt.

Mark: 'N 157' painted in grey enamel.

5.7 cm.   Private Collection.

349. CABINET CUP AND COVER   c.1798

Ogee form with two elaborately shaped handles and domed cover
surmounted by a ring finial.
Painted within a rectangular reserve outlined in gilt with a
monochrome landscape, set below a yellow and gilt border, a
similar yellow and gilt border round the cover.

14 cm.   Private Collection.

    Prov. Brig. Gen. E.S.D'E. Coke Collection.
    Lit. C.L. Exley, (Ed. F.A. Barrett & A.L. Thorpe), 1963,
          Pinxton China Factory, Derby, Pl.7a, and dust cover.

350. CABINET CUP AND COVER (Pair) c.1798

Trumpet form with angular moulded handles and slightly domed covers
surmounted by ringed finials.
Painted in sepia with landscapes, the rim and base of the cups
and the rim of the covers outlined in gilt.

12.5 cm.   Private Collection.

    Prov. Brig. Gen. E.S.D'E. Coke Collection.
    Lit. C.L. Exley, 1963, op. cit., Pl.8B.

351. SLOP BASIN   c.1797

Semi-spherical form set on a low foot rim.
Decorated on both sides with square reserves, outlined in gilt,
enclosing landscapes painted in enamel colours, with a band of
gilt foliage flanked by lines and a gold line round the foot rim.

Mark: '300' in gilt.

7.9 cm. D. 15.8 cm.   Private Collection.

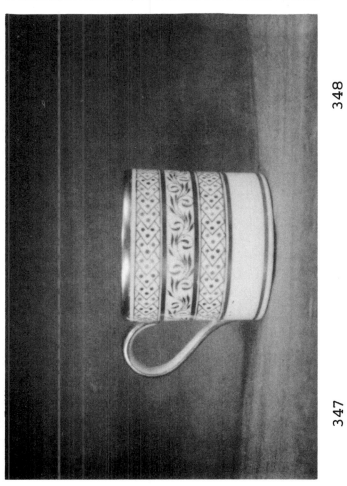

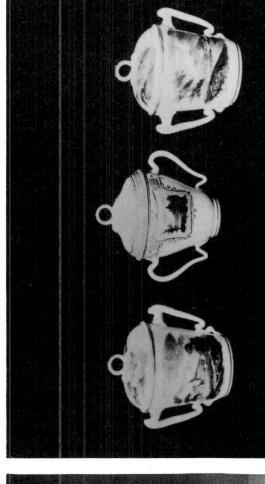

351

350, 349, 350

348

347

352. CREAM JUG   c.1796

    Oval boat-shape, with spiral fluting, a wide spout and a loop
handle with an inward pointing spur.
Decorated with three floral sprigs painted in enamel colours,
an iron-red line round the base, the shoulder and the rim of
the jug.

    9.3 cm.   Private Collection.

353. CREAM JUG   c.1798

    Bucket-shaped, with moulded flaring spout and angular shaped handle.
Decorated with a spray of roses and buds, painted in sepia enamel
colour, a sepia line round the base, the rim and the edge of the
spout.

Mark: '12' painted in sepia enamel.

    7.9 cm.   Private Collection.

354. CREAM JUG   c.1798

    Semi-spherical shape with concave shoulders and undulating rim,
with a wide flaring lip and an elaborate shaped handle.
Decorated with a broad band of stylised leaves and flowers painted
in grey enamel and gilt and set between gilt lines. The rim of
the jug outlined in gold.

    11.7 cm.   Private Collection.

      Note: The design known as Pattern No.275 also occurs in
            other colours.

355. CREAM JUG   c.1799

    Oval shape with slightly concave shoulders, wide spout, and
angular shaped handle.
Decorated on either side with oval reserves, outlined in gilt,
containing landscapes painted in naturalistic enamel colours, a
floral gilt spray under the spout. A gilt line round the base,
the shoulder, the rim of the jug, the spout and the handle.

    9.5 cm. L. 7.5 cm.   Private Collection.

354

353

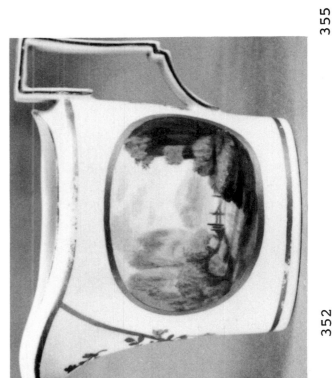

355

352

356. BUTTER TUB   c.1798

Oval form with slightly flaring sides.
Painted in polychrome enamel colours with scattered 'Angoulême'
sprigs and a floral leaf border, and a gilt line painted round
the rim of the tub.

    L. 12.5 cm. W. 8.9 cm.   Private Collection.

357. SUCRIER   c.1797

Open oval boat shape, with moulded handles rising at either end.
Decorated on either side with a landscape painted in naturalistic
enamel colours, and a gilt line round the rim and the foot.

    L. 20.3 cm.   Private Collection.

    Note: Known as Pattern No.218.
    Lit. W.D. John, 1963, William Billingsley 1758-1828,
        The Connoisseur, Feb.

358. SUCRIER AND COVER   c.1798

Oval ogee shape with broad shallow vertical flutes, applied
moulded ring handles, and a stepped domed cover surmounted by
a moulded finial.
Decorated with foliage in a band painted in enamel colours with
a row of dots, painted in alternate blue and green enamel and
set between gilt lines.
The cover painted in a similar style of decoration, the ring
handles and the finial painted in gilt.

Mark: 'Pinxton N.214' painted in blue enamel on the base.

    14 cm. L. 16 cm.   Private Collection.

    Prov. Haslem Collection.
    Note: A teapot from this service is in the Derby Museum &
        Art Gallery.

359. JUG   c.1798

Inverted baluster form, with tall cylindrical neck and pronounced
lip, angular shaped handle with moulded acanthus leaf decoration.
Painted in naturalistic enamel colours round the neck of the jug,
with a broad band of full-blown roses, a pendant loop chain
suspended from bows, painted round the shoulder. A narrow band
of stylised buds, in an undulating line round the middle of the
jug, scattered stars on the lip and the rim outlined in gilt.

    15.8 cm.   Western Park Museum, Sheffield.
                                (1972. 781).

358

359

357

356

360. BEAKER   c.1798

Trumpet shape.
Decorated with a powder blue ground, enclosing an oval medallion,
painted with a bouquet of flowers in enamel colours, a gilt border
to the reserve and the rim.

    8.9 cm.   Private Collection.

361. BEAKER   c.1798

Conical form with straight sides.
Painted in enamel colours with a landscape depicting a river
flowing beside a gabled house with a church in the distance,
enclosed within circular reserves outlined in gilt and surrounded
by stylised buds in a chain motif, with scattered floral sprays.

Mark: 'P' painted in red enamel.

    8.3 cm. D. 8.3 cm.   Private Collection.

      Exh. Trans. E.C.C., 1948, op. cit., (Exhib. Cat.) Pl.70,
          No.553.

362. MUG   c.1797

Large, plain straight sided, with ear-shaped handle with acanthus
moulding.
Decorated with a landscape painted in enamel colours, between
gilt sprigs and a line border. The interior rim decorated with a
gilt border of small husks and scallops, terminating in dots.

    13.5 cm. D. 12.5 cm.   Private Collection.

      Lit. W.D. John, 1963, op. cit., Pl.46c.

361

360

362

363. TANKARD   c.1797

Straight sided cylindrical form with ear-shaped handle with acanthus
leaf moulding.
Painted in naturalistic enamel colours with a bunch of English
garden flowers, a gilt line round the base and the rim.

    10 cm.   D. 9.5 cm.   Private Collection.

      Lit. W.D. John, 1958, <u>Swansea Porcelain</u>, Newport, Pl.21b.

364. TANKARD   c.1797

Shaped as No.363.
Painted in naturalistic enamel colours with a spray of peony flowers,
a gilt line round the base and the rim. A gilt border round the
interior rim as No.363.

    12.7 cm.   Western Park Museum, Sheffield.
                                     (1972.778).

365. TANKARD   c.1797-98   Colour Plate p.202.

Shaped as No.363.
The front painted with a square reserve outlined in gilt and
surrounded by a gilt chain leaf border enclosing a landscape
view painted in naturalistic enamel colours, on a yellow ground
adorned with classical urns, scrolls and drapery painted <u>en
grisaille</u>. A gilt line border round the rim and the base.

Mark: Inscribed on the base 'View of Brookhill Park from across
      the Lake'.

    12 cm.   D. 11 cm.   Private Collection.

      Prov. Brig. Gen. E.S.D'E. Coke Collection.

366. TANKARD   c.1798

Shaped as No.363.
The front painted with a square reserve outlined in gilt and
surrounded by a gilt chain foliate motif enclosing a bouquet
of flowers in naturalistic colours between two single sprays.

    10 cm.   D. 9 cm.   Private Collection.

      Prov. Brig. Gen. E.S.D'E. Coke Collection.

364 363 365 366

367. DESSERT PLATES   (Pair)   c.1798

   Plain shape with a wide flat flange.
   Painted in naturalistic enamel colours with a bouquet of flowers
   and two small sprays, the rim outlined in gilt.

      D. 20.3 cm.   Private Collection.

         Prov. Brig. Gen. E.S.D'E. Coke Collection.

368. DESSERT PLATE   c.1800

   Shaped as No.367.
   Painted with a landscape in sepia surrounded by a gilt line in a
   central reserve, the edge of the well and the rim of the plate
   picked out in gilt.

   Mark: Crescent and Star painted in puce. (No.368a)

      D. 23 cm.   Private Collection.

369. PLATE   c.1808

   Shaped as No.367.
   Painted with a floral spray in gilt surrounded by a gilt line in
   a central reserve, a broad yellow band edged with gilt lines and
   a red enamel scalloped motif painted round the flange.

   Mark: 'Pinxton' and 'N.202'.

      D. 21.6 cm.   Private Collection.

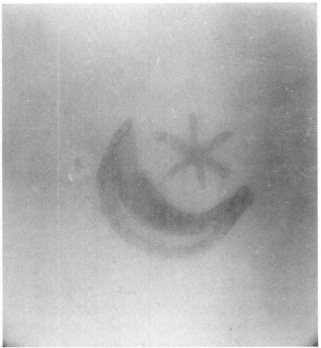

367   369   368a   368

370. DESSERT BOWL   c.1797

   Semi-spherical form set on a high foot rim.
   Painted in naturalistic enamel colours with a bouquet of mixed
   flowers, interspersed with three smaller sprays and a gilt line
   round the foot rim. An elaborate gilt border painted round the
   inside of the bowl with a bouquet of Summer garden flowers
   painted in enamel colours in the centre, the rim of the bowl
   outlined in gilt.

        11.5 cm.   D. 22 cm.   Private Collection.

           Prov. Brig. Gen. E.S.D'E. Coke Collection.
           Lit. C.L. Exley, 1963, op. cit., Pl.21a.

371. DESSERT BOWL   c.1798

   Large boat shaped bowl set on a flaring pedestal foot.
   Painted with an 'Imari' pattern, in imitation of the oriental, in
   overglaze enamel colours, a gilt leaf motif round the pedestal
   and a gilt line round the foot and rim of the bowl.

        14 cm.   L. 32.5 cm.   Private Collection.

372. INK WELL   c.1797

   Cylindrical form, with concave centre and separate ink well
   (missing), an ornate ring handle serving as a quill holder set
   on the side between two further quill holders and two moulded
   appendages for quill sharpeners.
   Decorated with scattered flower sprays and a blue enamel line
   round the base, the shoulder and the rim of the well, the quill
   holders and the appendages.

        5.2 cm.   D. 10.7 cm.   Private Collection.

370   371   372

373. **CROCUS POT AND COVER**   c.1797-99

Semi circular form, with flaring top and standing on a flared and
moulded plinth with elaborate rococo scroll feet. A shaped cover
fitting into the pot, with three raised necks for the crocus bulbs.
Decorated with an oval reserve, painted with a basket of flowers
in enamel colours, surrounded by stylised leaves and a gilt band,
on a pink ground.

        12.4 cm.   L. 17.8 cm.   G.Godden Reference Collection.

374. **CROCUS POTS AND COVERS (Pair)**   c.1797-99

Shaped as No.373.
Both pots decorated with a square reserve, painted with a basket of
flowers in enamel colours, surrounded by gilt ornamentation, and
flanked by lozenge shaped reserves, enclosing circular medallions,
painted with birds, on a salmon pink ground.

        13.5 cm.   L. 19.5 cm.   Private Collection.

Prov. Brig. Gen. E.S.D'E. Coke Collection.
Lit. R.J. Charleston, 1965, op. cit., Pl.49b.
      C.L. Exley, 1963, op. cit., Pl.18b.
      G.A. Godden, 1968, An Illustrated Guide to Pottery and
      Porcelain, (Second Impression) London, Pl.458.
      W.D. John, 1963, op. cit.,

375. **CROCUS POTS AND COVERS (Pair)**   c.1798

Shaped as No.373.
Painted round the centre, in naturalistic enamel colours, with a
continuous landscape, set between an elaborate gilt border
comprising of circles, lines and dots, painted on the flaring
shoulder and the plinth. A chain leaf band in gilt and a gilt
line round the rim.

        13.5 cm.   L. 17.5 cm.   Private Collection.

376. **CROCUS POTS AND COVERS (Pair)**   c.1798-99   Colour Plate p.203.

Shaped as No.373.
Both pots decorated with a rectangular reserve, painted with a
landscape in enamel colours, surrounded by a gilt line and flanked
by ornate gilt scroll-work, on a salmon pink ground, set between
an elaborate gilt border painted on the flaring shoulder and the
plinth. A chain leaf band in gilt and a gilt line round the rim.

Mark: Inscribed, 'Chepstowe Castle, Monmouthshire'.
      'Harlech Castle, Merionethshire', painted in red enamel on
      the base.

        13.2 cm.   L. 17.5 cm.   Private Collection.

Prov. The Coke Collection.
Note: The views of 'Chepstowe Castle' and 'Harlech Castle' are
      taken from 'The Virtuosi's Museum' containing select
      views in England, Scotland, and Ireland, drawn by P.
      Sandby, Esq., R.A., London 1778, printed for G.Kearsly,
      at No.46 near Serjeants Inn, Fleet Street.
Lit. W.D. John, 1963, op. cit., Colour Pl.7b, pp.82, 87.
      E.C.C., 1977, op. cit., (Exh. Cat.) No.218.
      G.Blake-Roberts, 1976, Sources of Decoration on an Unrecorded
      Caughley Desert Service, Trans. E.C.C., Vol.10, Pt.1, Pl.16
      for other engravings by Paul Sandby.
      Godden, 1968, op. cit., Pl.458.

376

373

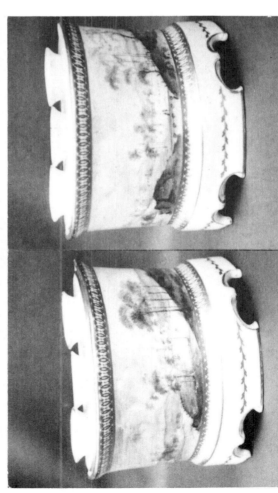

375

374

377. CACHE POT AND STAND   c.1798

Conical shape with ring handles and a hole in the base, fitting
on to a separate turned stand.
Painted in enamel colours with a domestic scene of a lady holding
a child, which is seated on the back of a dog, a gilt line round
the rim of the pot and the stand and the ring handles picked out
in gilt.

    11.3 cm.   Private Collection.

      Prov. R.S. Coke Collection. Formerly at Brookhill Hall.
      Note: Possibly the figure depicted, is a member of the
           Coke family.
      See. A similar cache pot, signed 'Billingsley, Mansfield',
           in the Derby Museum & Art Gallery.

378. VASE AND COVER (Pair)   c.1797

Flared conical form, and slightly spreading base with applied
scroll handles. and pierced domed covers.
Painted in naturalistic enamel colours with landscapes on one
side and on the other side, with bouquets of flowers, the rim
of the.pot, the cover and the pierced holes and the rim of the
stand outlined in blue enamel.

    17.2 cm.   Western Park Museum, Sheffield.
                              (1972. 783).

379. PLANT POT AND STAND   c.1798

Flared conical form, with applied ring handles and a hole in the
base, fitting on to a separate turned stand with spreading base.
Painted in enamel colours with, on one side, a bouquet of flowers
in a basket set in a circular reserve surmounted by a Duke's
coronet, and on the other side, a landscape view of 'Haddon Hall'
also set in a circular reserve surmounted by a Duke's coronet, on
a salmon pink ground painted with classical motifs en grisaille,
a stylised floral border around the rim and the base of the pot.
The stand painted en grisaille with classical leaf and pendant
husks, on a salmon pink ground with a gilt band round the base.

    16.5 cm. D. 15.7 cm.   Private Collection.

      Prov. Major Gen. John Talbot Coke Collection. Formerly at
           Debdale Hall.
      Lit. E.C.C. 1977, op. cit., (Exh. Cat.) No.217, for view of
           'Haddon Hall'.

377   378   379   378

WIRKSWORTH 1772-1777

The Wirksworth china manufactory was established in the grounds
of the Manor House, Wirksworth, in or about 1772, by Philip Gell.
In the Gell family papers, (Derbyshire County Records Office),
there are several documents relating directly to the construction
of the china works. Seven invoices dated between September 11th,
1772 and November 27th, 1772 are made out to the Wirksworth China
Works and issued by G. Bacon, the proprietor of a brick works at
Crich. These invoices also detail the supply of clay, apparently
four to six hundred-weight at a time, with one unusual entry for
six hundred-weight of slip clay.

A later document in the Gell papers dated November 9th, 1773, adds
a little to the knowledge of the works. It is headed 'P. Gell Esq.
debtor to John Symes' and refers directly to building work executed;
specifying brick and stone walling, six tunnels, (presumably flues
for the fire mouths), two chimney tops and paving a kiln floor.
These estimates were approved by Josiah Outram, who was possibly
Philip Gell's agent or perhaps the works manager.

Other bills concern charges from the local carrier between August
31st, and September 29th, 1774, seventy separate journeys were
made, some of which were for the transportation of coal to the
factory. The total bill for £9. 0s. 9d. was presented on February
21st, 1775, but not paid until June 26th, 1775.

Some isolated details add to the sparse picture of the manufactory;
a reference in Josiah Wedgwood's 'Common Place Book No.1' at the
Wedgwood Museum, Barlaston, dating from 1775, states, 'A china
works lately begun at Wirksworth by Mr. Gell of Hopton, who has
lately made some use of a fine white clay, found near Brassington
in Derbyshire, first in an estate of Mr. Haynes of Ashburn,
afterwards in other adjoining lands belonging to Mr. Cope of
Duffield and others. It is found in low lands, and a black soil -
about 12 yards, and at other depths - in small lumps, amongst
inferior clays and other earths - and so uncertain and such small
quantities, as to be worth £10 per ton raising. See my catalogue'.
The Brassington referred to, was only three miles due west of
Wirksworth. A cautious letter from James Maidment, a London
china dealer, written on December 5th, 1773, in reply to one
received from a Mr. Pennington relates to the possibilities of
retailing the chinaware to Maidment, indicating an attempt, though
tentative, to find a market for the wares already being manufactured.

A second and more interesting batch of documents relates to the
actual wares; they cover the relatively short period from January
12th, to October 30th, 1773, and appear to be a series of tally
sheets for the work carried out; they provide not only specific
details, but an indication as to the volume of the items produced
and, for the first time, the names of some of the work people are
indicated. The payments are varied; for teapot handling and spouting
in two sizes, a worker was paid at the rate of 'four and a half

dozen small teapots; at ten pence per dozen, eight and a half
dozen second size at twelve pence per dozen'. These rates were
paid to Samuel Parr and William Walker; they appear again on a
second payment, dated July 30th, 1773 for 6s. 6d. in respect of
'small and large sauce-boats and creams'.

Fourteen further bills, of May 29th, to October 9th, 1773 were
paid to Edward Jones, for casting and repairing a great variety
of wares, which are given as: 'Large water jars, guglets, large
flower vases, jardinieres, large and small beakers, jars,
flower pots, perfume jars, a drug jar, egg jars, swan jars and
stands for flower pots'. Further items were listed in greater
detail: '6 pedistals with rams heads, flower jars with faces and
handles, and flat round fluted jars'.

The details of the decoration are outlined in a series of invoices,
two of which are signed by a Mrs H. Smith, who is possibly the
Hannah Smith, referred to by Jewitt[1], as a decorator at Derby in
1778, and subsequently at Pinxton. She was receiving seven pence
per dozen for cups and saucers, and one and halfpenny each for
teapots and pint bowls, and one penny for half pint bowls. Similar
rates were paid to J. Jackson, who worked on a wider range of
objects such as, large and small plates, jugs, bowls, and boats,
a few teapots, cream jugs, pepper boxes and mustard pots. The
occasional reference to 'China in blue' is open to interpretation,
but most probably refers to a style of decoration, owing something
to the Chinese, and painted in underglaze blue cobalt, whilst the
higher rates recorded would indicate polychrome painting.

A separate section of bills in the Gell papers are from W.Underwood
to Mr. Steer and Co., and actually read, 'Ware printed and sent in
for Mr. Steer and Co., by me, Wm. Underwood'. The accounts cover a
week's work and are itemised on a daily basis, to quote an example,
'July 26th, 1773 - 20 dozen teacups at four pence per dozen',
while on the 28th of the same month, 20 dozen saucers were printed
at the same rate. On October 22nd, 1773, Underwood completed the
decoration on 20 dozen cups and saucers, 2 dozen pint basins, 1
dozen half pint basins and 2 dozen quarter basins, at 1s; 1s. 7d.,
and 4d. respectively. There is an interesting reference to 'Gleas'
ware presumably printed over the glaze; these items are listed as
2 dozen butter pots and milk jugs, 3 dozen quarter and half pint
basins, 6 dozen cups and saucers. A comparison in the prices
shows that the latter were nearly twice as expensive. For example,
cups and saucers were 7d. per dozen instead of the usual 4d. per
dozen, which perhaps reflects the extra care and difficulty in
printing 'on glaze'.

The relative anonymity of the names so far recorded amongst the
work-people at Wirksworth is not echoed by the modellers. Fourteen
papers bearing the name of Thomas Briand and all referring to
'Flower pots flowered' or 'Ornamented flower pots' at 1s. 6d. per
pot, whilst the Stephan family are also mentioned in the Gell
papers. (See Cat. Nos. 22, 23 and 43). Five invoices are simply

signed Stephan, which, when compared with the signature of Pierre
Stephan on Wedgwood documents appear to be identical. This is
corroberated by the completely dissimilar form of a second signature,
that of J.C. Stephan, (John Charles), thus establishing that both
father and son were working for Gell. Further evidence of their
stay at Wirksworth is found in the parish registers, for on
'October 24th, 1773, Frances, daughter of John Charles and Catherine
Stephan, was baptised', also a letter written to Josiah Wedgwood
from Pierre Stephan, dated May 9th, 1774, was addressed from
Wirksworth. The Stephans appear to have worked on prestigious
objects, such as water urns, two figures of dogs and a sphinx jar,
for which they received three guineas.

The manufactory was of short duration and a final sale was advertised
in the Derby Mercury on May 23rd, 1777, listing not only the wares,
but also the equipment, necessary for the production of china:

> 'To be sold
> On Wednesday the 28th day of this present month of May A
> great number of elegant plaster moulds for Tureens, plates,
> dishes, sauce-boats in sets, Tea services, and equipages
> with all other sorts requisite for the manufactory or pot
> works.
> A few very fine large figures, vases, urns, lamps, exquisitely
> moulded; throwing wheels, lathes, and all other instruments
> necessary. A quantity of zaffer, borax, red lead, lynn sand
> whiting Umber and salts with some fine frit ready made.
> Enquiries of Mrs Dickins, the Three Crowns, Wirksworth,
> where a person will attend to these, the above articles, and
> treat for the same'.

Some of the moulds were undoubtedly acquired by other manufacturers,
which adds to the complication of isolating the pieces manufactured
at Wirksworth during the five years of production between 1772 and
1777.

Only six fragments given to the Victoria & Albert Museum (Illustration
opposite) by Mr. Tudor remain as positive examples of Wirksworth
porcelain.

Gaye Blake-Roberts.

1. Jewitt, 1883, op. cit.

S H A R D S

from Wirksworth in

Victoria & Albert Museum.

COCKPIT HILL   1751-1779

The first detailed study of this factory was published by
Williamson, 1931[1], though it is claimed that the first reference
to the factory was in a guide by Wallis and Bemrose[2], 'For...
visitors to the Midland Fine Arts and Industrial Exhibition,'
held in Derby, 1870. Quoting from the Richardson Deeds No.12,
Williamson states that on November 11th, 1751, a partnership
commenced between William Butts, John Heath, Thomas Rivett and
Ralph Steane as potters at Cockpit Hill and this is generally
considered to be the start of the Pot Works. In an Agreement
dated January 1st, 1747, between Thomas Rivett and his brother
Francis Rivett, no mention is made of a pottery on the site of
Cockpit Hill Close. In March 1752 Thomas Rivett leased to
William Butts, the north end of a close with buildings on
Cockpit Hill for 21 (or 42) years from March Lady Day, 1752,
and in June of that year William Butts leased a Water Mill at
Darley Abbey near Derby for grinding flint for the pottery.

Little further is heard of Ralph Steane but the other three men
continued in partnership till the death of Thomas Rivett in
April 1763. He was buried in the Cathedral Church of All Saints
and there is a memorial plaque to him in the church. His share
in the partnership was taken over by his widow. On March 28th,
1764, William Butts died and in the Derby Mercury of March 30th,
he is quoted as 'Master of the Pot Works' and his share in the
partnership passed to his widow. It was not acquired by John
Heath until October 1767 and three years later, after he had
purchased the Rivett share he became the Sole Proprietor but at
a later date he took his brother Christopher into the partnership.

An advertisement appeared in Drewery's Derby Mercury, on Friday
March 4th 1774, under the heading, 'To be LETT and entered upon
immediately A Neat House with a good Garden and other conveniences;
situate on the Cockpit Hill in Derby. For further particulars
enquire of Messrs Heaths; or Ralph Walker at the Pot Works who
will show the premises'.

The joint partnership continued until both John and Christopher
were declared bankrupt in March 1779 and the Potworks were closed.
In the auction which followed, it was stated in the Derby Mercury
of February 29th, 1780, that the sale would include 'Earthen and
China Ware' which had been the stock in trade of Messrs John and
Christopher Heath, bankrupt. In later announcements in March and
April of that year, mention is made of an assortment of Enamell'd
and Blue and White useful China; a large quantity of Enamell'd
Cream Ware and plain Cream tentable (sic) Ware; a great quantity
of White, Stone and Brown Ware.

Donald Towner[5] points out that no mention was made concerning
transfer printing and suggests that this may have come under the
heading of Enamell'd Cream Ware. Referring to porcelain it is
suggested that although this was probably one of the primary

reasons for starting the Potworks, this probably ceased when the factory at St. Mary's Bridge began to develop and he goes on to quote Aubrey Toppin[3] that 'the theory of Cockpit Hill porcelain cannot be accepted as fact until some really circumstantial evidence has been found.' Franklin Barratt when summing up after the Derby Seminar in November 1976 re-echoed this point. However what is meant by the reference 'Useful China'? Could this describe the tureen and cover from the Allman collection No.382 which is of a porcellaneous nature, or the two shell moulded sweetmeats No.381 also of a hybrid paste. Neither of these pieces was made until long after the St. Mary's Bridge factory was well under way.

It has been pointed out by Norman Stretton that the floral transfers on the tureen were also used on the sauce-boats No.199 and 200. However, the date of the sauce-boats are slightly earlier, though the date of the plate No.212, where the transfers are also used, are thought to correspond, which would imply that the copper plates had been borrowed by Cockpit Hill from the St. Mary's Bridge factory. It has been suggested that the lobed dish No.380 was also produced at Cockpit Hill and again the question of borrowed copper plates arises. (see p. 92). This print of Sutton Hall was used on a Worcester teapot and the same print, with added electioneering slogans, a rebus 'anchor' and 'Derby' is on a barrel-shaped mug in the Derby Museum & Art Gallery[4]. Williamson[1], points out that the paste and the glaze of the mug are very different from any porcelain known to have been made at the Nottingham Road factory and that the shape would have made it more suitable for common earthenware than for porcelain, perhaps suggesting that Cockpit Hill was its home. However apart from the addition of a thumb rest on the scroll handle, the mug is exactly the same shape as Nos. 109, 110, 216 and the height of the mug, 15 cm., compares favourably with the 14.5 cm. of No.110 and is slightly smaller than the blue and white mug No.216 (17 cm.)

The electioneering references are associated with the occasion in 1768 when Mr. Godfrey Bagnall-Clarke, who lived at Sutton Hall, Sutton-in-the-Dale, fought and defeated Sir Harry Harper for the representation of the County of Derby in Parliament. It is suggested that the date of the lobed dish is c.1770, that is, after Holdship ceased his engagement with Heath and Duesbury, which would account for the anchor rebus being omitted.

A creamware teapot[3], inscribed 'Harper for ever/fow play and now/fair Dealings' now in the British Museum, was included in the Derby Exhibition, 1870, and Wallis & Bemrose[2] state 'it is a true specimen of Cockpit Hill pottery fabricated about that date' 1768. Donald Towner[3], considers that it comes from the Derby neighbourhood, although not from the Cockpit Hill works. If it were from the Cockpit Hill works it would appear that they supported both candidates in the election.

In the 1870 Exhibition was a two handled bowl-shaped mug, then in the Falke collection, 12.5 cm., inscribed 'JOSHVA HEATH 177-', the last figure being obliterated. Also, a porcelain mug, or beaker, then in the Wallis collection, with the initial 'R' in an oval border, which, in the notes stated had originally been bought from Alderman Heath's works on Cockpit Hill.

Unfortunately our present knowledge of the output of the factory remains very limited. Most of the shards from an early excavation of the site have been lost and nothing has been published concerning any of the finds made shortly before the whole site was redeveloped. Wallis & Bemrose[2], state 'it has always struck us as a curious circumstance, that, the existence of this factory should have remained so long unnoticed by writers upon the manufactures of Derby.' This tradition is still carried on by many modern writers.

H. Gilbert Bradley.

1. F. Williamson, 1930, The Derby Pot Manufactory, known as Cockpit Hill Pottery, reprinted from the Derbyshire Archeological Society, Trans.

2. A. Wallis & W. Bemrose, 1870. Pottery and Porcelain of Derbyshire, London.

3. A. Toppin, 1951, Holdship Transfer-printing at Derby. Trans. E.C.C., Vol.3, Pt.1. Pl.28b and p.68.

4. B.M.Watney, 1964, The Origin of some Transfer Prints on Two Derby Mugs Decorated by Richard Holdship, Ibid. Vol.5, Pt.5, Pl.267a.

5. D. Towner, 1967, The Cockpit Hill Pottery, Derby, Ibid, Vol.6, Pt.3, Pl.160.

380. **LOBED OVAL DISH**   c.1770

Twelve-lobed dish.
Transfer-printed in underglaze blue with a view of Sutton Hall,
set in a landscape, with two flower sprays, a moth and a butterfly,
printed in the lobed border.

    L. 21 cm. W. 18 cm.   Private Collection.

      See. Introduction to Cockpit Hill, p.235.
      Note: Sutton Hall, Sutton in the Dale, was the seat of
           Godfrey Bagnall-Clarke, M.P., for Derby 1768-1774.
      Lit. E.C.C, 1948, Miscellany, Trans. E.C.C., Vol.2, Pt.10,
           p.237.
           A.J. Toppin, 1951, op. cit., Pl.28a.
           Godden, 1966, op. cit., Pl.213, for a mug with identical
           print.
           Watney, 1973, op. cit., p.94.

381. **SWEETMEAT PICKLE-TRAY (Pair)** c.1765   Colour Plate p.237.

Shell-shaped dishes with deeply indented crimped borders, standing
each on three helical shell-like feet.
Painted in the interior in underglaze blue with flower sprays and
smaller sprigs, the frilled edge painted with a blue wash border
and the moulding on the scroll handle outlined in blue.
Translucent body. Hybrid paste.

    L. 18.5 cm.   Private Collection.

      Lit. E.C.C., 1976, Miscellany, Trans. E.C.C., Vol.10, Pt.1, Pl.35
           E.C.C., 1977, op. cit., (Exh. Cat.) No.152.

382. **TUREEN AND COVER**   c.1770

Tureen of porcellaneous nature, supported on three lion's mask and
paw feet, a moulded bead border round the shoulder, applied rope
twist handles, a high dome shaped cover with gadroon moulding
round the edge and surmounted by a rope twist handle.
Transfer-printed in underglaze blue round the body of the tureen
with four floral sprays interspersed with butterflies, four floral
sprays round the shoulder, and scattered butterflies printed on
the cover. Floral sprays printed round the inside rim of the
tureen and the 'open zig-zag fence' pattern in the centre.

    L. 30 cm. W. 23 cm.   Private Collection.
                              Ex. Ernest Allman Collection.

      See. Nos. 199, 200, 212, for floral transfers.
           No. 167 for the 'open zig-zag fence' pattern.
           No. 159 for the 'open zig-zag fence' pattern, in the
           'mirror' position.
      Lit. Towner, 1967, op. cit., Pl.188b.
           N. Stretton, 1975, A Ceramic Conundrum; A Porcelain
           Tureen from Cockpit Hill, Antique Collecting, July.

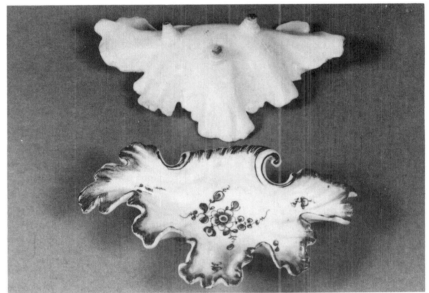

380   381   382

DERBYSHIRE CREAMWARE

Our knowledge of Derbyshire Creamware is of comparatively recent date. A small transfer-printed teapot marked in the print 'Pot works in Derby' was discovered by F. Williamson, curator of the Derby Art Gallery in 1931 and presented to the British Museum.

In 1955, Mr. Geoffrey Godden, in a paper to the English Ceramic Circle, drew attention to several other pieces inscribed in the same way. This formed a basis on which to work and it was not long before the wares, both painted and printed, of the Derby Pot works, also known as the Cockpit Hill factory, became familiar to us. There is no doubt that although the Cockpit Hill factory was one of the great English Creamware factories, its wares were not always of the highest standard and pieces of slovenly workmanship are frequent. On the other hand it produced pieces of great excellence and much of the ware is distinctive. Founded about 1750 by John Heath and others, its first productions seem to have been saltglaze, porcelain and porcelanous earthenware. Creamware was probably not produced till the early 1760's. By 1779 the works were closed.

Although some of the Cockpit Hill Creamware was decorated by Robinson and Rhodes of Leeds, most of the enamelling was executed by Derby painters. Particularly distinctive, is the painting of a large red rose surrounded by lilies, honeysuckle and cherries. The painting of Chinese figures was undertaken by the same Derby painter who painted on Derby porcelain and some Melbourne creamware. The engraving of transfer-printed pieces was largely the work of Thomas Radford who signed his name on a number of pieces.

Of even more recent date is our knowledge of the Melbourne Pottery.[2] Situated some eight miles south of Derby, its site was discovered accidentally and a large number of creamware and other shards were found, which formed a basis for establishing its wares in general. The Melbourne Pottery seems to have been started about 1760 and, as far as the creamware is concerned, came to an end about 1780. After this, different classes of ware were made, probably due to a change of ownership. Melbourne creamware is usually distinctive in design and of a high quality. Painted pieces are sometimes by an enameller who decorated some of the Cockpit Hill creamware. Others are clearly enamelled by Robinson and Rhodes of Leeds, while those in green or purple monochrome, seem to be peculiar to the factory. Transfer-printed pieces of Melbourne creamware also occur and, apart from the usual bird patterns the engravings are often distinctive and were probably done in Derby.

A creamware factory was started at the very end of the eighteenth century in the Nottingham Road, Derby, but lasted for a very short time only. Some good quality creamware decorated with flowers by a Derby porcelain enameller may be attributable to this factory.

There is no doubt that other creamware factories existed in Derbyshire besides those already mentioned. Creamware with distinct Derbyshire characteristics which fit in with neither the Cockpit Hill nor Melbourne factories, are sometimes found. Perhaps one day we may discover their place of origin.

Donald C. Towner.

1.   Towner, 1967, op. cit.,

2.   D.C. Towner, 1971, The Melbourne Pottery,
                    Trans. E.C.C., Vol.8, Pt.1.

CREAMWARE

COCKPIT HILL.

383. **TEAPOT AND COVER**   c.1760

Globular shape with a crabstock handle, S-shaped crabstock spout, with low domed cover, surmounted by a crabstock ring. Decorated with applied reliefs of prunus blossom.

   9.5 cm.   Private Collection.

      Note: Applied relief decoration on creamware is unusual.

384. **TEAPOT AND COVER**   c.1760-70

Globular shape with crabstock handle, S-shaped crabstock spout, with low domed cover, surmounted by a balluster-knop. Painted in iron-red, purple and green enamel colours with bouquets of roses, tulips and other garden flowers outlined in dark brown.

   11.1 cm.   Leeds Art Galleries.
                                              (CR4. 3.2/68).

      Note: A jug dated 1765 in the British Museum and a second
            jug dated 1773, in the Victoria and Albert Museum,
            are decorated in a similar manner.
      Lit. P. Walton, 1976, Creamware and other English Pottery
            at Temple Newsam House, Leeds, London and Bradford,
            No.722.

385. **TEAPOT AND COVER**   c.1765

Globular shape with a small rim round the base, scroll handle with slight ribbing and S-shaped spout, moulded with raised decoration of flowers and leaves. A slightly convex cover with a mushroom shaped knop.

   8.9 cm.   Private Collection.

      Lit. Towner, 1967, op. cit., Pl.165b.

386. **TEAPOT AND COVER**   c.1765

Shaped as No.385.
Painted in red, green and black enamel colours with exotic birds on one side, and flowers on the reverse.

   8 cm.   Private Collection.

      Lit. D.C.Towner, 1957, English Cream-coloured Earthenware,
            London, Pl.9b.
            Towner, 1967, op. cit., Frontispiece & Pl.166a.

385

383

386

384

387. TEAPOT AND COVER   c.1765-70

Globular shape, with faceted loop handle, S-shaped spout and
slightly convex cover with a pierced button knop.
Painted in green, red and black enamel colours with flower and
leaf sprays and scattered flowers on the cover.

    12 cm.   Castle Museum, Norwich.
                                              (361.70.946).

    Lit. Towner, 1967, op. cit., Pl.173a.

388. TEAPOT AND COVER   c.1765

Shaped as No.387.
Painted in red monochrome with a cartouche of scrollwork, foliage
and winding stems.

    10.2 cm.   Private Collection.

    Lit. Towner, 1967, op. cit., Pl.157, for similar shape.
          E.C.C., 1977, op. cit., (Exh. Cat.) No.81, for other side.

389. TEAPOT AND COVER   c.1765

Shaped as No.387.
Painted in iron-red and black on each side with cartouche of
scrollwork foliage and winding stems, inscribed on one side in
black 'Wilkes./& Liberty' and on the other side 'No.45',
scattered flower sprays on the cover.

    11.2 cm.   Leeds Art Galleries.
                                           (CR4. 10.6/38).

    Lit. G.A. Godden, 1955a. A Derby Teapot in the Leeds
          Collection. Leeds Arts Calendar, No. 5, 15, Pl.1a, 6.
          G.A. Godden, 1955b. 'Derby Pot Works, Cockpit Hill',
          Trans. E.C.C., Vol.3, Pt.4, Pl.686 b & C.
          Towner, 1957, op. cit., p.14 & Pl.9a.
          Towner, 1967, op. cit., Pl.169a.
          P. Walton, 1973, 'A Leeds Collectors Notebook', Leeds
          Arts Calendar, p.24.
          Walton, 1976, op. cit., No.709.

387   383   389

390. TEAPOT AND COVER   c.1765

Globular shape with a small foot rim, ribbed loop handle and
moulded spout, a slightly convex cover with a squat floral
knop.
Painted in red, green, blue and yellow enamel colours with a
full-blown rose in India red, and scattered floral sprays.

  13 cm.   Private Collection.

   Lit. Towner, 1967, op. cit., Pl.164b, for teapot with
     very similar decoration.

391. TEAPOT   c.1765

Globular shape with a small foot rim, crabstock handle with
slight ribbing S-shaped, rib moulded spout with an embossed
band round the middle and moulded flowers at the base.
Painted in red, green and blue enamel colours with a floral
spray, scattered flowers and insects. Replacement cover.

  10.3 cm.   Private Collection.

392. TEAPOT AND COVER   c.1765-70

Globular shape with a small foot rim, scroll handle with
moulded spurs and a spout shaped as No.391. A slightly convex
cover with a mushroom shaped knop.
Painted in naturalistic enamel colours with, on one side, roses
and floral sprays, and on the other side, fruits and flowers.
The cover is probably a replacement.

  13 cm.   Private Collection.

393. TEAPOT AND COVER   c.1765

Globular shape, moulded on either side with a pineapple and
leaves arranged in a basket, surrounded by a scroll cartouche
and basket work, a scroll handle with shaped terminal and a
spout, shaped as No.392, (restored). A slightly convex cover
with moulded basket work, surmounted by a finial (restored).
Painted in underglaze metallic oxide colours, made to resemble
'Wheildon-type' ware, with orange and blue on the pineapple,
the leaves green and the cartouche picked out in pink.

  14 cm.   Northampton Museum &
                    Art Gallery.
                    (1920-/d/-4).
   See. Nos. 397, 398, for similar moulded decoration.
   Note: A teapot with similar moulded decoration is in
      the Castle Museum, Nottingham (82.403).
   Lit. J.Draper, 1977, 18th Century Earthenware Tea & Coffee
     Pots in Northampton Museum, Northampton Museum, No.21.

392

390

391

393

394. TEAPOT AND COVER   c.1768-70

Globular shape with bead moulding round the rim and base of the
pot, S-shaped spout moulded with acanthus leaves and made to
resemble bamboo divided into bands, and a loop handle with acanthus
leaf moulding. A slightly convex cover with an onion knop.
Painted in dark orange and black enamel colours with a cartouche
of foliate scroll work and trailing stems, and inscribed on one
side 'Spencer Howe/And Liberty'.

    13 cm.   Northampton Museum & Art
                                                       Gallery. (D.1920-21. 1-120).

        Note: This teapot is connected with the 1768 'spendthrift
                  election' in Northamptonshire, during which it was
                  said that Lord Spencer spent £160,000 in order to get
                  his candidate Mr. Howe elected.
        Lit. J. Draper, 1975, Dated Post-Medieval Pottery in
                  Northampton Museum, Northampton Museum, Pl.20.

395. TEAPOT AND COVER   c.1768-1772

Globular shape with double intertwined loop handle with flower and
leaf terminals, S-shaped octagonal faceted spout, and heavy bead
moulding round rim. A low domed cover with bead moulding round
the edge and surmounted by a pierced button knop.
Painted in iron-red, purple and gold with, on one side, a Chinaman
with a parasol and a flower, and a vase of flowers on a table, and
on the other side, a Chinaman sitting on a chair, with a vase on
a table, behind him a woman, with a child on her back, and to his
left is another woman and a vase of flowers. The cover is painted
with vases of flowers.

    13 cm.   Leeds Art Galleries.
                                                       (CR4. 16.162/47).

        Lit. Godden, 1955, op. cit., Pl.4.
                  Barrett & Thorpe, 1971, op. cit., p.27
                  Walton, 1976, op. cit., No.777.

396. TEAPOT AND COVER   c.1770

Globular shape with double intertwined loop handle with flower
and leaf terminals, and S-shaped spout with moulded leaf
decoration at the base. A low domed cover with convolvulos
type knop.
Painted in purple, red, yellow and green enamel colours with,
on one side a Chinese lady nursing a baby and another Chinese
figure looking down at a rabbit on the ground, and on the reverse,
a spray of purple daisy-like flowers with elongated lower petals.
The outside edge of the convolvulus knop painted red.

    15 cm.   Private Collection.

        See. No.412 for work by the same enameller.
        Lit. Towner, 1967, op. cit., Pl.174a & b.

395   394   396

397. CREAM JUG   c.1765

   Inverted pear shape, with an undulating rim and wide lip, a
   broad strap loop handle with slight traces of ribbing and kick
   terminal.
   Decorated on either side with a moulded pineapple pattern, placed
   in a basket, set in a scroll cartouche surrounded by moulded
   basket work.

      8.9 cm.   Private Collection.

         See. Nos. 393, 398, for similar moulded decoration.
         Note: The oval ring moulded on the basket and the diagonal
               basketry.

398. SAUCE-BOAT   c.1765

   Sauce-boat with an undulating rim, wide lip and double intertwined
   loop handles with flower and leaf terminals.
   Decorated on either side as No.397.

      L. 12.7 cm.   Private Collection.

399. TANKARD   c.1765

   Cylindrical shape with spreading base and flat strap loop handle
   with kick terminal.
   Painted in orange-red, green, yellow, black and purple enamel
   colours with roses, honeysuckle, lilies, forget-me-nots and
   scattered cherries.

      17 cm.   Private Collection.

         Lit. Towner, 1967, op. cit., Pl.170.

400. TANKARD   c.1765

   Cylindrical shape with moulded bands and slightly spreading foot
   rim, moulded bead decoration set below the rim and round the
   foot rim, a broad strap loop handle with slight moulded ridge
   down the centre spine.
   Painted in red green and black enamel colours with a Chinese lady
   standing beside a fence and holding in her hand a flower, scattered
   flowers, a stylised weeping willow and fanciful clouds.

      15.7 cm.   Private Collection.

         See. Nos. 194, 195 for similar stylised willow tree.

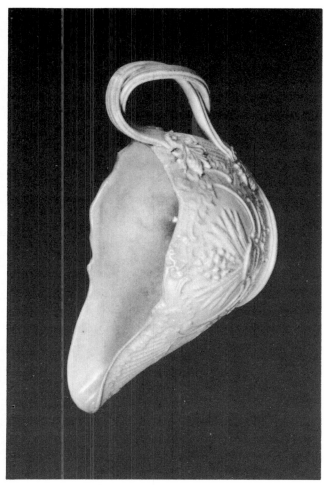

397   399   398   400

401. VASE   c.1765

Neo-classical urn shape, with high domed foot set on a square
plinth, rococo-shaped handles rising to spreading rim moulded
with acanthus leaves, a wreath of moulded leaves round the
shoulder and moulded with festoons of flowers, pendant from
goat masks.
Painted in purple, green and red enamel colours with traces of
gilding, depicting children playing 'blind-man's-buff' in a
garden, and on the reverse, painted in purple, red and yellow,
an allegorical figure riding a winged steed, with scattered
moths and insects. The wreath of leaves, the pendant festoon
and the goat masks all picked out in naturalistic colours.

    26 cm.   Private Collection.

        See. Colour Plate p.242 for reverse side.
        Lit. E.C.C., 1960, Miscellany, Vol.5, Pt.1, Pl.11 & 12.
              Towner, 1967, op. cit., Pl.178.

402. LOVING CUP   c.1765

Inverted bell-shape, set on a domed moulded foot and two scroll
loop handles with kick terminals.
Decorated with a formal leaf design set between a band of moulded
beads and a band of vertical fluting, a rouletted band below the
rim and the foot decorated with a formal leaf pattern and a band
of moulded beads.
The handles decorated with moulded acanthus leaves.

    16 cm.   Private Collection.

        Note: No other cup of this shape has been recorded.
        Lit. E.C.C., 1963, Miscellany, Trans. E.C.C., Vol.5,
              Pt.4, 1963, Pl.184.

403. BASKET   c.1765-70

Oval shape, with flared sides, moulded in panels, comprising
concave sections decorated with a moulded ladder design, set
between panels having moulded openwork patterns of scrolling
and formal acanthus leaves with cut-out floral sprays applied
to the panels on the inside of the bowl. The handles at both
ends of the basket (missing) ending in flower shaped terminals,
raised above the level of the rim.
Yellowish green coloured glaze, tending to run in long horizontal
lines, and finely crazed all over.

    9.5 cm. L. 31.3 cm. W.25.5 cm.   Private Collection.

        See. Saltglaze basket in the Victoria & Albert Museum,
              Schreiber Collection (Sch. II.154).
        Lit. Towner, 1967, op. cit., Pl.186a.
              Walton, 1976, op. cit., No.49, for similar cut out
              floral sprays.

401   403   402

404. TEA-CADDY   c.1770

Eight sided, with sloping shoulders and raised collar.
Transfer-printed in black with, on one side, 'The Tea Party' and
on the reverse a 'Round Tower' surrounded by buildings set in a
rural landscape with two men standing beneath a tree, a stork
and winged insect flying overhead.

    12.7 cm.   Private Collection.

      Note: 'The Tea Party' is taken from page 37 of an
            unidentified drawing book published 24th November,
            1756, for John Bowles & Son at the Black Horse in
            Cornhill.

            The 'Round Tower and buildings' is taken from the
            'Ladies' Amusement', by J. Pillement, Pl.152. The
            page is signed 'J. Roberts Sculp'.

405. TEA-CADDY   c.1770

Shaped as No.404.
Transfer-printed in red with 'Harlequin and Columbine' on one
side and on the reverse 'Sheep grazing' in a field with a
thatched cottage and tree in the background.

    10.8 cm.   Private Collection.

      Note: 'Harlequin and Columbine' is taken from page 37
            of an unidentified drawing book, published in
            November 1756, for John Bowles & Son at the Black
            Horse in Cornhill.

            'Sheep grazing' is taken from the 'Ladies' Amusement'
            1762, published by Robert Sayer in 1762.

404   405   404   405

406. VASE AND COVER   c.1770

Ovoid shape, with concave shoulders and slightly spreading
rim, a domed cover with a mushroom shaped finial.
Transfer-printed in overglaze black enamel with, on one side,
a Chinese lady standing beside a birdcage, with a parrot
perched on a pole above, with peonies and rockwork on the reverse
side. Floral sprays round the shoulder and four butterflies
scattered on the cover.

    27.3 cm.   Private Collection.

       Note: See Nos. 199, 200, 212, 382, for similar floral sprays,
            transfer-printed in underglaze blue.

       Lit.   K. Boney, 1955, <u>A Ceramic Conundrum</u>, <u>Apollo</u>, January.
            Towner, 1967, <u>op. cit</u>., Pl.187.
            G. Wills, 1969, <u>English Pottery & Porcelain,</u> London,
            p.156, Fig.145.
            N. Stretton, 1974, <u>Some Rare Prints on 18th Century</u>
            <u>Creamware</u>, <u>Antique Collecting</u>, July, Fig.6.
            Stretton, 1975, <u>op. cit</u>., Fig. 3 & 4.
            E.C.C., 1977, <u>op. cit</u>., (Exh. Cat.) No.87.

407. TEAPOT AND COVER   c.1765

Globular shape, with double twisted rope handle with flower and
leaf terminals, bamboo moulded spout with upside-down moulded
foliage at the base, a flat cover with convolvulus flower knop
and three leaves.
Painted in washed-out red and black enamels with, on one side,
a church and trees and on the other side, a bridge and trees.
The edge of the flower finial painted in red with a black centre,
the border outlined with a red wavy line with black dots.

    12.5 cm.   Castle Museum, Norwich.
                                              (Bulwer 633).

       Note: It is suggested by Donald Towner that the painted
             scene is a conventialised view of Melbourne Church.
       Lit. Towner, 1971, op. cit., Pl. 31a & b.
            D.C. Towner, 1974, 'Robinson & Rhodes, Enamellers
            at Leeds, Trans. E.C.C., Vol.9, Pt.2., Pl.76.

408. TEAPOT AND COVER   c.1765

Globular shape, with double twisted reeded loop handle with
flower and leaf terminals, fluted spout shaped as No.407, and
a flat cover with convolvulus flower knop and leaves. A single
row of beading round the rim, the base of the pot and on the
cover.
Painted in enamel colours with, on one side, a Chinese lady
standing in a garden beside a table, on which are placed two
vases. On the other side, a Chinese lady standing beside a
flowering plant in a tall vase. Trailing flower sprays round
the cover with traces of gilding on the painting and on the beading.

    11.8 cm.   City of Manchester
                                              Art Galleries.
                                              (1923-898).

       See. No.416 for similar style of painting.
       Lit. Towner, 1971, op. cit., Pl.35a.

407   408   408

409. TEAPOT AND COVER   c.1765

Cylindrical shape, with concave shoulder, the handle and the spout-
shaped as No.407, a low domed cover with convolvulus flower knop
and three leaves. A row of diamond shaped beads round the rim of
the pot and a double row round the shoulder and base of the pot
and round the cover. Light buff colour.
Painted in red and black enamel colours with an all-over flower
diaper pattern in red, interspersed by black dots, with red and
black dashes on the handle and a trailing floral design on the
spout. The edge of the flower finial painted red and traces of
gilding on the beading round the shoulder and the base of the pot.

   15.2 cm.   Castle Museum, Norwich.
                                            (Bulwer 446).

        Lit. Towner, 1971, op. cit., Pl. 32a & b.

410. TEAPOT AND COVER   c.1760-70

Cylindrical pot and cover (finial restored) shaped as No.409, with
handle and spout shaped as No.408. A row of diamond shaped beads
round the rim, the shoulder and base of the pot and round the cover.
Deep cream colour with a greenish-yellow glaze.
Painted in iron-red and black enamel colours with a pattern similar
to No.409, with the beaded moulding picked out in gilt.

   11.6 cm.   Leeds Art Galleries.
                                            (CR4. 427/46).

411. TEAPOT AND COVER   c.1775

Shaped as No.410 with a row of pearl shaped beads round the rim,
shoulder and base of the pot and round the cover.
Pale cream colour.
Painted in enamel colours with, on one side, a Chinese lady
standing in a garden holding a parasol beside a table on which
are placed two vases. On the other side a Chinese lady and a
boy are standing in a garden,with trailing flower sprays round
the shoulder of the pot and on the cover.

   14 cm.   Castle Museum, Norwich.
                                            (Bulwer 547).

        Lit. Towner, 1971, op. cit., Pl. 34a, for view of
              reverse side.

412. TEAPOT AND COVER   c.1773

Shaped as No.411.
Painted in red, green, yellow, black and blue enamel colours with
'Harlequin and Columbine' in a garden, on one side, and on the
reverse, a Chinese figure standing in a garden, with trailing
flower sprays round the shoulder of the pot. A fence with vases
and a prunus tree painted on the cover and the petals of the
flower terminal picked out in red.

   15.2 cm.   Private Collection.
        Note: The harlequin figures are taken from Comedia del Arte.
        Exh. Exhibition of Leeds Creamware, Kenwood, London, 1958.
        Lit. Towner, 1957, op. cit., Pl.31b. (as Leeds).
              Towner, 1971, op. cit., Pl.34b.
              E.C.C., 1977, op. cit., (Exh. Cat.) No.92.

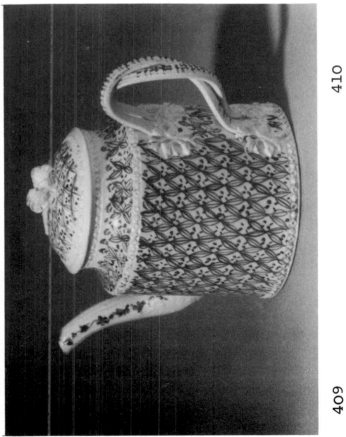

413. TEAPOT AND COVER   c.1770

Cylindrical shape, with straight spout and handle shaped as
No.408, but flower terminals only at the upper ends, a low domed
cover with an acorn finial. A row of pearl and diamond shaped
beads round the shoulder, the base of the pot and on the cover.
Pale cream colour with a pale green glaze.
Painted in purple monochrome colour with, on one side, exotic
birds in a landscape, and on the reverse, the sprays of flowers
and scattered flowers on the cover. The bead moulding picked
out in gilt.

          13.8 cm.   Leeds Art Galleries.
                                                (CR4.16.129/47).

          Note: All the moulded details on this pot have been
                excavated at Melbourne.
          Lit. J.R. & F. Kidson, 1892, Historical Notices of the
                Leeds Old Pottery, Leeds, Pl.13.
                Walton, 1973, op. cit., Pl.5, p.24.
                Walton, 1976, op. cit., No.699, & Colour Pl. p.184.

414. TEAPOT AND COVER   c.1770

Squat shape, with moulded reeding round the base, a straight
spout and handles shaped as No.407, but flower terminals only
at the upper ends, a low domed cover with reeding and flower
finial. A row of pearl shaped beads round the shoulder and the
rim of the pot.
Painted in red enamel colour with floral sprays and scattered
flowers on the pot and the cover, the flower terminal picked
out in red. The bead moulding picked out in gilt.

          11.5 cm.   Astley Hall, Chorley.
                                                (E.13).

413   414

415. COFFEE POT AND COVER   c.1770

Inverted pear shape, with a spreading foot, ribbed double intertwined loop handle with flower and leaf terminals, a long, slender,
curved, faceted spout moulded with leaves and the lip in the form
of a reptile's mouth.
A low domed cover with a baluster knop finial and beaded moulding
round the top of the pot and the rim of the cover.
Deep cream colour with a yellow glaze.
Painted in iron-red and green enamel colours with bouquets of
flowers and flower sprigs outlined in brown enamel.

  22.5 cm.   Leeds Art Galleries.
                    (CR4.4.43/46).

   Exh. Exhibition of Leeds Creamware, Kenwood, London, 1958, No.73.
       City Art Gallery, 1951, Handbook of Leeds Pottery,
       Leeds, No.16.
   Lit. Towner, 1971, op. cit., p.25.
       Walton, 1973, op. cit., p.24, ill, Fig.4.

416. COFFEE POT AND COVER   c.1770

Pot and handles shaped as No.415, a long slender curved spout with
reeded moulding and moulded leaves round the base. A domed cover
with three leaves and convolvulus knop and beaded moulding round
the top of the pot and the rim of the cover.
Painted in enamel colours with a Chinese lady, holding a parasol
and standing beside a table on which are placed two vases, with
scattered flowers on the pot and the cover. The leaves on the spout
picked out in green.

  24.3 cm.   Museum & Art Gallery,
                 Northampton. (D.20/1954-5).

   See. Nos. 408, 411, for a similar style of painting.
   Lit. Draper, 1977, op. cit., No.23.

417. COFFEE POT AND COVER   c.1768

Shaped as No.416 with small diagonal dots moulded round the top of
the pot and the rim of the cover.
Undecorated.

  23.5 cm.   Private Collection.

   Note: Flower knops pierced in a similar manner were found
        on the Melbourne site.
   Exh. Exhibition of Leeds Creamware, Kenwood, London, 1958.
   Lit. Towner, 1957, op. cit., Pl.28 (as Leeds).
       Towner, 1971, op. cit., Pl.30.
       E.C.C., 1977, op. cit., (Exh. Cat.) No.72.

418. COFFEE POT AND COVER   c.1770

Inverted pear shape, with fluted ribbing around the lower half of
the pot, a rope twist handle with an applied convolvulus flower
and trailing stem, florets and leaves. A slender curved reeded
spout with moulded leaves round the base, a high domed cover,
fluted on the upper part and surmounted by a rope twist handle
and applied pierced convolvulus flower. Bead moulding round the
rim and foot of the pot and the rim of the cover.
Deep cream colour.
Undecorated.

  24 cm.   Private Collection.

   Lit. Towner, 1971, op. cit., Pl.38.

415   417   416   418

419. DESSERT PLATE   c.1760-70

Circular shape, with a scalloped and fluted rim having the alternate
flutes pierced with a regular openwork pattern.
Deep cream colour with a greenish-yellow glaze.
Painted in green, monochrome, outlined in black, with a flower
spray in the centre and scattered floral sprays around the rim.

    D. 19.5 cm.   Leeds Art Galleries.
                                                 (CR4.11.122/69).

    Lit. Walton, 1976, op. cit., No.754.

420. DESSERT PLATE OR STAND   c.1770

Circular shape, with twelve-lobed rim and reeded with alternating
panels on the rim pierced with a design resembling a crown,
composed of circles, heart and diamond shapes.
Pale cream colour with a yellowish glaze.
Painted in purple monochrome with a floral spray in the centre
and scattered sprays on the alternate panels on the rim.

    D. 23.4 cm.   Leeds Art Galleries.
                                                 (CR4.16.238/47).

    Note: This type of pierced border has been excavated at
          Melbourne.
    Exh. City Art Gallery, 1926, Handbook of the Old Leeds
          Exhibition, Leeds.
    Lit. Towner, 1971, op. cit., Pl.20b, for a dish pierced
          with a similar design.
          Walton, 1976, op. cit., No.755, & Colour Pl. p.184.

421. FRUIT BASKET   c.1770

Circular shape, with flaring chamfered sides forming twelve
lobed panels, pierced with alternate openwork patterns of
geometric diamond heart and lozenge shaped piercing. Two cord
loop handles with briar terminals on the underside and with
fruit and foliage terminals on the upper side.
Deep cream colour with a yellowish glaze.
Undecorated.

    D. 19 cm.   Astley Hall, Chorley.
                                   Ex. Robert Grey Tatton Collection.

    Lit. Towner, 1971, op. cit., Pl.22b for a cake-basket with
          pierced crown design on alternate panels.
          Walton, 1976, op. cit., No.500, for a basket of similar
          shape, but different pierced design.

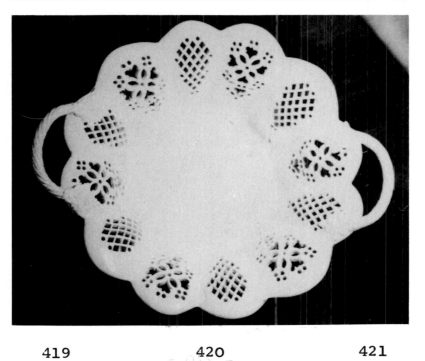

419   420   421

422. PLATE   c.1770

Circular shape, with scalloped rim and feather moulded border
(with seven barbs).
Deep cream colour.
Painted in green enamel with floral spray in the centre and four
trailing sprays around the rim.

Mark: Two nicks cut into the foot rim.

   D. 24.7 cm.   Private Collection.

      Lit. Towner, 1971, op. cit., Pls. 16b and 24b.

423. PLATE   c.1770

Octagonal shape, with a diamond-beaded moulded border.
Painted in purple monochrome with a floral spray in the centre
and four trailing sprays around the rim.

Mark: Two nicks cut into the foot rim.

   D. 20 cm.   Private Collection.

424. PLATE   c.1770

Shaped as No.422.
Transfer-printed in black with a Chinese lady fishing, printed in
the centre, and four prints of exotic birds around the rim.

   D. 24 cm.   Private Collection.

      Lit. Towner, 1971, op. cit., Pl.26b, for plate with slight
          variation in one of the exotic bird prints.

425. PLATE   c.1770

Shaped as No.423.
Transfer-printed in black with exotic birds printed in the centre,
and four prints of exotic birds around the rim.

Mark: Two nicks cut into the foot rim.

   D. 23.5 cm.   Private Collection.

      Lit. Towner, 1971, op. cit., Pl.26a, for plate with slight
          variations in two of the exotic bird prints.

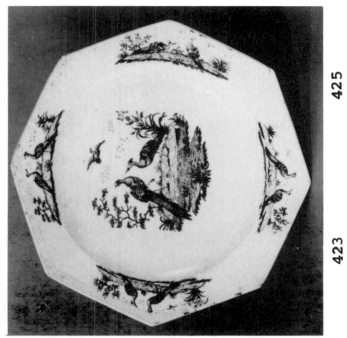

425

423

424

422

426. PLATE   c.1770

Shaped as No.423.
Transfer-printed in black with two dancing figures and a group
of spectators in a pastoral setting, printed in the centre, and
four prints of exotic birds around the rim.

    D. 23.5 cm.   Private Collection.
      See. No.427 for print used on the cover of the tureen.

427. TUREEN AND COVER   c.1770

Irregular octagonal form, on shaped dome foot with elaborate
scroll handles, a shaped dome cover with space cut out for a
ladle, and surmounted by a globular, foliate finial. Decorated
round the widest part of the tureen, the foot rim and the rim
of the cover, with a diamond-beaded moulded border.
Transfer-printed in black on the tureen, with two exotic bird
prints, and on the cover with a print of the two dancing
figures and another of exotic birds.

    14 cm.   Private Collection.

      See. No.426 for similar print of the two dancing figures.
      Lit. E.C.C., 1975, Miscellany, Trans. E.C.C., Vol.9, Pt.3,
            p.305, Pl. 200a & b.

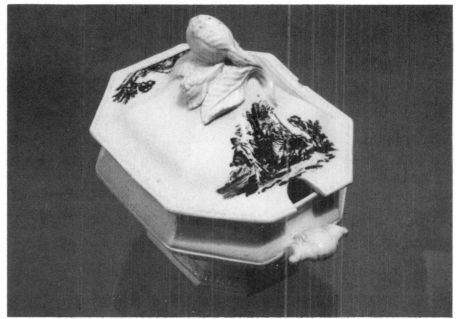

426 427 427

428. TANKARD   c.1770

    Cylindrical shape, with a spreading base and loop strap handle.
    Painted in iron-red enamel colours with a chinoiserie scene.

       12 cm.   Private Collection.

429. TAPER STICK   c.1765   Colour Plate p.243.

    After a silver original, with moulded irregular shaped, domed
    foot, double baluster stem and inverted bell-shaped nozzle.
    Deep cream colour.
    Painted in purple enamel monochrome with scattered floral sprays.

       17 cm.   Private Collection.

       Lit. Towner, 1971, op. cit., Pl.18.
              E.C.C., 1977, op. cit., (Exh. Cat.) No.74.

428   429

SALT-GLAZED STONEWARE

The sale announcements in the Derby Mercury dated March and
April 1780, stated that there was for sale a great quantity
of White Stone and Brown Ware, which had been made at the
Pot Works.

However very few specimens of these wares have been
identified. [1,2]

John Haslem in The Old Derby China Factory 1876, states that
much of the stock was bought by Duesbury and sold by him in
Ireland, and that the rest of the stock was removed to the
China Works where it remained until 1830, when it was sold in
a lump to a dealer in Derby.

Whilst carrying out dredging work in the river near St. Mary's
Bridge in 1973, workmen came across fragments of salt-glazed
plates, which differ from the usual Staffordshire pattern and,
although it cannot be proved, they may well have been part of
the stock removed from the Pot Works and stored at the China
Works near St. Mary's Bridge. The fragments are shown
opposite.

H. Gilbert Bradley.

[1] Towner, 1967, op. cit., Pl.186a, b & c.

[2] Walton, 1976, op. cit., Nos. 4, 5 & 49.

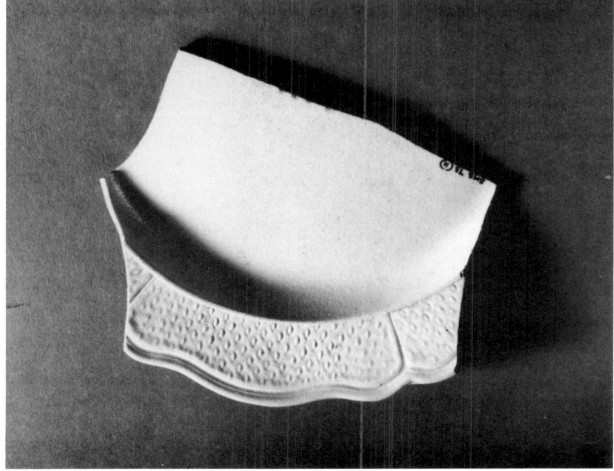

430. SAUCE-BOAT   c.1765

Moulded on either side with the 'pineapple' pattern set in a
basket with a moulded ring decoration, enclosed in a scroll
cartouche, surrounded by basket work, and a broad strap handle
with kick terminal.
Painted in underglaze metallic oxide colours, the pineapple
blue, the leaves green and the cartouche in pink.

       L. 15.2 cm.   Private Collection.

          See. Nos. 393, 397, 398 for similar style moulded
                decoration.
          Lit. Towner, 1967, op. cit., p.265, Pl.184, for a white
                salt-glazed example, with slightly different handle
                in the British Museum.

431. PEPPER POT   c.1765

Of inverted pear shape, on a high domed foot, with a perforated
domed cover, above an everted flange collar.
Decorated with scattered moulded seeds set between three wavy
combed lines, divided by one horizontal and four vertical lines.
The whole hollowed out with a cavity in the base for a cork to
be inserted.

       12.6 cm.   Private Collection.

          See. Introduction to Salt-glazed Stoneware, p.276.
          Note: The moulded decoration of seeds and three wavy lines,
                matches the fragments dug up in the river near St.
                Mary's Bridge in 1973.

432. BASKET   c.1765

Circular shape, with a foliate rim and outward sloping sides,
pierced with a design of intersecting circles, over which are
applied floral sprays.

       7 cm. D. 26.4 cm.   Private Collection.

          Exh. Burlington Fine Arts Club, 1914, Catalogue of an
                Exhibition of Early English Earthenware.
          Lit. Towner, 1967, op. cit., Pl.186b & c, for other examples.
                Walton, 1976, op. cit., No.49, for similar example.

431   430   432

DERBYSHIRE STONEWARE

The making of pottery in Derbyshire can be traced back many
centuries, even to A.D.98, when 'Derbyshire Ware' was not only
being produced, but also being exported from kilns at Hazlewood,
Holbrook and Little Chester. These were all in the vicinity of
what is now Derby and on prehistoric tracks, one of which was
known as Old Portway. But throughout the centuries it was
mostly a local industry, produced, no doubt, in conjunction with
farming and developed by families with a knowledge of the right
clays required which were to be found on their lands. It was of
the type that is described as plastic clay, which was suitable
for stoneware and when glazed with salt, is impervious to
liquids.

The use in the 18th Century of coal as a fuel, meant an expansion
of the mining area, which exposed new beds of clay and a corres-
ponding increase in the number of potteries. The Eastern part
of Derbyshire has always had an abundant source of the raw
materials required, particularly coal, since this part of the
county is on the Coal Measures. Also the stoneware clays were
suitable for salt-glazing, and even the rock salt required for
the glazing was easily obtained from the neighbouring county of
Cheshire, (on which a Salt Tax was levied by the Government).

The use of salt, causing a fall-out of hydrochloric acid on the
land, meant that new sites for the potteries had to be found
and these were developed on the outskirts of the towns, at
Brampton, Whittington Moor, Belper, Derby, Ilkeston and Codnor
Park.

The glaze of these 'pots' was an attractive light to dark brown
glassy covering, and the colour varied according to the use of
the minerals, such as lead or iron which are so prevalent in the
Derbyshire soils.

Most of the wares produced were simple domestic items, for use
in the kitchen, including stew, souse and hash pots, butter pots,
open and covered jars, jugs of all types and sizes, churns, bowls,
teapots and coffee pots, spirit kegs and water filters as well
as footwarmers and carriage warmers for use when travelling.
Amongst the more ornamental wares were puzzle jugs, with a wetting
for the unwary, well modelled toby jugs and money boxes. These,
like the tobacco containers which were kept on the mantle shelf,
were shaped in the familiar outline of the Toll House, with the
roof acting as a lid, often with a presser, in 'biscuit' to help
keep the tobacco down and moist. Ink pots, scent jars and cordial
flasks, were modelled with features made to represent well known
political figures. Mugs were fitted with handles in the shape of
greyhounds, and applied with all types of decoration; also
spitoons, so necessary in those days of tobacco smoking and
chewing.

The decoration is interesting, because, unlike the porcelains
and earthenwares of the period, there are no chinoiserie designs.
It is the one branch of English ceramics that was not influenced
by the Far East. The sprigged-on decoration includes oak leaves,
oak trees, windmills, hunting scenes and shooting scenes as well
as the Royal Family including Queen Victoria, Prince Albert and
even Queen Victoria's mother, the Duchess of Kent.

Thousands of stone bottles were mass produced that could be used
for ginger beer, blacking or furniture polish but the repeal of
the tax on glass in 1845 caused a decline in production.

Apart from the spirit flasks, which were marked with the name
of the firm and the place of manufacture, very few of the pieces
were marked until late in the 19th Century. This does not deter
admirers from collecting these items which were so essential to
the comfort of the majority of the British people in the 19th
century.

                                        R. B. Brown.

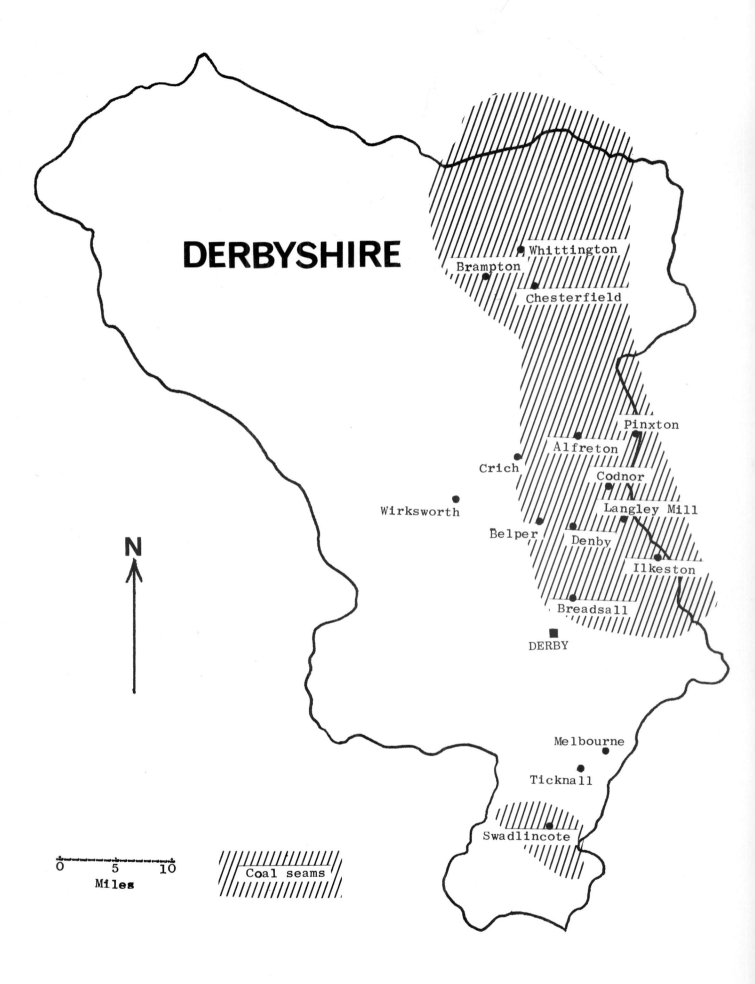

DERBYSHIRE

N

Whittington
Brampton
Chesterfield

Pinxton
Alfreton
Crich
Codnor
Langley Mill
Wirksworth
Belper
Denby
Ilkeston

Breadsall

DERBY

Melbourne

Ticknall

Swadlincote

0   5   10
Miles

Coal seams

BROWN SALT-GLAZED STONEWARE POTTERIES

ALFRETON   1750-1975

Built in King Street by George Bacon and carried on by his great
nephew; took over the pottery at Crich, after the bankruptcy in 1763.
In 1762 a man called Smith and a workman from Bacon's factory set
up in opposition in King Street.

Types of ware: The only vessel attributable to Alfreton is the
                Coffee pot No.435 a product of the Smith works.

BELPER   c.1740-1834

Acquired by William Bourne of Eastwood in the 1770's.
Succeeded by his son Joseph, who in 1812 took over the works at Denby.

Types of ware: Punch bowls, loving cups, mugs, jugs, blacking bottles,
                mineral water bottles and spirit bottles.

Marks: Impressed, Belper and Denby Potteries Derbyshire.
Lit: Jewitt, 1972, op. cit., pp.151, 152.

BRAMPTON

WELSHPOOL AND PAYNE POTTERY
Started in the late 18th century.
c.1835 taken over by Matthew Knowles, merged with Barker Pottery.
Closed in 1957.

THE POTTERY
Established in 1810 by Oldfield, Madin, Wright and Hewitt.
In 1838 Oldfield's nephew John Oldfield became sole owner.
c.1888 taken over by a member of the Pearson family and later merged
with Pearsons of Whittington Moor.
Marks: Impressed, Oldfield Manufactory, Chesterfield.

WALTON POTTERY
Started by William Briddon, c.1790. Continued by his son and
grandson. Taken over by Plowright.
Closed in 1957.

WHEATBRIDGE POTTERY
Built by William Robinson c.1750.
1769 sold to Edward Wright.
Closed in 1937.
Mark: later wares impressed Wright.(see No.439).
Jewitt states that this firm was making brown ware for the Dutch
market in 1887.

ALMA POTTERY
Started by S. Lowe, c.1854. Continued by his sons.
Closed early 20th century.

BARKER POTTERY
Started by S & H Briddon.
Bought by a Mr. Shaw and merged with Welshpool and Payne Pottery.
Closed in 1957.
Marks: Impressed S & H Briddon.

BRUNSWICK POTTERY
Merged with Alma Pottery. Closed early 20th century.

LONDON POTTERY
Started in 19th century by F. Lipscombe & Co. of London.
Types of ware: Water filters.

Taken over late 19th century by Oldfields and connected by a
railway line.
Closed early 20th century.

EASTMOOR POTTERY
Originally a brick and tile yard.
In 1833 the pottery was owned by John Anthony.
In 1846 owned by J. Taylor.
Closed c.1862.
Lit. Jewitt, 1972, op. cit., pp.154-156.

CHESTERFIELD See Brampton and Whittington Moor.

CODNOR PARK
1820 Built by Butterley Iron Company and managed by William Burton.
Closed in 1832.
1833 Taken over by Joseph Bourne of Denby.
1861 Business transferred to Denby.
Types of wares: Bottles, spirit flasks, butter churns.
Marks: Denby and Codnor Park, Bourne Potteries, Derbyshire.
Lit.   Jewitt, 1972, op. cit., pp.167-170.

CRICH
Pottery Farm, Moorwood Moor.
Started c.1690, operated by members of the Dodd family.
1763 Bankruptcy of Dodd family. Taken over by George Bacon.
Closed in 1799. Operated as brick works until 1810.
Lit. W.B. Honey, revised by R.J. Charleston, 1964, English
      Pottery and Porcelain, London, p.60.

DENBY
Started in 1809 by Mr. Jager.
1812 Taken over by Joseph Bourne from Belper.
Denby Tableware Ltd. still in production.
Mark: Bourne included in various forms.
Lit. Jewitt, 1972, op. cit., pp.172-174.

ILKESTON
1807 Founded by George Evans.
1832 Richard, son of George Evans succeeded to the business.
1880 Pottery closed.
Types of ware: Bottles, harvest barrels.
Mark: Evans Ilkeston. (see No.441).

LANGLEY MILL
1865 Founded by James Calvert.
Became Calvert & Lovatt.
1895 Lovatt & Lovatt.
1931 Lovatt Potteries Ltd.
1959 Acquired by J. Bourne & Son, Denby.
      Name changed to Langley Potteries Limited.
      Still in production, known as Denby Tableware Ltd.
Types of ware: Ginger beer, furniture and blacking bottles,
               mugs, jugs etc. also terra cotta wares.
Lit. Jewitt, 1972, op. cit., pp.198-200.

SHIPLEY

1825 Founded on the estate of E.M. Mundy, of Shipley Hall.
1829 Leased to five Shipley men.
      Taken over by Mr. Waite, from London, a blacking manufacturer.
1845 Taken over by Joseph Bourne.
1856 Business transferred to Denby.

Types of ware: Bottles, furniture and blacking bottles.

WHITTINGTON

WHITTINGTON POTTERY
Established in mid 17th century.
1810 Taken over by a member of the Pearson family.
Pearson & Co. (Chesterfield) Ltd. Still in production.

Types of ware: Stone bottles, jars, flasks, wine and spirit kegs.
             Full range of domestic wares.

STONE BOTTLE WORKS
1818 Established by Aaron Madin. Carried on by his son-in-law
Samuel Lancaster.
Closed in 20th century.

WHITTINGTON POTTERIES
1800 Old pottery site taken over by William Bromley.
1828 Taken over by Robert Bainbridge & Co.
Closed early 20th century.

Lit. Jewitt, 1972, op. cit., pp.244, 245.

433. TEAPOT AND COVER   BRAMPTON   Early 19th century.

Globular fluted shape, with a moulded band round the centre
of the pot, S-shaped spout and shaped handle, a flat cover
with flutes radiating from the centre and surmounted by an
ornate finial.

Mark: S. & H. BRIDDON impressed on the base.

   9 cm.   Derby Museum & Art Gallery.
                                                (1308).

434. TEAPOT   BRAMPTON   Early 19th century.

Globular shape, with a moulded band round the centre, decorated
with stylised daisies and arabesques round the upper portion
and stylised vine leaves moulded on the lower half, S-shaped
moulded spout and loop handle with curled thumb rest.
Lid not original.

   8 cm.   Private Collection.

435. COFFEE POT AND COVER   ALFRETON   c.1820

High baluster shape, moulded in relief with a hunting scene and
a band of flowers above five engine turned rings, an S-shaped
spout and elaborate handle. A flat cover fitting inside the
raised rim of the pot, with moulded flowers, surmounted by a
mushroom shaped finial.

   19 cm.   Derby Museum & Art Gallery.
                                              (876-1939).

        Note: This coffee pot was found on the site of the
              Alfreton Pottery in 1878.
        Lit. R.G.Hughes and A.Oswald, Trans. E.C.C., Vol.9,
              Pt.2, 1974, p.168 and Pl.101f, for view of reverse
              side of pot.

436. CUP   probably Mid-DERBYSHIRE   Early 19th century.

Straight sided with flared lip and rounded into the foot, with
an ear shaped handle. Decorated with an incised line below the
rim.

   5 cm.   Private Collection.

437. PUNCH BOWL   BELPER   Dated 1775

Large shallow bowl on a low pedestal foot. Adorned with panels
of rouletted decoration, with incised flowers and leaves, and
an incised border round the inside rim of the bowl.

Mark: 'ONE MORE AND THEN' inscribed on the inside of the bowl.

Inscribed, H ^{K} M   Made at BELPER. May 29th, 1775'.
         *

    16.5 cm.   D. 34.5 cm.   Derby Museum & Art Gallery.
                                              (681-13.1937).

438. LOVING CUP   probably BELPER   Dated 1798

Inverted bell-shape, with two loop handles with kick terminals.
Decorated with incised flowers, divided into panels round the
upper half, and incised diamond shapes with impressed catherine-
wheels round the lower section.

Inscribed, 'E.R. 1798'.

    22.8 cm.   Derby Museum & Art Gallery.
                                              (467).

    Lit. Hughes & Oswald, 1974, op. cit., p.162 & Pl.98d.

439. PUZZLE JUG   BRAMPTON   Dated 1775

Globular shape, with a high pierced neck and fretted rim, a wide
loop handle connected to a hollow band round the top, pierced with
three protruding spouts. Decorated with a band of beads at the
junction of the neck and bowl, and round the foot rim.

Mark: Inscribed round the bowl: 'Gentlemen come try your skill
                                 I'll hold a wager if you will
                                 You dont drink this liquor all
                                 Unless you spill or let some fall'.

    'JN. WRIGHT MAKER. 1775' inscribed on base.

    16.5 cm.   Derby Museum & Art Gallery.
                                              (707-1939).

    Lit. Hughes & Oswald, 1974, op. cit., p.170 & Pl.104h.

440. PUZZLE JUG   BRAMPTON   c.1775

Globular shape as No.439, with a high neck and pierced below the
hollow band. Decorated with applied relief decoration of 'Toby
Philpot', drunken men and pipe smokers, with applied moulded
flower sprays round the rim band, which is also decorated with
the addition of manganese oxide to the body.

    24.5 cm.   Private Collection.

437 438 439 440

441. HARVEST BARREL   ILKESTON   Dated 1817

Barrel shape, with concentric grooves incised round both ends
of the barrel, with a hole in the centre for the bung and
moulded attachment for the tap.

Mark: Inscribed on the side of the barrel: 'ROBERT WADE
                                         ILKESTON
                                         DERBYSHIRE
                                         APRIL 14th, 1817'

    L. 30.8 cm.   Derby Museum & Art Gallery.
                                         (707-5. 1939).

      Lit. Hughes & Oswald, 1974, op. cit., p.174, & Pl.101c.

442. MASK JUG   BRAMPTON   Early 19th century

Shaped jug, moulded to represent the 'Head of Neptune' with an
undulated rim, wide spout with applied handle, representing a
biting dolphin.

Mark: 'S. & H. BRIDDON' impressed on the base.

    17.5 cm.   Derby Museum & Art Gallery.
                                       (883-1940).

443. CORDIAL FLASKS   BELPER   1830

Flasks, moulded in the upper half as busts, with head and
shoulder, and with arms and hands, the crown of the head
pierced for a cork to be inserted.

Mark: Impressed on the side: 'THE SECOND MAGNA CARTA BROUGHAM's
                                         REFORM CORDIAL'
                        'THE PEOPLES RIGHTS GREY'S CORDIAL'
                        'WILLIAM IV th's REFORM CORDIAL'

Impressed 'BELPER & BOURNE POTTERIES'.

    19 cm.   Derby Museum & Art Gallery.
                                       (681-1937).

    Note: A similar example, impressed, 'DANIEL O'CONNELL IRISH
           CORDIAL' in the Victoria & Albert Museum (3691-1901).

444. FLASK   BELPER-DENBY Early 19th century

Shaped in the form of a percussion pistol.

    L. 25 cm.   Derby Museum & Art Gallery.
                                       (681-11-1937).

      See. Hughes & Oswald, 1974, op. cit., Pl.103c, for similar
           style flask.

441   442   443   444

445. BELLRINGER's JUG   BRAMPTON   19th Century

Inverted pear shape, with cylindrical neck and wide spout, a
large strap handle and an applied wedge on the front of the
jug, for assistance when carrying the vessel. Applied moulded
leaf decoration round the shoulder and neck of the jug and
scattered sprigged relief decorations of lions, dogs, trees
and knights on horseback.

48 cm.   Private Collection.

    Note: On November 20th, 1976, Mr. John Howell read a paper
          to the English Ceramic Circle entitled 'The East
          Anglian Gotch' describing some of the Bellringers'
          Jugs to be found in East Anglia.

446. APOTHECARY'S JAR   ILKESTON   19th century

Globular, on a raised pedestal foot, cylindrical neck, large
straight spout and applied loop handle.

15.5 cm. L. 21 cm.   Derby Museum & Art Gallery.
                                                    (111-74).

447. TOBACCO JAR   DENBY   19th century

Cylindrical form, with applied scroll handles, a raised dome
cover surmounted by a finial, shaped in the form of a flower
petal, and a plain shaped disc, with mushroom shaped knop,
for use as a liner.
Decorated round the barrel of the jar with applied decoration
depicting the Royal Arms, a basket and cornucopia with flowers,
and on the cover Sampson wrestling with a lion.

16.5 cm.   Derby Museum & Art Gallery.
                                                    (1317).

    Lit. Hughes & Oswald, 1974, op. cit., for a tobacco jar
          dated 1885 of similar style.

445   447   446

448. TOAST RACK   <u>BRAMPTON</u>   19th century

Rectangular shape, with wide flat handles, moulded in one with
the base, with five applied elaborately shaped triangular supports,
the centre one surmounted by a shaped ring finial.

    9.5 cm.   Private Collection.

      Note: Imitating a silver original.
      See. Similar example in the Victoria & Albert Museum (C3-1935),
            with the heads of Queen Victoria & Prince Albert,
            and therefore dating after the Royal Wedding in
            February 1840.

449. FERN POT   <u>BRAMPTON</u>   19th century

Manufactured in two sections, the lower of globular shape, with
applied moulded masks for handles, set on a rounded foot ring,
the upper section of flaring cylindrical form, with two scroll
handles.
Decorated on both sections with floral sprays and other applied
motifs.

    18.5 cm.   Private Collection.

450. ANIMALS   <u>BRAMPTON</u>   19th century

Moulded in the form of, a Camel,
                       a Cow,
                       a Cat,

all set on low moulded plinths.

Mark: 'S. & H. BRIDDON'

    5 cm. to 10 cm.   Derby Museum & Art Gallery.
                                    (1649-1).

451. ANIMAL   <u>BRAMPTON</u>   19th century

Moulded in the form of a goat, set on a low moulded plinth.

    6 cm.   Private Collection.

452. ANIMAL   <u>BRAMPTON</u>   19th century.

Pair of lions couchant, set on a rectangular bases.

    L. 19.3 cm. W. 10 cm.   Private Collection.

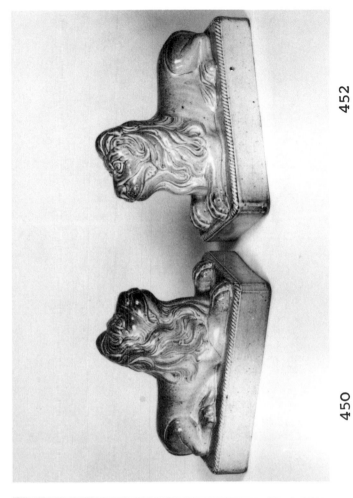

452

449

450

448

When the Exhibition was originally assembled it included a number of items thought to be of doubtful Derbyshire origin, which were, nevertheless, included in the exhibition and these have been grouped in this section. It will be seen that some have now been ascribed to other factories whereas others are still left unknown. It is hoped that more information will come to light which will help in their attribution.

UNDECORATED WARES

453. CUP   c.1755-60

Of fluted form, with scalloped rim, sprigged and moulded decoration and loop handles.

    6.4 cm.   Private Collection.

      Note: Although this cup has certain affinities with the early Derby period, it is, in many ways, nearer the 'Pomona' group, which may indicate a Staffordshire origin.

POLYCHROME WARES

454. MINIATURE TEA BOWL   c.1770   CAUGHLEY

Painted in enamel colours with a rose and a floral spray, the rim outlined in brown.

    2.3 cm.   Private Collection.

455. COFFEE CUP   c.1760-65   WORCESTER

Of flaring form with everted lip and grooved loop handle. Painted with enamel colours with a Chinoiserie scene and two cocks fighting.

    5.7 cm.   Private Collection.

      Note: Both the shape and the pattern differ slightly from No.72.

456. PLATE   c.1790

Of standard shape with shallow spiral fluting round the rim. Painted in the centre with a bouquet of flowers in enamel colours, alternate long and short floral sprays set within the flutes and the rim outlined in gilt.

    24.2 cm.   Private Collection.

      Note: This plate is marked with the 'Ting' or 'Potters stool' painted in puce, which is now considered to be an outside decorating factory mark. Although the shapes conform to the Derby patterns, pieces having this mark are usually of an inferior quality implying that they had been bought in the 'white'.

453   456   454   455

BLUE AND WHITE WARES

457. TEAPOT AND COVER   c.1775-80

Globular shape with S-shaped spout, ear-shaped handle with
acanthus leaf moulding on the upper surface, a low domed cover
with onion knop.
Transfer-printed in underglaze blue with a Chinese river scene on
both sides of the pot, and on the cover, flower sprigs printed on
the spout and a diamond shaped design on the handle, a double line
border round the shoulder of the pot and rim of the cover.

>   14.6 cm.   Castle Museum, Norwich.
>   (Bulwer -415).

>   Note: Col. Bulwer originally catalogued this teapot as
>   Church Gresley. His reasons were as follows :-
>   1. 'It had been in the possession of Lord Carnarvon, then
>   living at Bretby Park Derbyshire which was close to
>   the factory.'
>   2. 'Lord Chesterfield, who once owned Bretby, was greatly
>   interested in the factory and was a great friend of
>   the Gresleys of Drakelowe.'
>   3. 'It is very fine transparent china and resembles an
>   inferior Derby, which were characteristics.'
>   4. 'Coffee, a well known Derby painter, worked at Church
>   Gresley in 1795, and this pot is of a Derby shape with
>   a Derby handle.'
>   5. 'It is warped, cracked and blistered in the firing as this
>   piece has done. They could never get over this drawback.'
>   6. 'Church Gresley decorated with trees, etc., in a palish
>   blue like this one.'
>
>   "Col. Bulwer later withdrew the attribution, probably on
>   reading W.B.Honey's account of the factory in his 1928
>   Old English Porcelain, London, where he states (p.255)
>   'Church Gresley must therefore be considered to be
>   another myth'.
>   Whatever the truth about Church Gresley, the local
>   provenance of this pot and its similarity to Derby
>   porcelain, may point to a Derbyshire origin."

458. PLATE   c.1780-90

Broad rim with shaped and everted rim and shallow fluting in the well.
Transfer-printed as No.457 with a chinese river scene and four
transfer-printed vignettes placed round the rim.

>   D. 22.6 cm.   Private Collection.
>   Note: The body is badly discoloured, with blister marks in
>   the glaze.

459. SAUCER   c.1780-85

Shallow form with a slightly flattened rim.
Transfer-printed as No.457 with a double line border.

>   D. 12.5 cm.   Private Collection.
>   Note: The rim has warped badly, in the firing and, although
>   the under surface is well covered with glaze, the upper
>   face is almost matt biscuit.

458 457 459

BLUE AND WHITE (continued)

460. SAUCER   c.1778-82

Painted in thick underglaze blue with a Chinaman, sitting on a
rock beneath a willow tree, fishing: an island with a fence
barrier and a pagoda, two small sailing boats and floating
'cannon balls' with flights of birds in the sky. A painted
diaper border.

     13 cm.   Private Collection.

       Mark: Traces of stilt marks on the rim.
       Note: No other pieces from this service have been recorded.

461. DISH   c.1765   WORCESTER

Kidney shape, painted in underglaze blue, with a subject taken
from chinese porcelain, known as 'The eight Horses of Mu Wang'.

     L. 26.5 cm.   W. 19 cm.   Victoria & Albert Museum.
                                       (C. 114-1942).

462. SAUCE-BOAT   c.1772-75   WORCESTER

Shaped as No.204.
Painted in underglaze blue in a similar manner.

     L. 18.2 cm.   Private Collection.

460   461

463. MUG   dated 1779

Plain cylindrical shape, with a loop handle having a centre
ridge in the groove.
Painted with a continuous farm-yard scene in underglaze blue,
depicting a woman drawing water from a well, a three-storey
timber-frame farm house, with a woman feeding pigs in the
foreground and a herdsman and a milkmaid standing beside a
goat. A windmill set on a hill in the distance.

Mark: 'I ^{C} A' on the base in underglaze blue.
          1779

    14.5 cm.   G. Godden Reference
                                        Collection.

       See. Creamware jug, probably Wedgwood, painted in enamel
             colours with a farm-yard depicting a maid milking a
             cow, instead of drawing water or feeding pigs. Inscribed
             'JOHN BRIDGEN 1780'. Fitzwilliam Museum, Cambridge
             (Cat. Gl - 1055-1929).
      Note: Nearly opaque to transmitted light due to underfiring.
             Also there are faults in the glaze, leaving unglazed
             biscuit areas.
       Lit. Godden, 1974, op. cit., No.49, Pl.8.
             A. Smith, 1970, Illustrated Guide to Liverpool
             Herculaneum Pottery, London, p.24 & 35.

464. MUG   c.1780   NEW HALL

Plain cylindrical shape, with loop handle.
Painted in underglaze blue with a fence surrounding a house,
which is almost hidden by a tree, with scattered sprays of
flowers, and scroll decoration on the handle.

    13 cm.   G. Godden Reference
                                        Collection.

      Note: There are clear indications of spiral wreathing
             in the glaze.
       Lit. D. Holgate, 1971, New Hall & Its Imitators, London
             p.31.

464

463

465. SPILL VASE (pair)   c.1803-06

Pair of tall cylindrical shaped vases, with slightly spreading
base.
Painted in purple enamel colours with a continuous landscape, a
gilt scallop and husk motif border round the rim and base of the
cylinder and a gilt band round the spreading base.

    12.5 cm.   Private Collection.
                                 Ex. Brig. Gen. E.C.D'E.Coke
                                            Collection.

        Note: It is thought that these vases are possibly Minton
              rather than Pinxton.
        Lit. Charleston, 1965, op. cit., Pl.50b.

IRONSTONE

466. OVAL DISH   c.1770-80

Lozenge shape with a wavy border, the under-side flat without
a foot rim.
Painted in underglaze blue with two deer set in a stylised landscape with trees and flowering prunus, with a roll and arrow
border round the 'cavetto' and an elaborate border painted round
the rim.
Non-translucent, with a body intermediate between porcelain and
pottery, possibly an early form of ironstone.

    L. 26 cm.   Private Collection.

        Note: Pattern copied from a Chinese original.
        Lit. Watney, 1973, op. cit., Pl.68 D (2), for similar
              border design.

CREAMWARE

467. TEAPOT AND COVER   c.1764

Globular shape with moulded crabstock spout and crabstock handle,
a shallow domed cover and baluster knop, with pearl bead moulding
round the rim of the pot and round the slightly spreading base.
Painted in dark brown enamel colours with, on one side, 'WILKES/&/
LIBERTY/No.45' 'God Speed/The Plough'.

    12 cm.   Astley Hall,
                                 Chorley Borough Council.
                                   Ex.Robert Grey Tatton
                                            Collection.

        See. P.241. Introduction to Derbyshire Creamware.
        Note: Perhaps from another Derbyshire factory.
        Lit. Haslem, 1876, op. cit., p.32, mentions two works
              connected by a 'birdcage walk', and at one of them
              both creamware and earthenware were made for a
              short period.

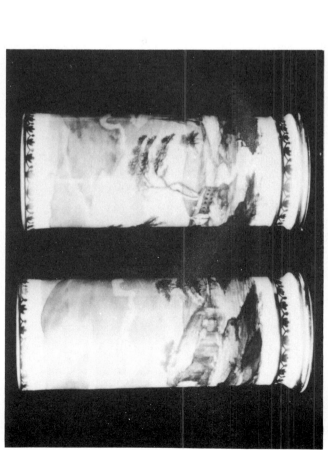

465

466

467

467

RED STONEWARE

In his paper on Melbourne, Donald Towner believed that the redware
teapot in the City Art Gallery, Manchester (No.468) and a teapot
in the Salisbury Museum were made at Melbourne by reason of the
convolvulus with three leaves on their covers.
Robin Price discussing redware considered that the impressed
pseudo-Chinese square seal on the base denotes a Derbyshire origin,
and on these assumptions the following three teapots were included
in the Exhibition at Morley College.
However, shards with these marks have now been excavated in Staffordshire which may prove these pots to be of Staffordshire origin.

> Lit. Towner, 1971, op. cit., p.30.
>   R.Price, 1959, 'Some Groups of English Redstone:'
>   Trans. E.C.C., Vol.4, Pt.5

468. TEAPOT AND COVER   c.1760-70
Globular shape with loop handle, straight spout and flat cover.
Decorated with stamped ornament, depicting, on one side, a seated
oriental figure holding a musical instrument and on the other side,
two figures at a tea stall. Fantastic birds to the left and right
of each scene and below, a festoon of scrolls and flowers, a
cartouche enclosing a griffin. The cover decorated with stamped
ornament in the form of scrolls and surmounted by a convolvulus
terminal, but only two and a half leaves remaining.
Mark: Chinese seal.   City of Manchester Art
                                           Galleries. (1923-675).
    15 cm.
        Lit. Towner, 1971, op. cit., p.30.

469. TEAPOT AND COVER   c.1760-70
Globular shape with S-shaped ribbed spout, moulded acanthus leaves
round the base, a rib moulded loop handle with an acanthus leaf
thumb rest, a slightly convex cover with a pierced ball knop.
Decorated on both sides with applied reliefs, on one side a seated
Chinaman playing the mandolin, and on the other side, a Chinese lady
standing up beside an exotic bird which is perched on a rococo stand,
scattered flower sprays round the top of the pot and on the cover
and incised lines also round the rim and the cover.
Mark: Chinese seal.   Castle Museum, Norwich.
    15.7 cm.   (Bulwer 185).
        Lit. Price, 1962, Trans. E.C.C., Vol.5, Pt.3, Pl.150x
              for similar mark.

470 TEAPOT AND COVER   c.1763-64
Cylindrical shape, with straight spout, loop handle, and slightly
convex cover with pierced ball knop.
Decorated on both sides with applied reliefs hanging as festoons
supporting a griffin set in a rococo cartouche and on one side, a
seated Chinese figure with a large bird on the left hand, set between
two heraldic roses, and on the other side, a seated figure of
Britannia with '45' on her shield, also set between two heraldic
roses. On the cover, a large and a small rose and a formal motif.
Mark: Chinese seal.   Castle Museum, Norwich,
    13.8 cm.   (Bulwer 272).
        Note: The '45' on the shield refers to copy No.45 of the
              'North Briton' published by John Wilkes in 1763.
        Lit. Price, 1959, op. cit., pp. 2 & 3, Pl.1c, Coffee Pot
              (Fitzwilliam Museum) and 2d teapot (British Museum)
              with applied Britannia relief decoration.

468   469   470

BIBLIOGRAPHY

E.Aslim & P.Atterbury, 1976, Minton 1798-1910, Catalogue of
          Exhibition at Victoria & Albert Museum.
J.C.Austin, 1977, Chelsea Porcelain at Williamsburg,
          Williamsburg, Virginia.
F.A.Barrett & A.L.Thorpe, 1971, Derby Porcelain, London.
W.Bemrose, 1898, Bow, Chelsea, & Derby Porcelain, London.
K.Berling, 1911, Königlich Säshsische Porzellan Manufactur
          Meissen 1710-1910, Dresden.
G.Bickham, 1739, Musical Entertainer, London.
W.Binns, 1906, The First Century of English Porcelain, London.
G.Blake-Roberts, 1976, Sources of Decoration on an unrecorded
          Caughley Dessert Service, Trans. E.C.C.10 (1).
R.W.Blunt, Ed.1924, Cheyne Book of Chelsea China & Pottery, London.
K.Boney, 1955, A Ceramic Conundrum, Apollo, January.
Bristol Museum Art Gallery, 1970, Bristol Bicentenary Exhibition
          Catalogue.
Burlington Fine Arts Club, 1914, Catalogue of an Exhibition of
          Early English Earthenware.
R.J.Charleston,Ed., 1965, English Porcelain 1745-1850, London.
City Art Gallery, 1926, Handbook of Leeds Exhibition, Leeds.
C.Cook, 1948, The Life & Work of Robert Hancock, London.
W.Coombe, 1813, The Life of Dr. Syntax.
J.L.Dixon, 1952, English Porcelain of the 18th Century, London.
W.Doenges, 1921, Meissener Porzellan, Dresden.
J.Draper, 1975, Dated Post-Mediaeval Pottery in the Northampton Museum.
J.Draper, 1977, 18th Century Earthenware Tea & Coffee Pots in
          the Northampton Museum, Northampton Museum.
Trans. E.C.C., 1948, Miscellany, Vol. 10, Pt. 2.
Trans. E.C.C., 1948, English Pottery & Porcelain, London, Exhib. Cat.
Trans. E.C.C., 1957, Miscellany, Vol. 4, Pt. 1.
Trans. E.C.C., 1960, Miscellany, Vol. 5, Pt. 1.
Trans. E.C.C., 1963, Miscellany, Vol. 5, Pt. 4.
Trans. E.C.C., 1973, Miscellany, Vol. 9, Pt. 1.
Trans. E.C.C., 1975, Miscellany, Vol. 9, Pt. 3.
Trans. E.C.C., 1976, Miscellany, Vol.10, Pt. 1.
Trans. E.C.C., 1977, English Ceramics 1580-1830, Exhibition Catalogue.
S.Erickson, 1974, Early Neo-Classicism in France, London.
C.L.Exley, (Ed. F.A.Barrett & A.L.Thorpe), 1963, Pinxton China
          Factory, Derby.
S.W.Fisher, 1947, English Blue and White Porcelain of the 18th
          Century, London.
T.Friedman & T.Clifford, 1974, The Men at Hyde Park Corner, Sculpture
          by John Cheere, Temple Newsam, Leeds & Marble Hill,
          Exhibition Catalogue, Twickenham.
F.B.Gilhespy and D.M.Budd, 1964, Royal Crown Derby China, London.
F.B.Gilhespy, 1965, Derby Porcelain, London.
G.A.Godden, 1955a, A Derby Teapot in the Leeds Museum, Leeds Art
          Calendar.
G.A.Godden, 1955b, Derby Pot Works, Cockpit Hill, Trans. E.C.C.
          Vol. 13, Pt. 4.
G.A.Godden, 1966, An Illustrated Encyclopaedia of British Pottery
          and Porcelain, London.
G.A.Godden, 1969, The Illustrated Guide to Lowestoft Porcelain, London.
G.A.Godden, 1970, Coalport & Coalbrookdale Porcelains, London.
G.A.Godden, 1974, British Porcelain, An Illustrated Guide, London
G.A.Godden, 1974, An Introduction to English Blue & White Porcelain,
          Private Publication.

Y.Hackenbroch, 1957, <u>Chelsea & Other English Porcelain in the</u>
          <u>Untermyer Collection</u>, Harvard.
R.T.Halsey, 1916, <u>Ceramic Americana of the 18th Century</u>, Pt.IV,
          Art in America.
J.Haslem, 1876, <u>Old Derby China Factory</u>, London.
D.Holdgate, 1971, <u>New Hall & Its Imitators</u>, London.
W.B.Honey, 1928, <u>Old English Porcelain</u>, London.
W.B.Honey, Revised by R.J.Charleston, 1964, <u>English Pottery and</u>
          <u>Porcelain</u>, London.
R.G.Hughes & A.Oswald, 1974, <u>Nottingham & Derbyshire Stoneware</u>,
          Trans. E.C.C., Vol.9, Pt.2.
F.Hurlbutt, 1926, <u>Chelsea, Bow & Derby Porcelain</u>, London.
L.Jewitt, 1883, <u>The Ceramic Art of Great Britain</u>, London.
L.Jewitt, (Revised by G.A.Godden), 1972, <u>The Ceramic Art of</u>
          <u>Great Britain, 1800-1900</u>, London.
W.D.John, 1963, <u>William Billingsley 1758-1828</u>, The Connoisseur, Feb.
J.R. & F.Kidson, 1892, <u>Historical Notices of The Old Leeds</u>
          <u>Pottery</u>, Leeds.
A.Lane, 1954, <u>Italian Porcelain</u>, London.
A.Lane, 1961, <u>English Porcelain Figures of the 18th Century</u>, London.
D.MacAllister, 1931, <u>William Duesbury's London Account Book</u>,
          <u>1751-1753</u>, E.P.C.Monograph, London.
F.S.MacKenna, 1952, <u>Chelsea Porcelain, The Gold Anchor Wares</u>,
          Leigh-on-Sea.
H.R.Marshall, 1954, <u>Coloured Worcester Porcelain of the First</u>
          <u>Period, 1751-1783</u>, Newport.
T.Martyn & S.Lettice, 1773, <u>The Antiquities of Herculaneum</u>, London.
M.C.F.Mortimer, 1972, <u>The Antique Taste: The Neo-Classical Vases of</u>
          <u>Derby in the 1774 Catalogue</u>, Antique Collector, August.
J.E.Nightingale, 1881, <u>Contributions towards the History of</u>
          <u>English Porcelain</u>, Salisbury.
J.Pillemont, 1760, <u>Ladies Amusements</u>, London.
R.Price, 1959, <u>Some Groups of English Redware</u>,Trans.E.C.C.,Vol.4,Pt.5.
R.Price, 1962, <u>Some Groups of English Redware of the Mid. 18th</u>
          <u>Century Part II</u>, Trans. E.C.C., Vol.5, Pt.3.
S.Renack, 1903, <u>Répétoire de la Sculpture Greque et Romaine</u>, Paris.
D.G.C.Rice, 1965, <u>Rockingham Ornamental Porcelain</u>, London.
D.C.Towner, 1962, <u>English Cream Coloured Earthenware</u>, London.
D.C.Towner, 1967, <u>The Cockpit Hill Pottery, Derby</u>, Trans. E.C.C.,
          Vol.6, Pt.3.
D.C.Towner, 1971, <u>The Melbourne Pottery</u>, Trans. E.C.C., Vol.8, Pt.1.
A.Troude, 1874, <u>Choix de Modeles de...Sèvres</u>, Paris.
A.Wallis & W.Bemrose, 1870, <u>Pottery & Porcelain of Derbyshire</u>, London.
P.Walton, 1976, <u>Creamware & other English Pottery at Temple Newsam</u>
          <u>House, Leeds</u>, Bradford & London.
B.M.Watney, 1963, <u>English Blue & White Porcelain</u> (1st Edition), London.
B.M.Watney, 1964, <u>The Origin of some Transfer prints on Two Derby Mugs</u>
          <u>decorated by Richard Holdship</u>, Trans. E.C.C., Vol.5, Pt.5.
B.M.Watney, 1967, <u>Pre-1756 Derby Domestic wares contemporary with</u>
          <u>"Dry-Edge' Figures</u>, The Burlington, 109, No.766, January.
B.M.Watney, 1972, <u>A Hare, Two Putti & Associated Figures</u>, Trans.
          E.C.C., Vol.8, Pt.2.
B.M.Watney, 1972, <u>Notes on Bow Transfer-Printing</u>, Trans. E.C.C.,
          Vol.8, Pt.2.
B.M.Watney, 1973, <u>English Blue & White Porcelain</u> (2nd Edition), London.
F.Williams, 1930, <u>The Derby Pot Manufactury known as the Cockpit Hill</u>
          <u>Pottery</u>, Reprinted from the Derbyshire Archeological
          Society Transactions.
W.Williams, 1973, <u>Early Derby Porcelain</u>, Exhibition Catalogue.

N O T E S

- 310 -

```
Lobed dishes,                                              97, 128, 238
Locker, William,                                                    181
London, Duesbury's decorating establishment in,          2,   8,  10
London Account Books,                                 1,  6,  10,  96
London Pottery,                                                    283
London Showroom, opening of, 1773,                                 144
Longton Hall figures,                                                6
'Louis XIV', Martin Desjardins,                                     14
Lovatt and Lovatt (later Lovatt Potteries Ltd.),                   284
Loving cups,                                             253, 283, 288
Lowe, S., and family,                                              283
Lowestoft:    Derby formerly attributed to,             97, 116, 118
              patterns common to Derby and,                        124
Lucas, Daniel,                                                     145
Lück, K.G.,                                                         42
Lygo, Joseph,                                             28,  36, 144
Lyttleton, George, Lord,                                            32

MacAlister, Mrs. Donald,                                        6,  10
Mackenna, F.S.,                                                     42
Madin, Aaron,                                                      285
Maidment, James,                                                   230
Mallet, John,                                                        2
Manganese oxide, decorative use of,                                288
Mansfield, Billingsley's decorating establishment at,             144
'Mansfield' pattern,                                          106, 112
Manufacturing techniques:    at Pinxton,                          201
                             difficulties, in blue and white,      96
                             for figures,                     2,  3,  4
        see also Glazes, Pastes, etc.
'Maria' figure, on garniture of vases,                             32
'Marine Society' print,                                            92
Marks:      absence, on stoneware,                                281
            anchor rebus and 'Derby',                   92,  94, 235
            'BELPER AND BOURNE POTTERIES',                         290
            'Belper and Denby Potteries, Derbyshire',             283
            Bloor period,                                         145
            'Bloor' in circle,                                    170
            'Bloor Derby' and crown,        42, 148, 164, 172, 178
            'Bourne',                                             284
            Bow and Arrow,                                       201
            circle surrounding triangle, lines and dots,          12
            crescent,                                         97, 112
            crescent and star,                               201, 222
            Crossed Arrow and '190',                             210
            crown, crossed batons,                               158
            crown, crossed batons, '8' painted,                 154
            crown, crossed batons and D,              156, 158, 176
            crown, crossed batons and D, '44' painted,          176
            crown, crossed batons and D, '236' painted,
                    'G' and 'H' impressed,                       156
            crown, crossed batons and D, 'No.372' and )(*,       36
            crown, crossed batons and D, '409',                 158
            crown, crossed batons, six dots and D,  150, 152, 156,
                 160, 162, 164, 166, 168, 170, 172, 174, 178
```

- 324 -

Marks (contd.):

Patterns, named, numbered, contd:

```
Phosphatic pastes,                                              70,    124
Pickle (sweetmeat) dishes,             96,  97, 118, 235, 237,  238
Pillemont, Jean,                                               156,   256
'Pineapple' pattern,                                      248, 252,   278
Pinks, (colour), use of,           2,  74,  92,   94, 154, 156,  158,
                                 174,   182, 184, 226, 228, 246,  278
Pinxton Factory: doubtful attribution of spill vases to,        304
                 location,                                      282
                 history,                         144,  200-1,  204
                 manufacturing techniques,                      201
                 marks,                                         201
                 modellers,                                40,  231-2
                 prices,                                        231
                 range, characteristics of wares,         200-28
                 sale of moulds,                               232
                 shards from,                                  233
Pipe clay, possible use of,                                     38
Pipe stopper,                                                   90
'Piping Faun',                                                  36
'Piping Shepherd',                                         4,   36
Planché, Andrew,                                      1,   2,   3,  6
Planché family,                                                  1
Planché period, marks,                                         178
Plant pot and stand,                                           228
'Plantation' pattern,                                          130
Plates:          cf undertain attribution,               296,  298
                 pattern used both at Nottingham Road
                       and Cockpit Hill,                       235
                 various examples, 72, 74, 130, 166-8,  179,  180,
                     182-8, 190, 222, 231,   268, 270,  272
Playing cards, on 'Hardy' plate,                              168
Plowright, of Walton Pottery,                                 283
Plumb, S.H.                                                   204
Plymouth, view of,                                            172
Political slogans,                    235,  250,  290, 304,   306
Polychrome wares: attribution of,                             296
                  cost of,                                     22
                  quantities produced,                        96
'Pomona' group,                                               296
'Poppy' pattern,                                              206
Pot-pourri vase,                                               84
Pots, stoneware,    see also different types of pot          280
Pottery, The, Brampton,                                      283
Pounce Pot,                                                    88
'Proposal, The',                                          4,   36
Price, R.,                                                   306
Prices, of Pinxton ware,see also under individual items,     231
Prince, Edward,                                              182
'Princess' pattern,                                          186
Puce (colour), use of,   48, 50,56, 58, 74, 92,  94, 154, 178, 206 .
            see also Marks
'Pug scratching its ear', flower modelling on,                47
Punch bowls,                                           283,  288
Punch jug,                                                    82
```

```
Punch pot,                                                    58
            with cover and stand,                             58
Purple (colour), use of,    14, 48, 50, 156, 186, 208, 240, 244,
                       250, 252, 254, 264, 268, 270, 274, 304
Putti:    modelling of,                          22,  24,  28
          painting of,                                       94
Puzzle jugs,                                        280, 288

Radford, Thomas,                                            240
Reds (colour), use of,  32, 50, 70, 76, 80, 82, 86,168, 222, 244,
                   246, 248, 250, 252, 254, 256, 260, 262, 264
            see also Crimson, Iron-red, Maroon, Puce
Red Stoneware,                                              306
Redstone, Dr. David,                                        96
Reform Bill slogans,                                       290
Reinach, S.,                                                36
Rice, D.G.G.,                                               40
'River scene with house surrounded by fence and six
            storey pagoda' patterns,                       110
Rivett, Francis,                                           234
Rivett, Mrs. Thomas,                                      234
Rivett, Thomas,                                            234
Robertson, George,                                    144, 158
Robins, Richard,                                          200
Robinson, William,                                        283
Robinson and Rhodes, Leeds, decorators,                  240
Rockingham, model of setter,                               40
Rock salt:    availability,                               280
              tax on,                                     280
Rococo models, adaptation to neo-classical taste,         34
'Rodney',                                                  38
Rossi, J.C.F.,                                             28
'Round Tower and Buildings design',                      256
Rowley, George,                                           182
Royal Crown Derby, use of prefix,  see also Derby ceramics 181
Royal Family, depictions of,            94, 181, 280, 294
'Royal Gadroon' shape,                             179, 184
Royal patronage,                                   144, 181
Rückert, R.,                                        16,  18
'Russian Shepherd Group',                                  36
Rutland, Duke of, collection,                            134
Ryland, W.W.,                                              32

Sadler, of Liverpool,                                      92
'St. Philip' figure,                                       2
'St. Thomas' figure,                                       2
Salter, W., Snr.,                                         176
Salt-glazed stoneware:  brown,       280-1, 283-5, 286-94
                        fragments,                     276-8
                        from Cockpit Hill,                240
Salts,                                         47,  97, 116
Saly, Jacques,                                             28
Sandby, Paul,                                             226
Sandon, H.,                                     92,  93, 104
Sarti, dealer in models,                                   3
```

Prepared by Brenda Hall, M.A., Registered Indexer
        of the Society of Indexers.

Peter and Heather Jackson
ANTIQUES

Specialising in English Porcelain, 18th and 19th Century

3 MARKET PLACE,
BRACKLEY, NORTHANTS
NN13 5AB

SHOP AT WOOLWORTH AND THE POUNDS WILL TAKE CARE OF THEMSELVES.

Wonderful Value. Great Quality.

THAT'S THE WONDER OF WOOLWORTH

KLABER-KLABER

A rare **DERBY** desk writing-set, fitted with pen-tray, taper stick, pounce-pot and ink-pot. Painted with a continuous landscape around the ink-pot and pounce-pot and on the pen-tray and insects on the taper stick. The scroll boarders painted in turquoise enamel colour and gilt. c. 1755

2b Hans Road, Brompton Road, Knightsbridge, London, SW3 1RX

Venner's Antiques
(Mrs. S. Davis)

Specializing in fine 18th and 19th Century Porcelain, Pottery. Also Paintings, Furniture.
ALSO AT A4 LITTLEWICK GREEN, NR. MAIDENHEAD, BERKS.
TEL: LITTLEWICK GREEN 2757/2588.

Superb Derby Coffee Pot painted with English Flowers
C. 1758.

China Choice
(Simon Spero)

A Large Selection of English Porcelain, 1750-80. Blue and White a Speciality. Also Watercolours.

Rare Blue and White Derby Ecquelle and Cover with Stand. C. 1765. Chinoiserie decoration.

Both at 7 New Cavendish Street, London W1.
Off Marylebone High Street.
Phone 01-935 0184. Open Mon-Fri. 10 am to 5 pm. Sat. 10 am to 1 pm

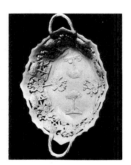